EUROPE AS THE WOULD-BE
WORLD POW[...]

D0771622

For fifty years European integration has been pursued according to an operational code based on rules which have never been publicly discussed. This book demonstrates the far-reaching consequences of the prioritisation of integration over competing values, fait accompli and other implicit rules of action. The willingness to sacrifice democracy on the altar of integration is demonstrated by the monopoly of legislative initiative granted to the non-elected Commission. Monetary union preceding, rather than following, political integration, is a striking example of fait accompli, and the reason behind many holes in the EU system of economic governance. Until now, academics have avoided radical criticism; Giandomenico Majone argues that only an open acknowledgement of the obsolescence of the traditional methods can stem the rising tide of Euro-scepticism.

GIANDOMENICO MAJONE is Emeritus Professor of Public Policy at the European University Institute in Florence.

EUROPE AS THE WOULD-BE WORLD POWER

WORLD POWER

The EU at Fifty

GIANDOMENICO MAJONE

CAMBRIDGE
UNIVERSITY PRESS

CAMBRIDGE UNIVERSITY PRESS
Cambridge, New York, Melbourne, Madrid, Cape Town, Singapore, São Paulo, Delhi

Cambridge University Press
The Edinburgh Building, Cambridge CB2 8RU, UK

Published in the United States of America by Cambridge University Press, New York

www.cambridge.org
Information on this title: www.cambridge.org/9780521758451

First published 2009

Printed in the United Kingdom at the University Press, Cambridge

A catalogue record for this publication is available from the British Library

ISBN 978-0-521-76528-2 hardback
ISBN 978-0-521-75845-1 paperback

CONTENTS

ACKNOWLEDGEMENTS

Chapter 8 in this book is a slightly rewritten version of an article published in the *European Law Review*:

Giandomenico Majone, 'Unity in Diversity: European Integration and the Enlargement Process', (2008) 33 E. L. Rev. August, 457–81.

I gratefully acknowledge prior publication, and consent by Sweet & Maxwell, the publishers of the journal, to publication in this volume.

Introduction

I have found that the word 'Europe' was always in the mouth of those
politicians who demanded from other powers that which they did not dare
to pretend in their own name.

Otto von Bismarck (1876)

The imposing structure of European laws, institutions, and policies has
been erected on the basis of a few operational principles that have
remained mostly implicit, but nevertheless have shaped the political
culture of the European Union. These principles – which taken together
form what may be called the operational code of the EU – are not
mentioned in official documents, nor discussed in the academic literature, but I submit that it is impossible to understand the current predicament of the European project – the EU's legitimacy crisis and the
growing alienation of the citizens from the European institutions –
without starting from them. Arguably the most important of these
implicit operational principles says that integration has priority over all
other competing values, including democracy. Hence the monopoly of
legislative initiative granted to the non-elected European Commission –
a sacrifice of basic principles of representative democracy on the altar
of integration. The rationale of this rule, the key element of what came
to be called the Community Method, will be explained in later chapters.
A second principle enjoins EU decision-makers to follow, wherever
possible, the strategy of the fait accompli – the accomplished fact
which makes opposition and public debate useless. This was, according
to insiders, Jean Monnet's approach: 'since the people aren't ready to

For cases and other legal information, see the Court of Justice of the European Communities
website: www.curia.eu.int/en/content/juris/index.htm. For treaties and secondary legislation (EC Regulations, Directives, and Decisions), see the Official Journal of the European
Communities: http://europa.eu.int/eur-lex/en/oj. For European institutions, policies, official statements, etc., see: http://ec.europa.eu/atoz_en.htm.

agree to integration, you have to get on without telling them too much about what is happening' (Pascal Lamy, cited in Ross 1995: 194).

A striking application of the strategy of fait accompli was the decision to proceed with monetary union before there was any agreement on political union; if anything, resistance to political integration has increased since the centralization of monetary policy. Hence the European Central Bank (ECB) operates in a political vacuum – a situation unknown to modern democracies. Hence, too, the absence of a politically legitimated authority capable of acting decisively for the entire EU in order to address the most severe financial crisis of recent decades. Even under less dramatic circumstances, if the Council of the twenty-seven finance ministers of the EU is unable to reach a common position on, say, external monetary action, authority over this matter would flow by default to the ECB. When the euro was introduced, an American scholar wisely wrote: 'Prudence might have counseled that the European Union take certain steps well before the creation of the euro area' (Henning 2000: 36). The problem is that prudential reasoning is foreign to the philosophy of fait accompli.

According to a third operational principle, ultimate ends are largely irrelevant: what counts are movement (the so-called bicycle theory of integration), procedures, and the expansion of European competences. This principle of irrelevance of ultimate ends – a distinctive feature of federalist revisionism, or cryptofederalism, as discussed in chapter 3 – explains the reluctance of the Euro-elites to discuss the finality of the integration process, except as an open-ended commitment to 'ever closer union'. It has been rightly remarked, however, that the conception of politics as an infinite process is in the long run uncongenial or incomprehensible to the human mind: the leader who wishes to mobilize the people and push them to political action is inevitably led to posit finite goals (Carr 1964: 89). The current Euro-fatigue has one of its roots in the indeterminacy of the final destination. The motto taken from Bismarck's papers suggests yet another implicit principle often used in interstate bargaining at EU level – the instrumental use of 'Europe' for national purposes – see the final section of this introduction.

Now, it is not difficult to deduce these and similar principles from the record of fifty years of European treaty- and policy-making. The question, therefore, is why scholars have been reluctant to examine the operational code of EU decision-makers, with all its disturbing implications, preferring instead to limit their investigations to legal, economic, or institutional technicalities. The reason, I believe, is that most students of the EU are not detached observers, but convinced supporters of

European integration. Hence they are afraid that fundamental criticism would jeopardize the attainment of the goals they support by sowing the seeds of discontent towards the Union in the minds of ordinary citizens. Having taught in the past several courses on environmental policy on both sides of the Atlantic, the following analogy has often occurred to me. When the law, politics, and economics of environmental policy-making were new academic subjects, students, and teachers tended to share a deep commitment to the environmentalist cause. They generally viewed environmental quality as an absolute value rather than an important, but not the sole, goal of public policy. As a consequence, the idea of discussing environmental policies in terms of trade-offs, opportunity costs, and cost–benefit ratios was anathema. Not only economic growth, viewed as the major cause of environmental degradation, but even the use of economic instruments like pollution rights to replace the traditional command-and-control methods of pollution regulation were regarded with deep suspicion. In spite of their commitment to democracy, and especially to public participation, the votaries of environmentalism were not troubled by the thought that their one-dimensional view of public policy hardly matched the preferences and priorities of the great majority of voters.

The fundamentalist phase of environmentalism did not last more than two decades, at least in the United States, while fifty years after the signing of the Treaty of Rome, the idea that European integration may have costs as well as benefits, or that the cost–benefit ratio may be shifting with changes in the size of the Union and in the international environment, is still foreign to many academic observers of the EU. The average citizen, on the other hand, is becoming increasingly aware that despite such ambitious projects as the single European market, Economic and Monetary Union (EMU), and 'big bang' enlargement – the simultaneous accession of all ten candidates except Bulgaria and Romania – the EU is apparently unable to do much about such everyday problems as unemployment, soaring prices of food and energy, or transnational crime – not to mention major financial crises. Instead of trying to understand the reasons for today's disenchantment with European integration, some scholars continue to express their admiration for 'the inherent ability of the EU integration process to constantly reinvent itself', (Szyszczak 2006: 487), and confidently assume that 'the approaches to integration that have been followed for half a century are still basically valid, and capable of evolving in response to changing pressures and new priorities' (Dougan 2006: 869).

Shortly before the French and Dutch voters rejected the Constitutional Treaty in 2005, a distinguished American student of European integration wrote that the 'constitutional compromise' embodied in the multi-level system of governance of the EU 'is unlikely to be upset by major functional challenges, autonomous institutional evolution, or demands for democratic accountability ... When a constitutional system no longer needs to expand and deepen in order to assure its own continued existence, it is truly stable' (Moravcsik 2005: 376). As a matter of fact, EU leaders are now so aware of the risk of systemic instability that they are haunted by the ghost of popular referendums. The Irish No to the Lisbon Treaty in 2008 has reminded people that the ghost is still in the machine. What these and other recent events teach is that total optimism and avoidance of radical criticism, far from promoting the integration process, make the arguments of the Euro-sceptics appear more realistic and relevant. This book offers a critical assessment of the traditional, Brussels-centred, approach to European integration precisely because its author believes that the idea of Europe united in its diversity must be saved from the rising tide of Euro-scepticism.

European Integration and its Discontents

Two shocks that recently hit the European Union – the rejection by popular referendums first of the Constitutional Treaty, then of the Lisbon Treaty – have revealed the fault in the foundations of the European structure: the chasm between elite and popular opinion on the scope, aims, and achievements of the integration project. France and the Netherlands, the two countries where the popular vote sunk the ambitious Constitutional Treaty in May/June 2005, were among the founding members of the European Coal and Steel Community (ECSC), established in 1951, and of the European Economic Community (EEC) and European Atomic Energy Community (Euratom), six years later. In different ways, both countries have always been in the forefront of the integration process – the first European Communities were largely a French invention, while Dutch governments have openly advocated federalist goals, notably on the occasion of the drafting of the Treaty on European Union (TEU). Ireland's rejection of the scaled-down version of the Constitutional Treaty, the Reform (Lisbon) Treaty, on 12 June 2008, was in some respects even more surprising than the negative votes of three years before. Ireland joined the European Community (EC) in 1973, after 80 per cent of the voters had approved their country's membership in a referendum.

Membership brought significant financial transfers under the Common Agricultural Policy (CAP) and the structural funds: almost €40 billion since 1973, net of contributions to the European budget. Irish industry and agriculture have undergone considerable adjustments since accession, although economists point out that causality is difficult to prove because of the influence of non-EC factors such as globalization and government policies – the shift in economic policy from protectionism and import substitution to free trade and foreign direct investment had already taken place at the beginning of the 1960s. Be that as it may, the shock of June 2008 was all the more surprising because of the conviction of the Euro-elites that four million Irish could not possibly stop the march of half a billion Europeans towards 'ever closer union'.

The French, Dutch, and Irish votes were not the first manifestations of popular discontent. Since the early 1990s referendums on treaty ratification have been used by voters to express their growing disillusionment with European integration. In 1992 almost 49 per cent of the French voted against ratification of the TEU, revealing surprisingly widespread resentment of deeper European integration. Earlier in the same year Danish voters had rejected the TEU, despite the fact that the political and economic elites of their country were in favour of, and campaigned for, ratification. In 2001 it was the turn of the Irish people to reject the Nice Treaty, again contrary to the indications of their national leaders. In the case of both the Danish and first Irish referendums, however, the process of parliamentary ratification continued in the other member states, and a few opt-outs and minor textual changes made it possible for the Danes and the Irish to vote again and in the end approve the treaties.

The situation turned out to be quite different in 2005. At first the heads of the European institutions tried to convince the other member states to continue with ratification in spite of the French and Dutch No, but their hopes were dashed by the British decision to postpone indefinitely the referendum originally planned for the first half of 2006. The Lisbon Treaty had been carefully drafted to avoid any reference, however remote, to terms like constitution, federalism, or political integration, and even failed to mention rather innocuous symbols of statehood such as the European flag and anthem. The treaty framers had also been generous in granting opt-outs in the hope of convincing the national governments that ratification by popular referendum was unnecessary, but all these stratagems failed to impress the voters – not only in Ireland, but probably also in many of the countries whose citizens were not given the same chance to voice their dissatisfaction.

The Irish Referendum and its Aftermath

After the Irish voters, including a large majority of young people and women, used the chance offered to them to vent their dissatisfaction with the European project, Euro-leaders remembered the lesson taught by the constitutional debacle of 2005. They resisted the first impulse to ask the other member states to continue with parliamentary ratification so as to isolate Ireland. Instead, it was decided to give the Dublin government time until mid-October 2008 to come forward with ideas on how to resolve the impasse. At the time of writing (early October 2008) it seems most unlikely that a solution will be found so soon. Although British prime minister Gordon Brown had promised to continue with ratification, the Czech Republic and Poland did not make similar pledges. In fact, Vaclav Klaus, the Euro-sceptic Czech president, declared that after the Irish No, the Lisbon Treaty was dead, while his prime minister was quoted as saying that he would not bet 100 crowns on a Czech Yes. The leaders of the larger member states unanimously declared that a substantive revision of the Lisbon Treaty was out of the question; but a survey commissioned by the European Commission, and released a few days after the Irish vote, indicated that almost two-thirds of those who voted No did so in the hope of forcing a substantive revision of the treaty. Unsurprisingly, at the time of writing nobody dares to predict what may happen in 2009, when the European elections are scheduled. According to the German social-democrat Jo Leinen, chairman of the constitutional committee of the European Parliament (EP), the crisis opened by the Irish vote is even more serious than the one of 2005 (quoted in Beste *et al.* 2008). Another European parliamentarian, the Christian-democrat Elmar Brok, did not rule out the end of the European Union as we know it. As reported by *Spiegel On Line*, the German politician, who is an influential advisor of Chancellor Angela Merkel on European affairs, envisages the possibility that the present Union may divide into a 'Small Europe', grouped around France and Germany, and a looser economic union including the member states which oppose a political union (Beste *et al.* 2008).

It is indeed difficult to see how the Irish voters could be induced to change their minds. European citizens had been told by their leaders that the Lisbon Treaty is necessary to give the EU a platform to project its influence more effectively on the world scene, in particular by means of the Common Security and Defence Policy – hence the emphasis placed by the treaty on the role of the European Defence Agency. The new treaty is also said to be necessary to start a new round of enlargements. But these are precisely the prospects which most alarmed Irish voters, strongly attached to the neutrality of their country, and so determined to retain full control of their national borders that they refused to join the Schengen Agreement on the abolition of all border controls. The issue of immigration from new member states also played a significant role in the rejection of the Constitutional Treaty, and continues to remain high on the list of public concerns in many member states. Hence, the announcement by the French and German leaders that the EU's plans to accept new members from the Balkans would be put on ice until Lisbon is ratified – 'No Lisbon, no enlargement' French president Sarkozy is reported as saying – could actually give many people, not only in Ireland, one more reason to oppose ratification (Volkery 2008). At the same time, what the French farm minister, and former EU commissioner, Michel Barnier, said after the referendum, namely that the Irish vote showed that Europeans were afraid of an EU 'without borders and limits', was immediately noted with preoccupation in the many countries, including Turkey, still waiting to be admitted to the Union (Cohen 2008: 5).

Right now Europeans have more immediate concerns than future enlargements of the Union. According to press reports, at their meeting of 16 June 2008, EU foreign ministers expressed fears that the Irish referendum might show that the Union had become too elitist and technocratic, and was losing touch with citizens on concrete issues (Castle 2008: 3). In fact, the concomitance of the Irish vote with protests across Europe against rising food and energy prices underlines a loss of confidence among significant parts of the electorate in the EU's ability to deal with everyday issues. Inflation and economic stagnation had also hit the European economy hard in the 1970s, yet few people at the time accused the EC of being unable to deal with everyday issues. The politically significant new factors in the present economic crisis are the end of what has been called 'permissive consensus' – when European voters took the integration project for granted, as part of the political landscape – and the growing divergence between elite and popular estimations of the value added by integration. 'Politics begins where the masses are, not where there are thousands, but where there are millions, that is where serious politics begins.' Lenin's dictum (cited in Carr 1961: 61) explains both the absence, in the present EU, of serious politics – as distinct from bureaucratic and institutional politics, and from political bargaining in camera – and the beginning of a necessarily messy process of politicization of the European project.

The Referendum Roulette

The current debate about alternative modes of treaty ratification is the first stage of this process of politicization. To understand the nature of the debate, one should keep in mind a fundamental difference between the EU and its member states, namely the absence of the traditional government–opposition dialectic at European level. Having been denied an appropriate political arena in which to hold European governance accountable, voters are almost forced to gradually transform popular referendums into contests for or against the EU. Given the present state of public opinion, such referendums represent a potential hazard for the integration process, not just in traditionally Euro-sceptic countries but in all member states – some authors go as far as to speak of a 'referendum roulette' (Trechsel 2005). It seems highly unlikely, however, that in the future it will be possible to force the referendum genie back into the bottle – or to stop the politicization of the European project. After the Irish No, demands for popular ratification of future European treaties have been advanced by leaders of different countries and political hues. In July 2008 Werner Faymann, the social-democratic candidate for the Austrian federal election to take place the following September, came out in favour of popular referendums for all future treaty amendments and on other important EU issues. The Austrian Parliament had already ratified the Lisbon Treaty in April of that year, but the social-democratic leader was obviously trying to improve his electoral chances by taking advantage of widespread EU-fatigue: according to recent Eurobarometer data, only 28 per cent of Austrian citizens still support the EU; in 1994, 66.6 per cent had voted in favour of joining the Union. In Italy, to mention another example, support for future referendums on Europe was expressed by the spokesman of the populist Northern League in the national parliament, just as that body was ratifying the Lisbon Treaty.

One of the favourite arguments against ratification of EU treaties by popular referendum is that voters cannot be expected to read and evaluate technically and legally complex texts running into hundreds of pages – 346 pages in the case of the Lisbon Treaty. This argument is flawed in several respects. First, it is not only the average voter who does not have the time, or the motivation, to peruse such documents. Brian Cowen, the Irish prime minister, admitted he had not read the Lisbon Treaty, and Ireland's EU commissioner, Charlie McCreevy, added that 'no sane person' would (Murray Brown 2008: 3). Justice Iarhlaith O'Neill, the High Court judge appointed by the Irish government to provide an impartial treaty analysis, admitted that parts of the text are difficult to understand (Murray Brown 2008: 3). It is reasonable to assume that not only the average citizen but also the average member of a national parliament – the body which would have to ratify a new treaty in the absence of popular referendum – would find it hard to understand what was unclear to a High Court judge. The difference is that the average parliamentarian is likely to vote according to party discipline, while the average voter uses the referendum as a rare occasion to express his or her assessment of the European project – voters' turn-outs at referendums are typically higher than at elections for the European Parliament. In sum, it is far from clear why parliamentary ratification of European treaties should be preferable to ratification by popular vote: it is certainly not more democratic, nor is it somehow more rational, or necessarily better informed.

According to an influential theory of democracy, moreover, even in national elections it is rational for the average voter *not* to become fully knowledgeable about public affairs. Anthony Downs was the first scholar to give serious attention to the problem of political information in modern mass democracies. Downs's argument is that the cost of becoming informed about the details of political issues generally outweighs the relative benefits to be derived from voting on an informed basis. The costs of becoming informed – the costs of gathering and selecting data; of undertaking a factual analysis of the data; and of evaluating specific goals in light of the factual analysis – are too high for most voters rationally to invest the time, attention, and resources needed to become politically informed. Rather, rational voters have strong incentives to develop methods of avoiding the high costs of information acquisition. They do so by developing a variety of principles of selection: rules employed to determine what to make use of and what not. These rules allow voters to make political decisions and form political preferences without becoming fully informed about the content and details of political issues: they focus their attention upon only the most relevant data. This 'will allow them to avoid the staggering difficulty of knowing everything the government has done during the election period and everything its opponents would have done were they in office' (Downs 1957: 217). In any case, since the rise of mass democracy nobody has proposed to use the 'rational ignorance' of the voters as an excuse to restrict the right to vote at national elections. Also from the viewpoint of democratic theory, therefore, the arguments of the Euro-elites, and of their academic sup-porters, against treaty ratification by referendum are flawed. Instead of

taking seriously the demands of modern mass democracy, such arguments reflect an old-fashioned conception of policy, in particular foreign
policy, as a virtual monopoly of cabinets and diplomats: the philosophy
of old-regime Europe applied to the post-modern system of governance
of the EU.

Legitimacy and Efficiency

A recurrent theme in the following chapters is the ineffectiveness of many
EU policies, and the implications of such ineffectiveness for the legitimacy
and stability of the EU system. In public discourse and in the academic
literature much more attention is given to the issue of the 'democratic
deficit' – the absence or incomplete development, at European level, of the
institutions and practices of parliamentary democracy – than to the question of suboptimal performance of the EU. In my opinion this is a mistake.
Suboptimal performance, I argue, is a more immediate threat to the
survival of the Union than the democratic deficit. Legitimacy, Martin
Lipset wrote, 'involves the capacity of [a] system to engender and maintain the belief that the existing political institutions are the most appropriate ones for the society' (1963: 64). Legitimacy is an evaluative
standard: 'groups regard a political system as legitimate or illegitimate
according to the way in which its values fit with theirs' (Lipset 1963: 64).
Like other evaluative standards (e.g. accountability) the modern notion
of legitimacy is derived from experience gathered at the national
level. Michael Shackleton, a reflective staff member of the European
Parliament, has rightly pointed out that it is not necessary for the EU
to meet the same level of legitimacy as its member states, provided it
delivers a reasonable level of benefits in terms of efficiency (Shackleton
1998: 134). The efficient delivery of benefits does not, per se, produce
legitimacy – efficiency is instrumental, not normative. As Shackleton
suggests, however, efficiency is particularly important for a polity that,
being new, still lacks popular support. A serious crisis is bound to occur,
sooner or later, if the new polity is unable to sustain the expectations of
major groups of the population for a long enough period to allow
legitimacy to develop upon a new basis.

There seems to be little doubt that disappointed expectations are one
important, if not the main, reason why the EU, instead of progressively
attracting the loyalty of its citizens, is becoming less popular and less
trustworthy with the years. Since its beginning, the process of European
integration has been driven essentially by economics. Indeed, the essence

of the Monnet method consists in pursuing political integration, not by frankly political means, but under the guise of economic integration (see chapter 3). The major risk inherent in this approach is that suboptimal economic performance over a period of years may impede the emergence of new sources of legitimacy, and thus further undermine the normative foundations of an elite-driven integration process. This risk was not sufficiently appreciated in the early stages of the process because the foundational period of the European Communities largely overlapped with the three 'glorious decades' 1945–75, when Europe experienced an unprecedented period of growth, macroeconomic stability, and high levels of social protection. Then the 'economic miracle' came to an end. After the phase of very rapid catch up with the United States, convergence in the levels of per capita income stopped at the beginning of the 1980s and has remained unchanged since. During the 1990s, growth of EU GDP was disappointing both in absolute terms and with regard to the US, in spite of ambitious projects such as the Single Market Programme ('Europe '92') and EMU. A few years ago the semi-official Sapir Report noted that 'the EU system has failed to deliver a satisfactory growth performance' (Sapir *et al.* 2004: 22), and the situation has not improved since then.

While the official rhetoric kept celebrating the economic achievements of European integration, the desire to improve poor economic performance has in fact driven EU policy for more than twenty years. The gap between official rhetoric and reality went largely unnoticed in the past because most EU policies were too remote from the daily problems of people to seriously concern public opinion. Monetary union and 'big bang' enlargement have changed all this. Unlike most policy decisions taken in Brussels, the decisions taken by the European Central Bank in Frankfurt are widely advertised, and their consequences – whether on home mortgages, on consumer credit, or on the availability of publicly financed services – have a direct impact on the welfare of all inhabitants of the euro-zone, indeed of the entire EU. Because of their impact on growth, also the Bank's non-decisions, e.g. concerning changes in the discount rate, are often discussed in the media. Similarly, the implications, true or presumed, of eastern enlargement on jobs, wages, social standards, and transboundary crime have become part of the daily concerns of the citizens of the older member states – and a hot topic of debate in national elections. For half a century Euro-elites could present integration as a positive-sum game; now people realize that integration entails costs as well as benefits, and that a positive net balance can no longer be taken for granted. This is why poor performance, in particular poor economic performance, poses more of a threat to the legitimacy and long-term survival of the EU than in the past.

Back to First Principles

It has been suggested above that many EU scholars refrain from questioning the principles on which the EU operates out of fear that criticism may endanger the integration process. Reluctance to go back to first principles, however, often means misunderstanding the nature of the problems, and hence proposing inadequate solutions. A striking demonstration of this is provided by the debate about the EU's democratic deficit. For years Euro-leaders and academics have been saying that a necessary, and perhaps sufficient, condition for solving the democratic-deficit problem is to give more powers to the EP. Yet, the steady growth of the powers of the supranational parliament has been accompanied by an equally steady decline in the turnout of voters at European elections – suggesting that the voters are less interested than the elites in the democratic-deficit problem, or at least that they are not convinced by the proposed solution. Other attempts to enhance the democratic legitimacy of the Union by such means as the development of 'Social Europe', or the allocation to regional policy of a growing share of the EU budget, have also failed, as shown in chapter 5. The fact is that most writers on the democratic deficit are reluctant to admit that the root cause of the phenomenon they deplore lies not so much in the failure to replicate at European level the legislative institutions or welfare policies of the nation state, as in the priority consistently given to integration over democracy. Less realistic than the founding fathers, the proponents of these pseudo-solutions would like to have both – more integration *and* more democracy – and grope for ways of resolving the basic dilemma without either questioning the logic of the received integration methods, or admitting the lack of popular support for a fully fledged federalist solution (if a majority of voters supported a European federal state, the democratic legitimacy problem would ipso facto be solved).

When, by the mid-1950s, it became clear that the federal solution was impossible because of the strong attachment of the people to the nation state, and their reluctance to be 'Europeanized' (see chapter 1), integrationist leaders were confronted with a stark choice between integration and democracy. As dictated by the operational code, the dilemma was resolved in favour of integration: Europe would be built without

Europeans, if necessary. That was the beginning of Monnet's method of integration by stealth: political integration was to be pursued under the guise of economic integration. As already mentioned, the clearest demonstration of the willingness to sacrifice democracy on the altar of integration is the monopoly of legislative initiative granted to the Commission under the so-called Community Method. The willingness to sacrifice democracy for the sake of deeper integration was again revealed at the time of the Maastricht Treaty, when it was decided to give quasi-constitutional status to the independence of the ECB. Before monetary union, the independence of the national central banks had only a statutory basis. This meant that in principle national parliaments could always change the rules if they thought that the central bank was using its independence in a manner with which they disagreed. In contrast, to change the rules under which the ECB operates requires a treaty revision acceptable to all the member states – a complex and risky procedure, as shown by the Irish referendum. The net result is that the national parliaments have lost control over monetary policy, while the EP has no authority in this area. The ECB is free to operate in a political vacuum since there is no true European government to balance its powers, and even the institutions of economic governance are poorly defined, as mentioned above and shown in detail in chapter 6. I conclude that the democratic deficit and many other still unresolved issues cannot be understood, let alone settled, without going back to the basic principles embedded in the operational code of the EU.

Between Soft Power and World Power

After World War I, wrote A. J. P. Taylor in *The Struggle for Mastery in Europe* (1971), what had been the centre of the world became merely 'the European question'. The federalist movement of the interwar period was driven by the ambition of restoring Europe to its former position at the centre of the world. This was to be accomplished by means of the economic and political integration of the continent. Ortega y Gasset devoted the second part of his *The Revolt of the Masses* (1932), one of the bestsellers of the 1930s, to the question, who rules the world? According to the Spanish philosopher only a united Europe could rule the world – neither capitalist America nor communist Russia were experienced and wise enough to do it. Besides, reconstructing Europe as a big nation state was the only project which could rescue Europeans from their depression and give them once more a sense of mission.

A well-known French intellectual, Julien Benda, dreamt of a sort of Holy European Empire (Holmberg 1994). These, or similar, goals were shared by other writers, and by a few political leaders, in the 1920s and 1930s. After World War II federalists could no longer share such neo-imperialist visions; still, the majority of the federalist movements then active in Western Europe viewed the united Europe of the future as a world power able to play the role of a third force between the super-powers of USA and USSR.

These geopolitical ambitions seemed to have been largely forgotten in the 1970s and 1980s, when the international role of the European Community was viewed by a number of Euro-leaders as that of a 'soft', 'normative', or 'civilian' power, based on dialogue, negotiations, and economic aid. As will be seen in chapter 7, many scholars enthusiastically championed the new doctrine. François Duchêne (1972), for instance, argued that the strength and novelty of communitarian Europe as an international actor were based on its ability to extend its own method of ensuring stability and security through economic and political, rather than military, means. Later writers expanded Duchêne's argument, claiming that the EU is a novel kind of power in international relations, not only because of its emphasis on non-military instruments of foreign policy, but also because of its promotion of multilateral solutions, its encouragement of regional cooperation, and because it assigns primacy to conflict prevention, negotiation, and peacekeeping. Contrary to the claims of these scholars, the practice of 'soft power' is hardly new. The historically minded reader may recall that a commitment to peace, and preference for economic means of conflict resolution were also key features of the foreign policy of the Republican administrations of Jefferson and Madison between 1800 and 1814. Thus, when Britain discriminated against American trade, James Madison argued that increasing commerce with other nations, and American counter-discrimination, would be sufficient to end British arrogance. He was convinced that, with perseverance, the United States could work its will on Britain without firing a shot. The actual result, however, was to leave the United States virtually helpless in a world it could not compel to accept its republican precepts. The great miscalculation of the Madison administration 'left a chasm between the principles it proclaimed and the powers and means necessary to give them effect' (Ketcham 1990: 471). The miscalculation became manifest when, on 24 August 1814, a British expeditionary force entered Washington practically unopposed, and deliberately set on fire all the public buildings of the federal capital.

For the EU the equivalent of the burning of Washington was the Balkan wars of the 1990s. The real tests of the EU's capacity to manage differences peacefully came after the implosion of the Soviet Union and the end of bipolarity. The limitations of the soft-power approach were clearly revealed, not in distant theatres of marginal interest, but in the EU's 'near abroad', in the former Yugoslavia. When the Yugoslav crisis broke out in June 1991, the president of the EU Council proudly – but, as it turned out, unwisely – proclaimed that this was the hour of Europe, not of the United States. In fact, the EU proved unable to enforce stability and peaceful coexistence among the peoples of the former federation. The civil war in Bosnia was ended only by the intervention of the American superpower, which mediated and guaranteed the Dayton Agreement of November 1995 between Serbs, Croats, and Moslems. Again, in 1999, this time in Kosovo, the EU was forced to ask for the military assistance of the United States – an assistance which President Clinton was reluctant to give, and which was finally provided only under the condition that the war should be conducted on American terms, i.e. only from the air. Even this limited commitment demonstrated the disparity between the sophisticated military arsenal of the US and the Union's own meagre contribution to the air war. This discrepancy had a shock effect on the military, the foreign-policy experts, and government leaders in most member states.

The failures in the former Yugoslavia explain why the vision of a united Europe capable of playing the role of a true world power – not only in economic terms – again became attractive at the beginning of the new century. Both Jacques Chirac in a speech to the German Bundestag in July 2000, and Tony Blair addressing the Polish Stock Exchange in Warsaw a few months later, proclaimed that the EU had reason and means to establish itself as a superpower on the international scene, albeit while avoiding the building of a super-state. The official contribution of the Prodi Commission to the Convention on the Future of Europe in 2002 stressed the need to consolidate and develop the EU so as to 'exercise the responsibilities of a world power'. Also the eastward and southward expansion of the boundaries of the EU was seen by some Euro-leaders as part of a strategy to 'create a superpower on the European continent that stands equal to the United States' (Winkler 2005: 15). In December 2003 the European Council approved the first-ever European Security Strategy, and in 2004 the member states decided to 'commit themselves to be able by 2010 to respond with rapid and decisive action ... to the whole spectrum of crisis management operations covered by the Treaty on the European Union' (W. Wallace 2005: 447). Later in the same year the EU Council established the European Defence Agency, which has among its tasks to promote and enhance armaments cooperation, and to strengthen the technological and industrial base of European defence.

Once the memory of the Kosovo conflict faded, however, it proved difficult to maintain the momentum. The budgetary constraints imposed by the Stability Pact of EMU do not allow any substantial increase in defence spending, and, in addition, in most member states the majority of voters are opposed to plans to project power outside Europe. Financial restrictions and public opinion are not, however, the only, or even the main, obstacles to the EU playing a leading role in international affairs. The structural flaw of EU foreign policy is the pretension to be one of the players at the table of world politics without having first reached a common understanding on what ought to be treated as vital European interests. The EU Council of 14 December 2007 was a forceful reminder of the difficulty of reaching agreement on delicate foreign-policy issues. The Council was supposed to define a common position in the event that Kosovo unilaterally proclaimed its independence from Serbia. The majority of member states favoured recognition of the new state, perhaps with a compensation for Serbia in the form of a fast-track membership of the Union. In fact, no common European position could be defined, except for the decision to send a civilian mission composed of judges, police, and administrators. The most determined opposition to agreement on the main political issue came from Spain – always very sensitive about problems of separatism – and from Cyprus, which was worried about the implications of an official recognition of Kosovo's independence for its own relations with the Turkish part of the island. Also opposed to the recognition were other new members of the EU with significant internal problems of secession or ethnic conflict such as Slovakia, Romania, and Greece.

E Pluribus Unum?

In spite of recurring problems, repeated disappointments, and outright failures, the official position of the national governments is that all members of the EU should advance together towards 'ever closer union' – a position reaffirmed with special emphasis by both the German chancellor and the French president after the Irish referendum. Various models of differentiated integration have been proposed since the first enlargement in

1973, but they were always ignored by the national governments. Even the possibility of 'closer' or 'enhanced' cooperation – a limited and tightly constrained form of differentiated integration – has never been made use of since it was first offered by the 1997 Treaty of Amsterdam. Different countries have different reasons for supporting the official position. Small countries, in particular, see in common institutions and common deliberations the best protection against the risk of domination by the larger member states. Sheer vanity is another possible reason. The idea of being the president (albeit for only six months) of a Community/Union of several hundred million people is heady stuff for most political leaders, especially for the leaders of small or medium-sized countries.

A more basic explanation, however, is suggested by the motto prefixed to this introduction: Bismarck's cynical reflection on a long diplomatic experience which included his own role as Prussia's representative at a time when political unification was the major issue confronting the representatives of the German states assembled in Frankfurt. The comment of the chancellor of German unification (cited in Gall 1981: 93, my translation), on the use of 'Europe' to obtain advantages not otherwise available, seems also to be applicable to the method of bargaining in the EU. According to one of the best-known historians of European integration, for French leaders 'integration was an attempt to restore France as a major national force by creating an integrated area in Western Europe which France would dominate politically and economically' (Milward 1992: 17). Thus, de Gaulle viewed common European programmes in atomic and space research as convenient ways to tap foreign contributions for the improvement of French national competitiveness rather than as ways for France to contribute to European unity. He also insisted on farm subsidies as a non-negotiable condition for accepting the EEC. Thanks to the CAP, the citizens of other member states help support the income of French farmers by paying higher prices than they would pay otherwise. For his part Adenauer eagerly accepted de Gaulle's leadership in order to complete Germany's post-war rehabilitation and retain the common market for the booming German industries. Again, in the bargaining for the formation of the ECSC, the Belgian government was able to use European integration to protect its coal industry not only from competition external to the Community but from competition within the common market as well. It has been calculated that the cost of preserving employment in coal mining, in subsidies alone, was US$141.42 million between 1953 and 1958, of which slightly more than

US$50 million was contributed by other Community members, mainly by Germany. Milward and Sørensen (1994: 11) conclude that 'The integration solution was used to sustain levels of welfare and employment in Belgium which would have been much less easily sustainable [without European integration]'.

Such instrumental use of 'Europe' for national purposes is by no means limited to the early history of communitarian Europe. While EMU was seen by federalist leaders like Jacques Delors as the point of no return on the road to political integration, many member states supported the idea mainly because of their dissatisfaction with the dominant role of the German central bank in the European Monetary System. In particular, France's call in 1987 for the creation of a European central bank and a single European currency was an attempt to recapture some of the influence lost to the Bundesbank. Countries like Italy and Portugal, on the other hand, were mostly interested in reducing the costs of servicing their huge public debt. By joining the euro-zone – if necessary with the help of a flexible interpretation of the Maastricht criteria, and some assistance from the European Statistical Office – they expected to borrow financial credibility from the more fiscally virtuous members, and thus pay lower interest rates on the international markets. Finally, Germany secured the full inclusion of the former German Democratic Republic in the EU in exchange for its agreement to give up the D-mark in favour of the common currency.

In order to be conducted in the name of Europe, such complex interstate bargains must involve the whole membership of the Union. Moreover, it is easier to put together attractive package deals if there are more possibilities of political exchange, more potential quid pro quos, than in a thin political market. Again, blame avoidance, in case something goes wrong, works well only when the decision-making group is large. There are thus several reasons why EU leaders insist that all members of the EU should advance together – even at the cost of slowing down the march. Now, a system of interstate bargaining that manages to give, or at least to promise, something to everybody should be quite stable. In fact, the scholars who praise the stability of the EU base their arguments on the capacity of the system to satisfy a variety of demands through a series of package deals both within and across issue areas. It has also been pointed out that since not all demands can be satisfied simultaneously, an agreement on x today may be exchanged for the promise to discuss y tomorrow. The participants who receive such IOUs acquire an interest in the maintenance of the bargaining forum itself; they become 'locked in, and socialized by the intensity and rewards of their interactions' (Hayes-Renshaw and Wallace 1997: 254–5).

Despite its obvious attraction for the political elites, however, the method of collective bargaining in the name of Europe cannot be expected to continue indefinitely, because of the politicization of the integration process. Politicization means the end of permissive consensus and growing resistance to deals made in camera, often for the benefit of narrow interest groups. As European integration becomes politicized, political entrepreneurs seize the opportunity to differentiate themselves from other parties in EU terms, so that bargains struck in Brussels may now be contested at national level. The politicization of European issues is already evident in several member states. During the campaign for the Austrian national elections of September 2008, for example, both the social-democratic leader and the leaders of the two parties of the extreme right appealed to widespread anti-EU feelings in the population to steal votes from the pro-EU Volkspartei. One can also see that certain issues which used to be kept out of the public debate are beginning to be discussed along partisan lines. An increasingly significant topic of partisan debate is the mismatch between the priorities of the EU budget and those of the great majority of citizens – for instance the fact that 40 per cent of the EU budget still goes to agriculture, which EU-wide employs less than 5 per cent of the labour force. The regressive nature of the CAP, whose benefits flow mostly to the richest farmers and landowners, makes it even more difficult to keep decisions on agricultural policy out of public debate. As shown in chapter 5, the perverse redistributive consequences of the CAP, once the topic of a few academic studies, are now debated in some national parliaments.

The question, then, is whether the idea that all member states should take part in all projects still makes sense. The answer given by the present work is a definite No: the world in which the EU operates today has changed so much since the 1950s that it seems highly unlikely that the old operational principles and working hypotheses may still be valid. The view of straight-line evolution towards European integration emerged at a time when the EC comprised a small group of fairly homogeneous West European states. In the early stages of the integration process it was not unreasonable to assume that the entire Community would evolve, sooner or later, into a politically unified bloc, perhaps even into something like a nation. That assumption is no longer tenable in a Union of twenty-seven – and in the future more – members at vastly different stages of socioeconomic development, with different geopolitical concerns, and correspondingly diverse policy priorities. Under today's conditions, the appropriate metaphor is not evolution along a single developmental path, but evolution with several side-branches.

The economic theory of clubs, sketched in the last chapter of this book, suggests that in an increasingly heterogeneous polity the multiplication of voluntary associations, or 'clubs', tends to be welfare enhancing: not only because it facilitates the design of institutions and policies more closely tailored to the resources and preferences of the members of the various clubs, but also because institutional and policy innovations are more likely to flourish in a decentralized system. Thus, policies that prove to be politically unfeasible in the EU at large, such as the full liberalization of the services sector (see chapter 4), might be acceptable to the members of a smaller, more homogeneous subset. Instead of compromise solutions that do not really satisfy anyone, genuine innovations would become possible – albeit on a smaller scale – and other members of the Union could later draw lessons from the practical experience of the pioneering states. In this way the clubs forming within the Union could effectively become political laboratories, without the bureaucratic complications and background noise that necessarily arise when all the thirty or so member states must participate in all the initiatives. This is the idea of differentiated integration, interpreted in terms of the theory of clubs. The idea itself is hardly new – it was proposed, in different versions, after the first enlargement of the EC in 1973 – but, as already mentioned, it has not been taken too seriously so far: on the one hand, the early formulations lacked a sound conceptual basis; on the other, until recently the Union was reasonably homogeneous so that the cost of common rules was not too high relative to the reduction in transaction costs made possible by EU-wide harmonization.

The kind of differentiated integration advocated in this book does not of course mean the end of European integration – only the abandonment of open-ended commitments and indefinite goals. While rejecting the traditional view of integration along a single trajectory to an unspecified destination, this model of differentiated integration aims to give substantive meaning to the twin notions of unity in diversity and competition with cooperation. Both notions presuppose a body of rules accepted by every member state, and an agreement on the level of integration which their citizens are willing to support at any given time. All available data indicate that few people in Europe are willing to give up the level of market integration achieved so far. If the opinion polls were confirmed by popular referendums to be held in all countries, preferably at the same time, then this would be the concrete goal which every member state of the Union must be prepared to sustain and promote. Note that to make this commitment credible it may even be appropriate to strengthen the role of the Commission and of the European Court of Justice (ECJ) in certain respects.

More advanced goals could be pursued by those national governments which can count on the support of their public opinion. What is especially needed today is a practical demonstration that it is not wholly unrealistic to aspire to a more incisive role for Europe in the governance of the new world order. Actual proof that a group of European countries are able to reach a common definition of vital interests, and are willing to provide the resources needed to protect those interests, could exert a powerful demonstration effect on the other members of the Union. If, on the other hand, such an experiment were to fail, we could at least draw the lesson that mere rhetorical announcements of high-sounding initiatives only undermine the credibility of the EU as an international actor. The abandonment of overly ambitious aspirations, no matter how painful initially, would facilitate a more realistic and experimental approach to European integration.

1

An Elitist Project

The Failed Europeanization of the Masses

A politically integrated Europe, a continent finally united in spite of its diversity and of the internecine wars of the past, was – and continues to be – an elitist project. Unless this point is clearly understood and constantly kept in mind, the development of European integration – from the founding treaties in the 1950s to the Irish No to the Lisbon Treaty in 2008, only three years after the French and Dutch rejections of the Constitutional Treaty – remains largely unintelligible. Of course all key ideas of modern history, from popular sovereignty to the ideas of nation, nation state, and citizenship, were initially advanced by intellectual and political elites – were 'invented', in the terminology used by Edmund Morgan in his classic study of the rise of popular sovereignty in England and America. Thus, James Madison's 'invention' of an American People distinct from, and superior to, the peoples of the thirteen former colonies turned out to be a decisive move in the struggle to replace the Articles of Confederation by a strong federal constitution. To quote Morgan: 'As the English House of Commons in the 1640s had invented a sovereign people to overcome a sovereign king, Madison was inventing a sovereign American people to overcome the sovereign states. It was not one of those inventions for which the world was unprepared, but an invention crying out for realization' (1988: 267). Such timely conceptual inventions prove their vitality by their ability to mobilize the people and push them to political action.

The idea of a politically and economically united continent has been propagated by some of the most distinguished intellectual and political leaders of twentieth-century Europe. Names like Richard Coudenhove-Kalergi, Aristide Briand, Gustav Stresemann, Denis de Rougemont, the Spanish philosopher Ortega y Gasset, and two Nobel Prize-winning economists – Maurice Allais and Lionel Robbins – come to mind. Determined to realize the ideas of these men, after World War II a new generation of federalists became convinced that only by appealing directly to the peoples of Europe would it be possible to build a federal state against the resistance of the national governments. Federalism was to be the new orthodoxy superseding the ideological cleavages of the past (see chapter 2). Unfortunately, despite some promising signs in the years immediately following the end of the war, federalist ideas proved to be untimely, and thus unable to mobilize the people. In the course of half a century a certain Europeanization of intellectual, economic, and political elites has taken place, yet this process hardly touched the vast majority of citizens. All attempts to induce a transfer of loyalties from the national to the supranational level – by such measures as the direct election of the European Parliament, various social-policy measures, a common agricultural policy (CAP), or policies of regional aid and social cohesion – failed completely in this respect, when they did not increase the degree of conflict among the member states of the European Union (EU), as in the case of the CAP.

Political symbolism – which had been so important in rallying mass movements in support of the cause of national unification in the nineteenth century – did not help. A European logo and flag, an EU anthem, a standardized European passport and driver's licence, EU citizenship, Brussels-sponsored games and sport events, an official 'Europe Day' public holiday: these and other 'cultural actions', meant to create a new kind of European consciousness, do not appear to have caused any transfer of loyalties to the European level. In an opinion survey conducted in March 2007 by the German publicly owned television network, ZDF, on the occasion of the fiftieth anniversary of the signing of the Treaty of Rome, 60 per cent of respondents even doubted the existence of a common European culture (*Spiegel On Line* 2007). In fact, all those culture-building initiatives seemed to echo many of the techniques and methods used in the past by nationalist elites to forge Europe's existing nation states – precisely the model EU supporters seek to transcend (Shore 2006). In sum, no 'Europeanization of the masses' has taken place even remotely comparable to the 'nationalization of the masses' perceptively analysed by George Mosse in the case of Germany, but which occurred in all countries of Western Europe during the nineteenth century. After the 'war of liberation' against Napoleon in 1813–14, what was before an elite movement in favour of German unification became 'a mass movement and as such embraced many different classes in propagating a fervid belief which became a major force of its own' (Mosse 1975: 15).

The irony of the predicament in which European federalists find themselves may be appreciated with the help of another historical parallel. Gordon Craig has suggested a quite plausible argument to the effect that the German empire of 1871 was the creation of the German people, or at least that the Reich would never have come into being without the persistent and growing popular desire for unification. Bismarck knew how to use the pro-unification sentiments prevailing both in Northern and Southern Germany after the great victory over France, but he did not want the broad masses to get any outlandish ideas about popular sovereignty. Hence the Iron Chancellor not only gave the princes – the heads of the eighteen German states forming the empire – the privilege of offering the imperial crown to William I of Prussia; he also built over this contrived gesture a constitutional theory that held that the Reich was the creation of Germany's rulers, not of the German people (Craig 1978: 43–4). The integrationist Euro-elites of today face the reverse situation. As already noted, early federalists were convinced that only a vast popular movement could overcome the resistance of national governments to the political unification of the continent. Actually, whatever progress has been made in the direction of closer integration could be achieved only with the agreement of the national rulers – with the indifference, and recently even against the opposition, of their voters.

Although fifty years of European integration have not produced any significant Europeanization of the masses, some scholars have recently claimed that the integration process has a 'transformative impact' on the national institutions. A body of literature focusing on this more limited type of Europeanization tries to explain how interactions with European institutions 'socialize' domestic agents and alter their behaviour over time (Eilstrup-Sangiovanni 2006: 397–9). In fact, the available evidence suggests that the influence of the European level on national institutions, never as significant as some authors imagined, is decreasing. A reason for this trend is the comparative advantage of national policy-makers in terms of cognitive and material resources. In addition to a greater potential for institutional and policy innovation, greater resources, and vastly superior implementation capacities, national policy-makers have at their disposal policy instruments unavailable to European policy-makers. For instance, EU environmental policy lacks a key instrument like taxation – as shown by the failure of the proposal to introduce a European carbon/energy tax.

Again, today many national regulators are at least as competent as their counterparts at the European level. Take the case of competition (antitrust) policy. When the Treaty of Rome was drafted, Germany alone had a well-developed competition policy and an effective competition regulator. The other founding members of the EEC had to develop this policy almost from scratch, largely following European competition rules. At present most member states have antitrust authorities with a satisfactory degree of technical expertise, and the power to impose tough remedies: the EU no longer sets the pace in this policy area. The Directorate General for Competition is by and large considered the most expert among the Commission services, as well as the one with the strongest treaty-based powers. Nevertheless, serious doubts about its expertise have been raised when the Directorate suffered several consecutive defeats at the Court of First Instance (CFI) in high-profile cases over merger decisions (Goyder 2003).

On the other hand, member states have always resisted any true Europeanization in economic/sectorial regulation. The broad discretion of the national regulators is often the price that has to be paid in order to get the Council's approval of the regulations presented by the Commission. For instance, the liberalization of the electricity industry became politically feasible only after the possibility of nationally differing regulatory regimes was allowed. A Commission proposal to establish a European regulator to police access to the national grids was flatly rejected by the energy ministers of the then twenty-five member states at a meeting on energy problems held in Brussels in March 2006. On that occasion the German representative stated explicitly that no new European agency was needed in order to improve competition: better cooperation among the national regulators would be sufficient. Thus, half a century of integrationist efforts has not simply failed to Europeanize the masses, but even to stabilize the influence of the European level on national policies and institutions. Indeed, the influence of the member states on the European institutions has lately grown to such an extent that the guiding principle of institutional reforms of the Union is now the protection of states' rights (Dehousse 2005).

Making Europe without Europeans

In a sense, this book is an attempt to understand the reasons for the failure of both declared federalists and cryptofederalists to convert to their cause a sufficient number of Europeans. The main purpose of the present chapter, however, is more limited: namely to help the reader appreciate how far-reaching the consequences of this failure are. Surprisingly, the implications of the failed Europeanization of the masses have always been minimized, when not completely ignored, by students of European integration. The explanation of this lack of sensitivity to such a relevant, and obvious, phenomenon can only be the elitist bias of traditional European studies. The authors of the first social-scientific analyses of the integration process – Ernst Haas and his neofunctionalist school – argued that the bureaucratized nature of European states entailed that all crucial decisions are made by elites: public policy-makers, as well as economic elites, trade unions, professional associations, business lobbies, etc. Public opinion at large, on the other hand, was deemed to be unimportant (Haas 1958: 17; Eilstrup-Sangiovanni 2006: 93). Andrew Moravcsik has aptly summarized this elitist stance: 'Elite groups most intensely concerned with an issue, Haas asserts, have the greatest impact on national decision-making, which is why a majority, in the strict sense, is not required to make policy' (2005: 352; see also chapter 4 in this book). Like cryptofederalists à la Monnet (see chapter 3), but unlike the post-war generation of federalists, Haas and his school thought that the basic problem was not how to 'Europeanize the masses'; rather, the problem was how to make 'Europe without Europeans' (Schmitter 2005). In the words of Pascal Lamy, former European commissioner and erstwhile lieutenant of Commission president Jacques Delors: 'Europe was built in a St. Simonian [i.e. technocratic] way from the beginning, this was Monnet's approach: the people weren't ready to agree to integration, so you had to get on without telling them too much about what was happening' (cited in Ross 1995: 194).

Neofunctionalism was meant to be a theory of regional *political* integration, but its practitioners badly underestimated the importance of broad popular support for the long-term viability of the integrationist project – a mistake Bismarck, hardly the model of a democratic politician, carefully avoided in the case of German unification – while overstating the effectiveness of supranational institutions. The superior problem-solving capacity of these institutions was supposed to produce a sufficient normative basis for the integrationist project by inducing the progressive transfer of the loyalties and political demands of social groups from the national to the European level. This is what Haas meant by political integration: 'Political integration is the process whereby political actors in several distinct national settings are persuaded to shift their loyalties, expectations and political activities to a new centre, whose institutions possess or demand jurisdiction over pre-existing national states' (Haas 1958: 16). As observed in the preceding section, the effectiveness of the supranational institutions is increasingly questioned. Rightly or wrongly, 'Brussels' is perceived less as a potential source of solutions than as a cause of some of the problems – e.g. crime and unemployment allegedly linked to immigration from the new member states – that most concern the citizens of the EU. The EU budget plays a role in the widespread disillusionment because it hardly reflects the needs of the citizens – 40 per cent of spending still supports agriculture, which EU-wide employs less than 5 per cent of the labour force. At the same time, outlays for research and innovation are too small to be effective, and this striking contradiction with the priorities continuously reiterated by the European Council, in particular since the Lisbon summit of March 2000, affects the credibility of the EU's entire growth strategy (Micossi and Gros 2006). Again, the mounting awareness that an ever widening and deepening integration process has proved impotent to arrest the decline of Europe's economy relative to its major competitors (see chapter 3) contributed to the dissatisfaction that found dramatic expression in the French and Dutch rejections of the draft Constitutional Treaty in mid-2005, and in the Irish No to the Lisbon Treaty in June 2008.

Now, the factor neofunctionalists had not anticipated – the limited effectiveness of the supranational institutions – can have serious normative consequences. As explained below, effectiveness is important to systemic stability because it gives a new polity the time necessary for loyalty and legitimacy to develop. A traditional political system can survive, at least for a while, even if it performs less than optimally; but a serious crisis is likely to ensue if a new polity appears to be unable to deliver the results that had been promised. If prolonged effectiveness – which today means primarily satisfactory economic growth – may give legitimacy to a new polity, a breakdown of effectiveness for a long period of time will endanger even a legitimate system's stability (Lipset 1963: 64–70). The fatal mistake of the neofunctionalists was to assume, without empirical evidence or theoretical reasons, that the advantages of supranational institutions relative to their domestic counterparts – their central position, superior information, capacity to act as 'honest broker', and, not least, their assumed policy expertise – were such as to guarantee their effectiveness, and thereby a progressive transfer of loyalties and political demands from the national to the supranational level. They did not realize that the strategy they were trying to theorize – Jean Monnet's idea of pursuing political integration 'by stealth', i.e. under the guise of economic integration – was bound to lead to systemic ineffectiveness, with all the consequences mentioned above. The reasons why integration by stealth is bound to produce unsatisfactory results will be discussed in later chapters (see in particular chapters 3 and 4), and a concrete example is provided below. At this point it suffices to remind the reader of a principle well known to economists, namely that the attempt to pursue several objectives using the same policy instrument generally produces suboptimal outcomes.

A number of other idiosyncratic characteristics of decision-making in the EU can be shown to follow from the elitist nature of the integration process – in particular, from the absence of public debate about European issues, and of a sufficiently developed sense of public accountability. I have in mind such features as the pervasive phenomenon of goal displacement, leading to the confusion of means and ends, of process and outcome; the habit of making commitments without calculating either the risks these commitments entail or the resources necessary to make them credible; a political culture of total optimism, often bordering on self-delusion and always preventing the preparation of contingency plans for the event of failure; further, and a direct consequence of total optimism, a style of policy-making that pays little attention to actual results, and refuses to draw lessons from past mistakes. These (and related) elements of EU policy-making will be discussed at some length in later chapters, but for the sake of concreteness let me briefly give here an example displaying many of the above-mentioned features. This is the conservation part of the Common Fisheries Policy (CFP), a case rather unimportant economically, but methodologically instructive.

The regime for conserving and managing the biological resources of the sea forms the cornerstone of the CFP, a European policy established in 1970 on the basis of three principles: free access for member states' vessels, common market organization, and structural aid to poorer member states. In 1983 a regulation setting a common regime for fisheries resources was adopted. Over its more than twenty-year history this regime has largely failed in its conservation aim, despite its seeming institutional advantages over other, actually more successful, international fisheries regimes. The reason is that the underlying principles of the CFP have more to do with promoting the cause of European integration than with the effective management of a seriously depleted resource (Symes and Crean 1995). Under the CFP, all EU fishermen can fish in the offshore waters of any member state, so that the international-commons problem (which the UN Law of the Sea attempted to solve with the introduction of the 200-mile Exclusive Economic Zone) was perpetuated. In turn, the perception that equal access causes overfishing has led to the loss of the CFP's legitimacy, especially among British and Irish fishermen. These fishermen are inclined to see the CFP as a policy aimed at redistribution across member states rather than conservation of marine resources, and fear that their compliance with quotas will simply result in their European competitors catching the fish. For similar reasons, Iceland has been reluctant to apply for full membership of the EU; and in 1973 Norway decided not to join the European Community following a negative referendum where fisheries played an important role. The situation would be different if the EU had the means to monitor implementation of its rules and quotas. Although the Commission's Directorate General responsible for fisheries (DG FISH) has had its own corps of inspectors since 1983, EU regulations do not allow them to carry out autonomous controls – they can only accompany national authorities in their land and sea investigations. At the same time, European law, as interpreted by the European Court of Justice, makes it impossible for the British authorities, say, to prevent overfishing in British waters: from the point of view of conservation, a no-win situation.

The conclusion is that the conservation objective of the CFP, as in the case of the declared objectives of most other EU policies, is largely epiphenomenal – the by-product of actions undertaken to advance the integration process, expand Community competences, promote 'social cohesion', and facilitate intergovernmental bargaining. In June 2006 the EU fisheries ministers adopted a new industry aid package worth almost €4 billion over the following six years. The decision fuelled accusations from environmental groups that the EU had joined Japan in dragging its heels on a World Trade Organization pact to outlaw subsidies encouraging overfishing. Environmentalists also complained that the EU had backtracked on its pledge to tackle overcapacity under pressure from Poland and the Baltic states – which joined the EU in 2004 – for more money to renew their aging fleets. Once more, the attempt to use the same policy to pursue several objectives simultaneously has led to suboptimal results.

This example also provides an illustration of the unwillingness of EU leaders to learn from experience. In spite of the well-documented failure of the common policy for the conservation of the marine biological resources, the framers of the now defunct Constitutional Treaty included this part of the CFP among the few exclusive competences of the EU. Under present conditions, the goal of conservation would be better served not by maintaining an exclusive European competence in this area, but rather by renationalizing the policy (Majone 2005: 111–14).

Policy failure is of course a well-known phenomenon at the national level too, but there voters can express their dissatisfaction by changing the governing majority at election time. European Parliament elections are not about the actual outcomes of EU policies, however, and no clearly identifiable policy-maker is accountable for results. Except on the rare occasions where people are afforded the opportunity to vent their dissatisfaction in a referendum, direct democratic controls are largely missing at EU level. Hence, suboptimal policies can survive, unscrutinized and unchallenged, for decades – as in the case just discussed.

Integration versus Democracy

The EU's 'democratic deficit' is the main consequence of the elitist nature of the integration process; more precisely, of the failure to convert a majority, or at least a significant minority, of Europeans to the cause of political integration. The reason is fairly straightforward: in the absence of popular support for the political unification of the continent, the founding fathers of communitarian Europe, and all integrationist leaders after them, were faced with a fundamental trade-off between democracy and integration – which they consistently resolved in favour of integration. Pascal Lamy's characterization of the Monnet approach, reported in the preceding section, gives a good idea of the atmosphere prevailing not only in Brussels, but also in most national capitals. The prime example of how the integration/democracy dilemma was resolved is provided by the so-called Community Method, which is discussed in chapter 6. From a normative point of view, the paramount feature of this method is the monopoly of agenda-setting enjoyed by the non-elected European Commission: where the method applies – roughly, in all matters related to market integration – only the Commission can make legislative and policy proposals. The Commission also proposes the legal basis for the measure under discussion, which basis determines the required majority in the Council.

This monopoly of legislative and policy initiative granted to a non-elected body represents a violation of fundamental democratic principles that is unique in modern constitutional history, and fairly rare even in ancient history. The model is not Athens but Sparta, where the popular assembly voted Yes or No to the proposals advanced by the Council of Elders, but had no right to propose measures on its own account. If we consider non-democratic polities in modern Europe, then there is the illustrious precedent of the French Constitution of 1799, under which

Napoleon, as First Consul, enjoyed a monopoly of legislative initiative. On the other hand, even the Constitution of the German empire of 1871 granted no right (let alone a monopoly) of legislative initiative to the executive headed by Bismarck; only the two legislative branches, Bundesrat and Reichstag, could initiate legislation, at least formally.

It is of course true that in contemporary parliamentary systems most legislative proposals are introduced to parliament by the executive as draft legislation. Once legislators receive such proposals, however, they are free to change or reject them. This is not the case under the Community Method, where as a rule the member states represented in the Council of Ministers may modify Commission proposals only under the stringent requirement of unanimity. In parliamentary systems, moreover, the executive cannot pre-empt the right of initiative of parliamentary parties and of individual members of the legislature. For example, during the eighth session of the legislature of the German Federal Republic (1976–80), the federal government introduced 322 bills, 52 bills were initiated by the federal states through the Bundesrat, but the Parliament (Bundestag) still managed to introduce 111 bills (Pilz and Ortwein 1995). In a separation-of-powers system like the United States, on the other hand, not only do legislators have the final word over the form and content of bills but, further, only they may introduce bills. In the course of a typical congressional term, members of Congress will introduce several hundred bills on behalf of the president or of executive-branch agencies. During the same period they will introduce on their own behalf as many as fifteen or twenty thousand bills (McCubbins and Noble 1995).

In addition to violating a basic principle of parliamentary democracy, the Community Method also violates the constitutional principle of separation of powers. Besides playing a key role in the legislative and policy process of the Union by virtue of its monopoly of agenda-setting, the non-elected Commission exercises considerable executive powers in the implementation of Council decisions, and quasi-judicial functions when it acts in its capacity as guardian of the treaties. That the framers of the 1957 Treaty of Rome, all good democrats, were willing to infringe basic democratic and constitutional norms for the sake of European integration is something requiring more attention than it usually receives in the scholarly literature. For the founders, the Commission's monopoly of legislative and policy initiative was a means of credibly committing the member states to the process of European integration (Majone 2005). If the Council had also been granted an autonomous power of legislative initiative, then the integration process could be arrested, and perhaps reversed, in response to changing national preferences, or for short-run political gains at the domestic level. Without the Commission's monopoly of agenda-setting the whole idea of an *acquis communautaire* – the ever expanding body of rules and regulations mandated by the Community law – becomes meaningless. Yet, such functional justifications underline the importance of limiting, rather than extending, the range of application of the Community Method. In particular, it is hard to see why the Commission's monopoly should be maintained in areas where the expertise of the Brussels bureaucracy has not been satisfactorily established, for instance in the area of Justice and Home Affairs (JHA). If the aim is to find the best possible solutions to problems of common interest, then what is needed is a competition, not a monopoly, of policy ideas. In the long run, the priority given to implicit integration aims over explicit policy objectives – a priority made possible by the unique position of the Commission in the institutional architecture of the EU – is bound to further undermine the legitimacy of the European project.

Some years ago a sympathetic American observer wrote: 'It is unimaginable that Americans would grant such political power as the Commission staff enjoys to a career bureaucracy. Not surprisingly, the people of Europe increasingly expect democratic accountability by Community political and bureaucratic leaders' (Rosenthal 1990: 303). These words were written a few years after the Single European Act (SEA) greatly extended the Community's competences. It is indeed significant that the issue of the democratic deficit was hardly ever raised before the SEA. The delegation of important policy-making powers to a non-elected body could be normatively justified as long as the Community's powers remained limited. Also at the national level, after all, certain technical tasks are delegated to non-elected bodies ('non-majoritarian institutions') such as independent central banks and regulatory authorities. As is shown in chapter 6, delegation of powers to non-majoritarian institutions may be reconciled with the theory and practice of representative democracy as long as the objectives of such institutions are clearly and narrowly defined, and policy discretion is strictly disciplined by means of efficient ex ante and ex post controls. Now, most EU policies are regulatory in nature, and in this respect the Commission may be considered a sort of super-agency (Majone 1996). However, it has been assigned a variety of other executive, legislative, and quasi-judicial tasks. Moreover, the institution has become increasingly politicized over the years – albeit in the sense of bureaucratic, rather than democratic, politics. In modern democracies the main aims of the political struggle are the control of political power and the formulation and implementation of public policy. In the EU there is no central power to conquer in a competition among political parties, while Union policies are not decided upon by a majority government, but by political exchange among the three law-making institutions – Council of Ministers, European Parliament, and Commission. In such a context, the language of democratic politics – government and opposition, party competition, accountability to the voters – is largely unintelligible.

The multiplicity of functions and objectives assigned to the Commission expands the scope of this institution's discretionary choices, complicating the task of evaluating the overall quality of its performance. The collegial nature of the Commission compounds the difficulty: in spite of the power of dismissal introduced by the 1997 Treaty of Amsterdam, the European Parliament is understandably reluctant to dismiss the entire college in order to sanction a single commissioner. Since the Commission performs a large number of different tasks, it is extremely costly to dismiss it even when there is intense dissatisfaction with how it carries out one particular task. Thus the real normative issue is not so much the delegation of certain functions to a non-elected body like the Commission, as the scope and open-ended nature of the delegation. Surprisingly, the limitation and more precise definition of the powers transferred to the European level are seldom, if ever, mentioned among the possible solutions to the EU's legitimacy problem. An extensive body of academic literature on the democratic deficit has produced a number of possible remedies – greater transparency, more participation, better communication, a deeper 'social dimension', and especially, more powers for the European Parliament – which so far have failed to improve the situation. Thus, for example, the steady increase of the powers of the EP turns out to be perfectly correlated with the *decrease* of voters' turnout in EP elections: from 63.0 per cent in 1979 to 61.0 in 1984, 58.5 in 1989, 56.8 in 1994, 49.4 in 1999, and 45.7 in 2004. In Germany, the largest member of the Union, and traditionally considered to be a strongly pro-integration country, the turnout in European elections declined from 65.7 per cent in 1979 to 43.0 in 2004; while in the member states from Central and Eastern Europe, which in 2004 took part in European elections for the first time, the turnout varied between 28.3 per cent in the Czech Republic and in Slovenia, and 17.0 per cent in Slovakia. These decreasing participation rates in European elections in spite of (or because of?) the continuous growth of EP powers suggest, at the very least, that the popular view of 'creeping competences' continues to play a role in the steady loss of legitimacy of the Union (see the following section).

Before discussing the normative implications of the continuous expansion of the competences of the Union, and of its geographical boundaries as well, let us briefly note that the priority given to integration over democracy is not an exclusive feature of the early stages of the integration process. Monetary Union, endorsed by the 1992 TEU (Maastricht Treaty) provides another striking example of the same ranking of the two values. In deciding to grant quasi-constitutional status to the independence of the European Central Bank, the framers of the TEU accepted a democratic and constitutional monstrosity – a central bank operating in a political vacuum – for the sake of 'deepening' the integration process, indeed, of making it irreversible (see chapter 6). Possibly even more revealing of the priority assigned to integration is the fact that the EP has never disputed the legitimacy of the Commission's monopoly of legislative initiative. The reluctance of this body to claim the birthright of a true parliament – the power to initiate legislation – proves that half a century after ratification of the Rome Treaty, and in spite of all official declarations about the democratic nature of the EU, the European institutions still consider integration a higher value than democracy.

The willingness of Euro-elites to sacrifice policy effectiveness and even democracy on the altar of integration naturally raises the question whether the expected benefits of an ever expanding Union are so certain and so significant as to justify the sacrifice of other important values. As will be seen in later chapters, this is the doubt behind the feeling of alienation from the EU's work felt by a growing number of Europeans. Also the end of the permissive consensus hints at a more sober assessment of benefits once taken for granted. Though seldom openly debated, the question of the benefits and costs of integration is hardly new. It was raised and answered in the past when the voters of some countries decided that European integration was not worth the sacrifice of what they considered more fundamental values. While many countries, many of them poor and newly democratized, line up to join the Union, it is easy to forget that the citizens of a few European states, affluent and with impeccable democratic credentials, have stubbornly refused to do the same. Both Swiss and Norwegian voters refused to follow the indications of their political and economic elites and decided by popular referendums to stay out of the EC and its successor, the EU: Norwegians in 1972 and again in 1994; the Swiss in 1992, when they rejected membership of the European Economic Area (EEA) which would have combined European Free Trade Association (EFTA) countries and EU member states. Iceland too has always been reluctant to apply for full membership of the EU. A variety of economic, political, and cultural factors explain these choices, but in both the Norwegian and the Swiss cases, and possibly in the Icelandic one as well, the overriding consideration appears to have been the fear that the limitations on sovereignty entailed by EU integration would mean a sacrifice, not only of certain commercial advantages and of policy flexibility, but also of basic political and cultural values. With growing socioeconomic and geopolitical heterogeneity, it seems likely that the calculus of the benefits and costs of integration will become a political issue even in some of the older member states of the Union. At the same time, the increasing recourse to opt-outs from treaty obligations, in order to avoid popular referendums, points in the direction of selective exit; see the following section and chapter 8.

From Permissive Consensus to the Revolt of the Masses

The elitist nature of the European integration movement was strikingly revealed by the results of the referendums by which in early summer 2005 the French and Dutch voters rejected the Constitutional Treaty drafted by a convention supposedly representing all segments of civil society, but in fact dominated by integrationist groups (Norman 2003). The negative outcome of the Dutch referendum was particularly shocking because the Dutch traditionally had a reputation for being strong supporters of European integration. As this public consultation made clear, such a reputation was more in the nature of a convenient assumption made by integrationist elites than a realistic assessment of the popularity of the European cause. True, the creation of the European Economic Community was inspired by a 1955 memorandum prepared by the Dutch foreign minister Beyen; the Dutch multinational company Philips played an important part in the Single Market project; and it is also true that the draft Treaty on European Union submitted in 1991 by the Dutch government – but rejected by all the other member states except Belgium – had strong federalist features. 'Nonetheless', writes political scientist Jan Klabbers, 'Dutch enthusiasm for Europe has been the result of a pragmatic assessment of national interests rather than an unmitigated commitment to federalism. Indeed, the federal route is quickly dismissed when it may conflict with Dutch interests' (1998: 355).

The Germans also used to enjoy a solid reputation as eager supporters of European integration; but even in Germany – where for historical and geopolitical reasons support for European integration has indeed been stronger than in most other countries – popular consensus never went beyond passive acceptance of the agreements reached in Brussels by the national government. This was the essence of the notion of 'permissive consensus' already mentioned in the introduction: consensus in the sense that the political elites agreed that European integration should be furthered; and it was permissive in the sense that high levels of trust in the national authorities implied that there was almost always during the early years deference to their commitments (Mair 2007). From the present viewpoint the most important consequence of this condition, as long as it lasted, was the excision of politics from the integration project. Unfortunately for the integrationist elites, it did not last very long. By the mid-1970s perceptive analysts could already detect the first signs of the crumbling of permissive consensus, and of some Euro-fatigue (Hrbek 1981). An indicator of the changing mood of the public was the growing opposition to the traditional role of Germany as 'pay-master of Europe'. Thus, if in 1973 77 per cent of West Germans expressed their willingness to help a member state of the Community in serious economic difficulties, five years later the percentage had dropped by fourteen points, to 63 per cent. Another telling indicator was the decrease in the number of those who supported an expansion of Community powers.

The economic problems and anxieties that characterized the 1970s and beyond – inflation, recession, energy shortages, international monetary confusion – partially explain the declining public support for European integration, in Germany and elsewhere. Then, as today, when confronted by serious international crises, people tended to look to their national government, not to supranational institutions, for effective problem-solving and a sense of collective security. The growing alienation of the people, if not from the European project then from the methods followed so far for its realization, can be explained by the apparently unstoppable extension of Union powers, as argued in the preceding section. During the 1960s the integration process moved, so to speak, underground, being visible only to small groups of experts and politicians, and to particular interest groups; but since the SEA, the impact on people's interests in decisions taken at the European level has become increasingly obvious. This awareness reached its peak with monetary union and the continuous expansion of the EU's borders (see chapter 4).

Since no Europeanization of the masses has taken place in any member state, popular referendums on European issues always represent a potential hazard for the integration process. In June 1992 50.7 per cent of Danish voters rejected the Treaty on European Union, proving that 'after more than twenty years of membership that brought Denmark uncounted billions of ecus in economic benefits, the nation's elites and ordinary citizens were almost as divided on the question of European integration as they had been in 1972' – when Denmark held its first European referendum to decide whether or not to join the European Community (Rasmussen and Hoekkerup 1998: 135–6). The Nice Treaty was rejected by Irish voters in a referendum held in June 2001. In both cases, however, the ratification process in the other member states continued, while in Denmark and Ireland it sufficed to make a few concessions, and again to ask the questions in a somewhat different form, for consent to eventually be elicited. The fact that no easy way to elicit consent could be found after the French and Dutch voters rejected the draft Constitutional Treaty shows how much the general situation has deteriorated in recent years. Never before had the gulf separating elite and popular opinion appeared as large as in these two founding members of communitarian Europe. The major political parties – on the left and on the right, in government and in opposition, the vast majority of members of the national parliaments, economic leaders (in the Netherlands also trade union leaders), major newspapers and other media, the European Parliament and Commission – all supported ratification. In the Netherlands two-thirds of members of parliament voted for the Constitution; almost the same proportion of voters rejected it. The negative vote did not come as a surprise, either in France or in the Netherlands, having been predicted by virtually all opinion polls. What *was* surprising in both cases were the high voter participation (compared with all previous European elections) and the size of the negative vote: almost 55 per cent against ratification and 45 per cent in favour in France; 61.5 and 38.1 per cent, respectively, in the Netherlands.

In an extraordinary meeting in Brussels, in early June 2005, the presidents of the Commission, of the European Parliament, and of the EU Council at first tried to minimize what had happened. They insisted that the ratification process continue, so that at the end of 2006, when it was scheduled to be completed, a general reassessment of the situation could be made. As already mentioned, their hopes were dashed by the British decision of 6 June 2005 to postpone indefinitely the referendum originally planned for the first half of 2006. Denmark, the Czech Republic, and

Poland soon followed the British example, reinforcing the impression of many commentators that the Constitutional Treaty – which was supposed to provide the institutional framework for the enlarged Union – was effectively dead. The last popular referendum was held in Luxembourg on 10 July 2005. As was to be expected in a country benefiting enormously, both politically and economically, from EU membership, the Yes did prevail, but the shock came from the 40 per cent who voted against ratification in spite of massive support for the draft Constitution by all political parties, trade unions, and economic interests, and despite the threat made by Prime Minister Juncker that he would resign in the event of a negative outcome. According to informed observers, the draft Constitution would not have passed popular consultations, not only in 'Euro-sceptic' countries like the UK, Denmark, the Czech Republic, and Poland, but even in Germany.

The title of Ortega y Gasset's manifesto – *The Revolt of the Masses* – may be fairly applied to these developments. According to the Spanish philosopher, masses revolt whenever average citizens refuse to follow the lead, or abide by the decisions, of the traditional elites. In the EU context such a refusal means not simply the end of permissive consensus, which had made it possible for the Euro-elites to take the issue of European integration out of the political arena, but also a growing feeling that the EU is unable to deliver a reasonable amount of benefits in terms of efficient solutions to the problems concerning the average citizen (see below). Analysts agree that the causes of the French and Dutch votes on the draft Constitution were socioeconomic rather than political or ideological. Among them: fears of soaring unemployment allegedly caused by the 'big bang' eastern enlargement, and the possible admission of Turkey; concerns about the low rate of economic growth and high rate of unemployment in the euro-zone; strong disappointment about the failure of monetary union to produce the economic growth, greater international competitiveness, and price stability promised by national and European leaders. The common currency was cited by one-third of Dutch voters as one major reason for their No to the European Constitution.

The French and Dutch pronouncements were not the only indications of widespread malaise. Doubts about the stability of the euro-zone were raised with increasing frequency in the international press. In particular there was speculation that Italy – a country with one of the largest public debts in the world – could decide to leave the euro-zone in order to recover the competitiveness of the national economy. National competitiveness was seriously compromised by the appreciation of the euro, which was not balanced by a moderate growth of labour costs: in 2006, labour costs in Italy were 30 per cent higher than in Germany (Cingolani 2006: 21–4).

Such rumours were promptly and officially denied. The reaction of the European Commission was typical: 'it is impossible to divorce from the euro', 'there is no possibility of leaving the monetary union', and similar statements intended to stress the irreversible nature of the integration process, but in fact masking the lack of serious contingency plans (see chapter 3). One thing at least was new: the debate about the wisdom of a politically, rather than economically, driven Economic and Monetary Union – a debate which should have taken place before the final decision to proceed with monetary union – had moved beyond the narrow circle of central bankers and finance ministers to become public. The rhetorical strategy of the European Central Bank changed accordingly: while previously the monetary authority had dismissed doubts about EMU merely by insisting that the euro – like a De Beers diamond – 'is forever', now it started to argue more analytically about the costs of leaving the euro-zone.

The Desertion of the Elites

How did the political elites react to the constitutional debacle of mid-2005, and to the loss of legitimacy of the European project so dramatically demonstrated by the results of the French and Dutch referendums? As we saw, the signs of dissatisfaction, if not outright opposition, had been accumulating for some time before those events. What happened after the constitutional debacle, however, showed the depth of the Union's twofold crisis: of legitimacy and of leadership. According to Ortega y Gasset, the revolt of the masses is typically accompanied by the desertion of the elites, by which term the Spanish philosopher meant the leaders' lack of plans, objectives, and ideals. The confusion reigning in Brussels and in the national capitals after the French and Dutch votes, and the persistent inability to formulate a credible contingency plan are evident manifestations of the crisis of Euro-leadership. As we saw, the presidents of the Commission, of the European Parliament, and of the EU Council met in Brussels, to accomplish nothing more than issuing a joint statement claiming that the Constitutional Treaty was still alive, and vainly urging the other member states to continue with the ratification process. The lack of clear ideas about what to do next was actually emphasized by the Commission president's announcement of a 'Plan D', where 'D' stood for democracy, dialogue, and discussion. In addition, the European summit of 16 and 17 June 2005 proved unable to do anything more than postpone any decision, waiting for the French and Dutch elections in 2007, and in the meantime hope for improvements in the general economic climate. One year later, the European summit of June 2006, under Austrian presidency, again postponed any decision concerning which parts of the Constitutional Treaty, if any, could be salvaged.

In the first half of 2007 the German presidency of the EU succeeded in getting a fragile agreement on how to restart the ratification process. The rather disappointing 'Berlin Declaration' prepared by the German chancellor Angela Merkel on the occasion of the fiftieth anniversary of the Community/Union, reiterated the commitment to create 'a new common foundation' for the EU in time for the 2009 European elections. The document carefully avoided any reference to a European Constitution because of the firm opposition of several countries, especially new members from Central and Eastern Europe such as Poland and the Czech Republic. In the dramatic EU summit of late June 2007, a tentative agreement to move forwards could be achieved only by scaling down the Constitutional Treaty to a 'Reform Treaty', by granting to the UK and Poland opt-outs on an important matter like the Charter of Fundamental Rights, and by satisfying Polish demands concerning voting rules in the Council of Ministers.

Even so, at the time of writing, final ratification of the Reform (Lisbon) Treaty remains quite uncertain, not only because of the Irish No, but also because the conclusion of the process still depends on future judgments by the Czech and German Constitutional Courts, and on the decisions of the Euro-sceptic presidents of Poland and of the Czech Republic. Most member states favour a second Irish referendum, but to stage another popular vote the government in Dublin would need some concessions. In his speech to the European Parliament at the beginning of the French presidency of the EU, President Sarkozy categorically ruled out any further modification of the Lisbon Treaty. According to him, either it is possible to rescue the treaty in its present form, or the EU must continue to function under the current Nice Treaty – in which case, however, any further enlargement of the EU would be impossible: 'No Lisbon, no enlargement'. To add to the confusion, Croatia, which hopes to join the EU in 2011 at the latest, said it had received assurances after the Irish vote that its accession would not be derailed. Thus, it remains to be

seen which concessions may be offered to Ireland, whose foreign minister ended all hopes of a quick resolution of the crisis when he ruled out
that his government would be in a position to offer a solution by the next
EU summit in October 2008. The Lisbon Treaty was due to come into
force on 1 January 2009, but at this time delay seems to be virtually
certain.

Coming back to the aftermath of the French and Dutch rejection of the
draft Constitution, one of the most obvious, and most disturbing, consequences was the return to brutal methods of defence of the national
interest. Of course, national interests always become highly visible in
critical situations. Still, an implicit rule had developed over the years,
according to which the defence of the national interest should not
exclude concessions to the other member states, and at least a formal
acknowledgement of the existence of a higher common interest. De
Gaulle, Chirac, and Mrs Thatcher – leaders who did not feel it necessary
to defend the national interest by appealing to Europe – are the
exceptions that confirm the general rule. As already mentioned, 'con-
structivist' theorists of European integration argue that European rules
and norms shape the behaviour and the very preferences of member
states: 'European integration has a transformative impact on the
European state system and its constituent units. European integration
has changed over the years, and it is reasonable to assume that in the
process agents' identity and subsequently their interests have equally
changed' (Christiansen *et al.* 1999: 529). Alas, no such transformative
impact could be detected at the Brussels summit of 16–17 June 2005,
where the financial framework for the period 2007–13 was to be defined.
On this occasion, the mode of interaction among the national leaders
reached a degree of brutality seldom, if ever, experienced before. Thus in
his advocacy of a narrowly construed national interest, the Dutch prime
minister Jan Balkenende was as immovable as the British, Spanish,
Swedish, and Finnish prime ministers, or the French president. His
country was tired, Balkenende effectively said, of being the main pay-
master of the Union – on a per capita basis, the Netherlands' net
contribution to the EU budget was then €120, against the €106
of Sweden, and Germany's €97. Unless the net contribution of the
Netherlands was sensibly reduced, there would be no long-term financial
framework. This from the leader of a country which had previously been
considered a champion of European integration.

Spain's attitude at the Brussels summit was particularly revealing of
the resurgence of naked national-interest thinking in the wake of the

constitutional debacle. After his unexpected electoral victory in April 2004, Prime Minister Zapatero repeatedly proclaimed his intention of placing Spain 'at the centre of Europe', together with France and Germany. Indeed, by abandoning the rigid position of the preceding Aznar government concerning the distribution of votes in the Council, the Spanish leader made possible the signing of the Constitutional Treaty in Rome, on 29 October 2004. At the Brussels summit of June 2005, however, Zapatero presented himself as the most strenuous defender of a narrowly conceived national interest. To appreciate the extent of this volte-face one should keep in mind that since becoming a member of the European Community in 1986, Spain has profited from a continuous flow of EC/EU funds, amounting to more than €93 billion. It has been calculated that such funds have created about 300,000 jobs year after year. In 2004 per capita income grew by 3 per cent, of which one-third could be attributed to EU transfers. In sum, Spain is the country that has benefited most from European largesse, so that its per capita income is by now above the EU average. Zapatero was well aware of the economic advantages his country derived from EU membership, and in his first visit to Berlin as prime minister he announced Spain's willingness to share with poorer member states the help so generously provided by the Union. But at the Brussels summit, instead of coming up with construc- tive ideas on how to solve the constitutional crisis, he presented a list of rigid conditions for Spain's acceptance of the 2007–13 financial frame- work: payments to Spain from the cohesion funds to go on for five more years at least, and an absolute refusal that Spain become a net contributor to the EU budget before 2014. In the end, the Spanish prime minister sealed the failure of the summit by rejecting the last compro- mise proposed by EU Council president Juncker. The agreement on the 2007–13 financial framework finally reached in December 2005 was made possible only by postponing any serious discussion about the Common Agricultural Policy, and by the decision of Chancellor Angela Merkel to increase her country's contribution to the EU budget – a return to the 'chequebook diplomacy' of Helmut Kohl that had been abandoned because of the parlous state of Germany's public finances.

Legitimacy, Efficiency, and Systemic Stability

It has been argued, correctly, that it is 'too much to expect the EU to meet the same level of legitimacy as its member states; it may not even be necessary for it to do so, provided it delivers a reasonable level of benefits in terms of efficiency' (Shackleton 1998: 134). In a previous section of the present chapter it was pointed out that efficiency is especially important for a polity that is new and still lacks popular support. Shackleton acknowledges the fact that the efficient delivery of benefits is particularly important for a new polity like the EU. Indeed, integrationist elites always hoped that superior economic performance would induce people to transfer their loyalty from the national governments to the European institutions, thus eventually legitimating the integration process. This hope did not seem to be too far-fetched in the foundational period of the European Communities, when Europe experienced an unprecedented period of economic growth and stability. Although these results had little to do with the common market – as will be shown in chapter 3 – the impression was created that the Monnet method could be used to pursue simultaneously two different objectives: more integration for the elites, and greater prosperity for the masses. Unfortunately, after the phase of very rapid catching up with the United States, convergence in the levels of per capita income stopped at the beginning of the 1980s and has remained unchanged since. While the American economy was generating employment as well as maintaining working hours, Europe's employment performance was weak and working hours fell consistently (Sapir *et al.* 2004). Given such disappointing results, it is not surprising that the desire to improve poor economic performance has driven EU policy for more than twenty years: from the Single Market Programme, which was meant to provide a response to perceived 'Euro-sclerosis' in the mid-1980s – a term popular at the time to denote the loss of competitiveness of the EU economy with respect to the US and Japan – to EMU in the 1990s; and, at the beginning of the new century, the Lisbon Strategy, which was supposed to boost growth and employment, and make the EU the most advanced, knowledge-based economy in the world – just when the budgetary restrictions imposed by EMU reduced the resources available for research and development.

Rather than opening a public debate on the reasons why the Union as a whole – in spite of the single market, monetary union, and the continuous expansion of its geographic boundaries – seems to be unable to match the economic performance of its major competitors, EU leaders prefer to repeat slogans which are at best half-truths, as will be shown in chapter 3. 'European integration has delivered 50 years of economic prosperity, stability and peace. It has helped to raise standards of living, built an internal market and strengthened the Union's voice in the world.' These opening lines of the Commission's White Paper on

European Governance (Commission of the European Communities 2001a: 9) were repeated almost verbatim by Chancellor Angela Merkel, as rotating president of the European Council, on the occasion of the fiftieth anniversary celebrations in Berlin of the signing of the Treaty of Rome, in March 2007. Such official rhetoric went unchallenged in the past because of the veil of ignorance covering European policies. While the implications of domestic policies are reasonably understood by the citizens affected by them, until recently most EU policies were too technical, too uncertain in their actual outcomes (because of their dependence on national implementation), too remote from the daily problems of people, to seriously concern public opinion. True, policies such as the CAP, or particular regulatory measures, have been questioned and criticized often enough, but controversies and contestations always remained confined within fairly narrow academic and political circles, or within particular interest groups. EMU and eastern enlargement have changed all of this. Unlike most policy decisions taken in Brussels, the decisions taken by the ECB in Frankfurt are immediately effective and widely advertised, and their consequences, whether on home mortgages, on consumer credit, or on the availability of social services, have a direct impact on the welfare of all inhabitants of the eurozone, in fact of the entire EU. Similarly, the implications, true or presumed, of the Union's enlargement on jobs, wages, social standards, and law and order have become part of the daily concerns of West European citizens.

This awareness of the consequences of European integration is not only a new, but also an ominous development. For half a century Euroelites could present integration as a positive-sum game. Now everybody can see that surrendering monetary sovereignty and losing control of the national borders entail costs as well as benefits. This realization is bound to induce greater popular resistance to future transfers of powers to the European level, and a much stronger demand for accountability by results – precisely what is foreign to the political culture of the EU, as will be discussed in chapters 3 and 7. Future European policies will be evaluated not primarily in terms of their contribution to the integration process – the criterion favoured by the European institutions – as by their actual impact on the welfare of the average citizen. This implies that poor performance will pose more of a threat to the credibility and legitimacy of the EU. Legitimacy involves the capacity of a political system to engender and maintain the belief that its institutions are capable of resolving the major problems facing society. Conversely, Martin Lipset reminds us, a breakdown of effectiveness in the provision of a satisfactory level of law and order, and of economic growth, will eventually endanger even a legitimate polity's stability (1963: 67–8). It is this connection between effectiveness, legitimacy, and systemic stability which makes so worrisome the unsatisfactory economic performance of the last decades, and the growing security problems of a Union without well-defined boundaries. Unless the EU can demonstrate (by deeds, not by words) that it can add value to what individual member states, or subsets of member states, can achieve on their own, it will be impossible to resolve the legitimacy crisis threatening the Union's stability. A long series of in camera agreements among Euro-elites were sufficient to expand European competences well beyond the limits envisaged by the founding fathers; they are not sufficient to provide a normative basis robust enough to support the structure erected in half a century of federalist and cryptofederalist efforts.

2

Federalism Old and New

'Federate or Perish'

Altiero Spinelli is probably the best-known representative of that particular type of apodictic federalism which flowered for some years after
the end of World War II, and which is well expressed by the phrase then
popular among federalists: Europe must federate or perish. For the
Italian Spinelli and his many followers in continental Europe, it was
impossible to rebuild a democratic, prosperous, and powerful Europe
starting with the nation states. Only a strong federation could solve the
great problems of the post-war period: the re-establishment of democratic regimes; the many dramatic economic and social issues facing the
continent; the German question; the security and autonomy of Europe
with respect to both the United States and the Soviet Union. The establishment of a federal super-state, Spinelli argued (cited in Paolini
1988: 12 and *passim*), would have to precede the political and economic
reconstruction of the member states, the former being the necessary
foundation of the latter. In turn, the European federation would open
the way to a world federation. It is of some interest that the majority of
the thirty or so federalist movements existing at the time in Europe
also claimed to be working towards a world federation. The idea of
an eventual world government was more than an exercise in utopian
thinking; it was needed in order to meet the telling argument that a
purely European federation would simply reproduce, on a larger scale,
the geopolitical ambitions and aggressive tendencies of the traditional
nation states. In any case the majority of the federalist movements then
active in Western Europe viewed the future European federation as a
world power, able to play the role of a third force between the two
superpowers. Some contemporary observers see the continuous expansion of the borders of the present EU, despite the severe problems raised
by large-scale enlargement, as part of the geopolitical legacy of old
federalism (see below).

46

The final resolution of the conference of European federalists held in Paris from 22 to 25 March 1945 – the first such conference to be held legally in liberated Europe – asserted the need for a federal army, since nothing short of a strong federal state would be sufficient to preserve peace, as demonstrated by the failure of the League of Nations. The government of the future federal state was supposed to be responsible not to the governments of the member states, but directly to the peoples of the states of the federation. Indeed, since the construction of a European federal state should precede the reconstruction of the national governments, the federalist ideology would necessarily supersede the ideological divisions of the past. Thus, the struggle for European unity would create a new watershed between left and right, between democracy and reaction. As Spinelli wrote in the *Ventotene Manifesto*, which became a basic document for the post-war federalist movement:

> The dividing line between progressive and reactionary parties no longer coincides with the formal lines of more or less democracy, or the pursuit of more or less socialism, but the division falls along a very new and substantive line: those who conceive the essential purpose and goal of struggle as being the ancient one, the conquest of national political power ... and those who see the main purpose as the creation of a solid international State, [which] will direct popular forces towards this goal, and who, even if they were to win national power, would use it first and foremost as an instrument for achieving international unity.
>
> (cited in Eilstrup-Sangiovanni 2006: 40)

This wing of federalism has been called 'Hamiltonian' because it was based on principles allegedly derived from the Founding Fathers of the United States – including their dislike of 'factions', or political parties, as the above quotation from Spinelli shows. Hamiltonian federalism became particularly influential among the elites of Germany, Italy, and the Netherlands.

Another enduring legacy of old federalism is the idea that European integration is too important to be left to the uncertainty of democratic politics. Commission president Romano Prodi exemplified this attitude when he presented his new team to the European Parliament on 21 July 1999. On that occasion he said: 'This new college ... provides a fair balance between the political complexion of the national governments and the European Parliament, and I welcome this. But let us be clear. The Commission does not function along party lines. This Commission is a college and commissioners are no more extensions of political groups than they are representatives of national governments' (cited in Magnette 2001: 300).

Already by 1946, however, the prediction that the European nation states would all collapse, leaving the people free to design their political future on a clean slate, had been conclusively refuted. The federalists attributed the responsibility for this failure to the interest of the super-powers in preserving the old state structures, except in the case of Germany. The truth is that Spinelli like many other intellectuals, then as now, underestimated both the amazing ability of European states to react to the catastrophes of the twentieth century, and the depth of popular attachment to the nation state. Just as the Napoleonic wars stirred the sense of nationality in all the countries occupied by the French army, so resistance to Nazi occupation – in the Soviet Union as in Poland, in France, Belgium, and the Netherlands as in Denmark, Norway, and Yugoslavia – was popularly perceived as a *national* war of liberation. Even in post-fascist Italy, all political parties – the Communists and Socialists no less than the Christian-democrats and Liberals – appealed to the value of national independence in order to incite armed resistance to the former German allies. In our own days, integrationist Euro-elites again underestimated the strength of popular attachment to the nation state when in their eagerness to expand the geographical boundaries of the Union they overlooked that the former communist countries of Eastern Europe are unwilling to sacrifice any part of their newly recovered national sovereignty for the sake of European integration.

In the years following the war, pride in the enormously successful reconstruction of the national economies of continental Europe could only increase popular attachment to the national institutions. In the same years the British government developed such an extraordinary activism in the social sphere that historians writing some thirty years later considered the foundation of the welfare state Britain's greatest post-war achievement (Sked and Cook 1979). As soon as the work of economic reconstruction was completed, the British model was imitated, more or less closely, by all democratic states of Western Europe. By the mid-1950s, perceptive analysts could already see that throughout the western part of the continent the nation state, far from withering away, was in the process of becoming the omnicompetent welfare state of later decades. Writing in the early 1980s, Walter Laqueur summed up the situation in the following terms: 'Despite the astonishing economic recovery, the interim balance sheet of the movement for European unity drawn in the late fifties was ... bound to be disappointing to the federalists. A large measure of cooperation between the West European governments had been achieved, but the federalists wanted unity, not just collaboration' (1982: 138). The assessment of this historian has to be qualified in one respect, however. The federalists were disappointed not despite, but *because* of the astonishing economic recovery of all democratic countries of Western Europe. The brilliant economic performance of the 1950s and 1960s – before the integration of the national markets of communitarian Europe could make its effects felt – disproved conclusively the federalists' claim that it was impossible to reconstruct a democratic and prosperous Europe starting with the nation states. Far from being a relic of the past, the European nation state proved to be not only highly resilient, but also quite effective. The fact that all the major problems – economic and political reconstruction, even the German question, and the defence of the western part of the continent – were somehow being resolved without any radical constitutional innovation may explain why by the late 1950s, to quote Laqueur again, 'the original impetus of the European idea had run out' (1982: 138). In Germany, for example, enthusiasm for the European idea had already peaked by the first half of the 1950s (Hillgruber 1981). Europe did not federate, but it did not perish either.

The Vision of the Founding Fathers

The federalist persuasion was never more than the belief of fairly small intellectual and political elites. Most political leaders were convinced that even after two catastrophic wars the European nation states remained viable, and that the problem was to adapt the traditional states system to the new situation, in particular by intensifying cooperation among national governments. The founding fathers of communitarian Europe belonged to this second camp. Unlike dogmatic federalists à la Spinelli, they never made the mistake of underestimating the depth of popular attachment to the national institutions. Some of their public statements, especially if taken out of context, might suggest a federalist stance, but it is important to keep in mind that 'federation' is not a technical term, but rather an omnibus label which, as its Latin root suggests, includes various forms of association among states. True European federalists, as we saw, used the term in the strong sense of a supranational sovereign state, independent from and superior to the member states, yet this was not the view of leaders like Konrad Adenauer, Alcide de Gasperi, or even

Robert Schuman. For the German, Adenauer, as for the Italian de Gasperi, a European federation in no way entailed the end of the sovereign nation states – on the contrary, they viewed European integration not as an end in itself, but as a means of rescuing their respective countries from defeat by reinserting them in the European and international states system. What these two leaders had in mind was perhaps something similar to the German Zollverein, the Customs Union established in 1834, that included most of the members of the German Confederation. Especially Adenauer was convinced that only the *national* parliaments could provide democratic legitimacy to the integration process. According to the German chancellor, politicians operating at the supranational level also derive their legitimacy exclusively from the domestic democratic process – something, he warned, they should never forget (Schwarz 1994: 855). Even a 'European saint' like Robert Schuman understood very well that 'our European states are an historical reality; it would be psychologically impossible to do away with them' (cited in Milward 1992: 327). Actually, the French foreign minister and founder of the European Coal and Steel Community (ECSC) thought that the competence of the supranational institutions should not extend to functions involving the sovereignty of the nation state, but be limited to technical problems (Milward 1992: 327).

As mentioned, the German question was one of those burning issues which, according to the federalists, only a fully fledged European federal state could resolve. In fact, a number of factors, having nothing to do with the federalist project, contributed to its settlement – from America's Marshall Plan, one of whose main objectives was the reconstruction of the part of Germany not occupied by the Soviet Union, to the project French leaders conceived as a counterweight to the American initiative: the Schuman Plan for pooling the coal and steel resources of Germany and France. As we know today, the economic results of the ECSC were rather modest (Gillingham 1991). The real significance of the ECSC is to be found in the political and diplomatic sphere, and the results achieved in this respect are due at least as much to Adenauer and the German government as to the French and American governments. For the German chancellor the ECSC was, above everything else, a means for ending the status of Germany as an occupied country. He entertained few illusions about the first European Community, which he considered an instrument of French control over German heavy industry (Schwarz 1994). Nevertheless, he accepted the 1951 Treaty of Paris establishing the ECSC, since its ratification served to eliminate the control of the allied powers over the resources of the Ruhr basin. Hans-Peter Schwarz, Adenauer's authoritative biographer, concludes that the chancellor thought European integration useful primarily as a means of settling the German question and, generally, of protecting the national interests of the participating countries.

The Window of Opportunity Closes

Still, Western Europe never seemed to be so close to being recast into some kind of federation as in the early 1950s – the years of lost opportunities according to those federalists who correctly sensed that the window of opportunity would remain open only for a short time. Among the factors which might have made possible a transformation of the European Communities into a politically integrated entity were the Soviet threat – true or imagined – and the existence of the 'Iron Curtain', which for the first time since the collapse of the Roman *limes* gave a precisely defined and stable boundary to the European heartland. Beyond the Iron Curtain, communitarian Europe formed an island of democracy, with borders as sharply drawn as the Atlantic and Pacific coasts of the United States. Such a well-defined territory could have favoured the development of a true European identity and, in time, even of something like a European nationality. Shared history and a common territory are generally thought to be the essential preconditions for the formation of a sense of nationality (Tilly 1975). But, Jean-Marie Guéhenno has pointed out, one of the unanticipated consequences of the collapse of the Soviet empire has been the discovery that Europe can no longer become a nation, even a federal one. For this would require a definite boundary to the east, hence the permanent exclusion from the EU of the Russia of Tolstoy and Dostoevsky (Guéhenno 1993: 76–7). The current debate about the accession of Turkey shows once more the difficulty of reaching agreement about the finality of the integration process.

The early federalists could not have foreseen these late developments, but their complaints about lost opportunities become understandable when one compares the project of a European Political Community (EPC) worked out in 1953 by an ad hoc Assembly of the Coal and Steel Community, with all subsequent federally inspired projects, including the draft treaty produced by the EP in 1984 (see below). The EPC was meant to provide a common institutional framework for both the ECSC and the European Defence Community (EDC). It would have had extensive competences in defence and foreign policy, as well as in economic and social policy, its own armed forces, and own resources provided by direct taxation of the citizens of the Community. In the EPC the supranational parliament – rather than the national governments meeting in the Council, as in the present EU – would be the ultimate decision-maker. However, these developments towards a federal Europe were stopped in their tracks when the French National Assembly rejected the proposal to ratify the EDC Treaty – a rejection received with a sigh of relief not only in Paris, but also in Bonn and Rome, not to mention London.

The failure of the EDC and the abortion of the Political Community suggested the need for a radical change in the federalist strategy. Leaders of the movement like Altiero Spinelli concluded that it was necessary to abandon the approach that had been followed ever since it was realized that the nation states were not going to wither away; namely to advance the federalist cause by relying on cooperation with the national governments, on the one hand, and on persuasion of the economic and intellectual elites, on the other. What was needed, instead, was a mobilization of the peoples, which federalists thought could be achieved by means of a popularly elected constituent assembly with the task of drafting a new European Constitution. The draft Constitution would be approved, not by parliamentary ratification but by popular referendums to be held in all the member states. Spinelli having been elected to the European Parliament in 1979, on 9 July 1981 the EP passed by a very large majority a resolution – proposed by the Italian federalist leader and a group of similarly minded members of the EP organized in the 'Crocodile Club' – establishing a commission to formulate the necessary institutional reforms. The final draft, although it proposed a significant expansion of Union powers, was much less ambitious than the EPC project: the politically most sensitive issues were left for further consideration by the Union's institutions. In spite of this cautious attitude, the project was rejected by the national governments, which traditionally preferred to proceed by piecemeal treaty amendment rather than by bold constitution-drafting. Indeed, after the ill-fated experiment with a Constitutional Treaty resulting in the negative French and Dutch referendums in 2005, the traditional, piecemeal approach to treaty amendment has been resumed. Alas, even this scaling down of integrationist ambitions has not prevented the Irish rejection of the Lisbon Treaty in June 2008.

One by one all the predictions so confidently made by the first generation of post-war federalists were refuted by history, their apodictic certainties shattered by the stubborn refusal of the nation states to wither away, and of the peoples to support federalist goals. Yet it would be neither fair to deride these failures with the benefit of hindsight, nor perhaps worthwhile to recall them here, were it not for the fact that a number of attitudes and beliefs of old federalism have helped to shape the political culture of the EC/EU. This legacy manifests itself in a variety of more or less conscious reactions to developments which seem to threaten the unidirectional and irreversible nature of the integration process, as will be seen in the following pages and chapters.

Manifest Destiny?

For the early federalists the United States of Europe were just around the corner. Today nobody shares their optimism, but a number of intellectuals and a few political leaders are still convinced that the EU is undergoing a steady process of federalization. The idea that the final stage of the integration process can only be a fully fledged federal state is of course not new, nor is it distinctly European. Among the first to advocate the idea that the establishment of a federal union was the top priority of (Western) Europe after the war were American policy-makers such as George Kennan, Dean Acheson, William Clayton, and George Ball. It was natural enough for Americans to repeat with reference to Europe Thomas Paine's cry to his adoptive countrymen 170 years earlier: 'Now is the seed-time of Continental Union' (cited in Rostow 1982: 79). Also Winston Churchill, in his famous Zurich speech of 19 September 1946, said: 'we must build a kind of United States of Europe … The process is simple: all that is needed is the resolve of hundreds of millions of men and women to do right instead of wrong and to gain as their reward blessing instead of cursing' (cited in Rostow 1982: 150–51). However, Sir Winston's enthusiasm for cutting national sovereignty down to size did not extend to Britain and its empire: 'we are with Europe but not of it' he had written in a 1930 article in the *Saturday Evening Post* endorsing European unity (cited in Barnett 1983: 98).

On the continent the idea of a federal destiny for Europe was particularly attractive to the elites of the countries that had lost the war, and academic commentators saw this federal destiny already inscribed in the founding treaties. In the 1960s some German legal scholars claimed that the institutions of the European Communities had been designed with the idea of replicating the model of the Federal Republic of Germany. The Council of Ministers, the organ for the participation of the member states in the decisions of the Communities, was said to correspond to the

German Bundesrat; the European Commission, the body responsible for implementing the Council's decisions, and would-be kernel of the future government of a united Europe, was the analogue of the federal executive; finally the European Court of Justice was simply the Constitutional Court of the future European federation. In an early, highly original presentation of European law, Hans Peter Ipsen warned about the risk of taking these analogies too seriously. In a purely structural or organizational perspective, Ipsen wrote, one may compare the institutions of the European Communities with certain institutions of the German federal state: if such comparisons are not very useful, neither are they dangerous. What *is* methodologically wrong is the tendency to derive from such analogies conclusions about the federal, or pre-federal, nature of the Communities – to argue that the founding treaties contain an inherent, automatic tendency towards a federal outcome of the integration process (Ipsen 1972: 190–91).

The notion of a federalist end-state prefigured by the European institutions is still alive today, although the belief in an ongoing process of federalization derives its intuitive appeal less from structural similarities with existing federations than from recent developments like the steady extension of the powers of the European Parliament, the equally steady expansion of the geographical boundaries of the EU, and monetary union. We shall come back to these developments in later chapters, where it will be shown that actual outcomes tend to diverge widely from federalist expectations. Monetary union, for instance, has not turned out to be the decisive move in the direction of a politically unified Europe some of its advocates had envisaged. Although 'One Market, One Law, One Money' was among the slogans coined by the Commission in the 1990s, one of the unexpected consequences of monetary union has been the splitting of the EU into two, and in the future possibly three, camps: the current members of the euro-zone; the 'opt-outs' (United Kingdom, Denmark, and Sweden); and possible 'dropouts' – countries with a large public debt and unable to reduce it sufficiently (see chapter 4). Again, the centralization of monetary policy has so far failed to bring about a closer coordination of the economic and fiscal policies of the members of the euro-zone, let alone agreement on international monetary governance and the external role of the common currency.

Furthermore, large-scale eastern enlargement, with the consequent dramatic increase in socioeconomic heterogeneity within the Union, has created serious problems for the Single Market project, especially in the services sector (refer again to chapter 4). The issue to be examined here is whether the enlargement process – which in slightly more than a decade has almost doubled the membership of the EU, and is still ongoing – is compatible with the alleged federalization process of the EU. Practically everybody agrees that after the collapse of the Soviet Union, Western Europe had a moral obligation to assist the former satellite states of Eastern Europe. There is much less agreement about the best method to provide the needed assistance. A good argument could be, and has been, made that financial and technical assistance on an adequate scale would have been more helpful than the sort of second-class membership that was eventually granted. The gap between the expectations of the Central and East European countries (CEEC) and the EU's offers became clear soon after the beginning of accession negotiations. Deep dissatisfaction on the CEEC's part led to two periods of deadlock in the negotiations with the Commission, culminating in the refusal of the Polish government in July 1991 to send a high-level delegation. A consensus about the big bang enlargement was only reached in November 2002, with Bulgaria and Romania due to become members a few years later. The accession negotiations were structured through bilateral Accession Partnerships setting timetables for alignment in various areas of EU laws and regulations (the so-called *acquis communautaire*), closely monitored by the Commission. This approach left little scope for the candidates to set their own pace and priorities, and caused considerable criticism about the language of 'partnership' being a euphemism for the imposition of EU priorities. As was foreseeable, negotiations on the Common Agricultural Policy and the structural funds were most controversial. The final agreement deeply disappointed the CEEC negotiators. Transfers from the structural funds would be much lower than for the older members of the EU (EU-15), and direct payments from the CAP to CEEC farmers would be initially limited to a measure of 25 per cent, to rise to 100 per cent after a ten-year transition period – by which time, incidentally, the CAP might be largely renationalized. The CEECs also had to accept transition periods of up to seven years for their workers to enjoy full freedom of movement in the single European market (Sedelmeier 2005: 421–4). The explanation for the unwillingness to provide more substantial help is simple: the major recipients of the EU's largesse refused to surrender their benefits in favour of the new, much poorer, members, while the net contributors to the EU budget opposed any increase of the financial resources available to the Union, as we saw in chapter 1.

The selfishness of the older member states suggests that the sense of moral obligation towards the unfortunate CEECs cannot have been very strong, and hence cannot be the sole, or even the main, explanation of eastern enlargement. A more likely explanation is that the eastward and southward expansion of the boundaries of the EU was seen by some Euro-leaders as part of a strategy to 'create a superpower on the European continent that stands equal to the United States' (in the words of Commission president Romano Prodi, cited in Brenner 2002: 22). This geopolitical dimension of enlargement has been strongly criticized by Heinrich August Winkler. The distinguished Berlin historian sees the continuous geographical expansion of the EU as an expression of 'European Bonapartism' (the title of his article in the *Frankfurter Allgemeine Sonntagszeitung*, Winkler 2005: 15). In this article he was extremely critical of Germany's European policy, which consisted in maintaining that there was no contradiction between widening and deepening, in fact that widening would necessarily lead to deepening – an illusory doctrine advanced in 1997 to justify the large-scale enlarge-ment of the Union. What Europe does not need, wrote Winkler, are ahistorical utopias, such as the end of the nation state, the existence of a European nation, and 'the wish of geostrategists like Joschka Fischer, Volker Ruehe and Guenter Verheugen to push the domain of the EU to the borders of Syria, Iraq and Iran, so that Europe may finally become a world power' (Winkler 2005: 15).

Whatever the rationale of the steady expansion of the EU – geopolitical, moral, ideological, economic, or a combination of all these motives – its geographic indeterminacy may remind some readers of the American gospel of Manifest Destiny – the movement of public opinion launched by John L. O'Sullivan in the 1840s. 'Manifest Destiny' meant expansion over an area not precisely defined: over the region from the Mississippi to the Pacific, over the North American continent, or even over the hemi-sphere. This expansion was presented as an opportunity for neighbour-ing peoples to gain admission to the American Union. Any neighbouring people capable of democratic self-government would be permitted to apply for membership: if properly qualified, they would be admitted. Some might have to undergo schooling in the meaning and methods of self-government, and this could take considerable time. But while any forced admission would be unthinkable – actually, a contradiction in terms – the people of the United States had the duty to admit all qualified applicants (Merk 1963: 25–7). Critics raised the possibility that 'expan-sionism would produce an unwieldy Union, a Union likely to collapse of its own weight, as Rome had done, in the process of empire building' (Merk 1963: 47). The preachers of the gospel of Manifest Destiny replied that a view of this sort was unduly pessimistic: by the 1840s the Union had doubled the number of the original states, and it had doubled its strength, too, in the process. In the end, the Atlantic and the Pacific, not the Arctic Ocean and the Isthmus of Darien, became the actual boundaries of the United States – Canada and Mexico never joined the American federation, as some preachers of the gospel had expected.

Despite a few intriguing similarities, there is an important difference between the American and the European versions of Manifest Destiny. For all its vast geographic ambitions the old American doctrine was singularly restrained in relation to the domestic policies and institutional arrangements of the future member states. The advocates of the doctrine presented it in the attractive form of states' rights, implying that the new members would be free to control all their internal affairs – including slavery. Under the US Constitution, as interpreted in light of the philosophy of states' rights, not only did the states preserve all governmental powers not specifically delegated to the Union; but, more crucially, the peoples of the separate states were the final judges of what they considered legitimate use of federal powers. They would possess an ultimate right to leave the Union, that is, to secede, if that were necessary to preserve their freedom. The peoples possessing these rights were both the citizens of the original thirteen states of the American federation and all those who subsequently entered the Union. Important public figures like John Quincy Adams and John C. Calhoun considered states' rights the most appropriate constitutional foundation for purposes of territorial expansion, and this was also the view of the votaries of Manifest Destiny (Merk 1963).

The doctrine of states' rights was considered the most appropriate foundation for purposes of territorial expansion because it could accommodate a great variety of institutional arrangements, different policy priorities, and therefore a high level of socioeconomic diversity among old and new member states. It did not require any prior harmonization of state laws and regulations, nor did it presuppose anything analogous to the EU's notion of an *acquis communautaire* binding all member states to the same body of legal rules and principles. The explicit acknowledgement of the right to secede emphasized the contractual basis of the federal union, and this right, perhaps more than anything else, made 'Manifest Destiny' both plausible and distinct from other expressions of nineteenth-century imperialism. Such flexibility is in striking contrast to the rigidity of the EU enlargement process and, more generally, of the traditional unitary approach to European integration (see chapter 8).

The idea of the irreversibility of the integration process has never been seriously challenged, but a debate about alternative approaches to the final goal started with the Maastricht Treaty on European Union (TEU). In preparation for the Maastricht summit, in September 1991, the Netherlands presidency proposed that both the Common Foreign and Security Policy and Justice and Home Affairs be brought within the sphere of application of the Community Method. As so often in the history of the EC/EU, the attempt to establish an explicit commitment to a federal Europe produced a backlash and sharpened conflicts among the then twelve member states. The proposal of the Dutch presidency was enthusiastically supported by the European Parliament and by the Commission, but was rejected by all the other member states, except Belgium. As a result, the negotiations leading to the TEU were pursued on the basis of the Luxembourg scheme of a Union founded on three separate 'pillars', with the Community Method largely confined to the first (economic) pillar. The perceived loss of unity of the Community legal order, and the likely effect on the *acquis communautaire* of the many opt-outs and derogations contained in the Treaty, attracted much critical comment. One of the severest criticisms was expressed by Deirdre Curtin in an essay entitled 'The Constitutional Structure of the Union: A Europe of Bits and Pieces' (1993). Professor Curtin concluded her analysis with pretty strong words:

> The result of the Maastricht summit is an umbrella Union threatening to lead to constitutional chaos ... at the heart of all this chaos and fragmentation, the unique *sui generis* nature of the European Community, its true world-wide historical significance, is being destroyed. The whole future and credibility of the Communities as a cohesive legal unit which confers rights on *individuals* and which enters into their national legal systems as an integral part of those systems, is at stake.
>
> (1993: 67, emphasis in the original)

The loss of legal unity – a worrisome indication of which was what Curtin called the 'hijacking' of the *acquis communautaire* by the treaty's drafters – was said to be fatal because 'Built into the principle of an "ever closer union among the peoples of Europe" is the notion that *integration should only be one way*' (1993: 67, emphasis added).

Those who, like Professor Curtin, believe that European integration must move along a single path, in a federal direction, were naturally alarmed by the loss of unity symbolized by the pillar structure of the Maastricht Treaty. It is by now obvious, however, that the differentiation and flexibility appearing in several forms in the treaty were no momentary aberration, but the indication of an emergent strategy for achieving progress in politically sensitive areas, even at the price of a loss of the overall coherence of the system (Craig and de Búrca 2003). As will be seen in greater detail in chapter 8, the movement away from a strictly unitary approach to European integration, initiated by the Maastricht Treaty, gathered momentum with the Amsterdam and Nice treaties (concluded in 1997 and 2000, respectively). The aim of greater flexibility was given official recognition and constitutional status by both treaties, which included a separate title on closer, or 'enhanced', cooperation among subgroups of member states. The framers of both treaties were aware that, in an increasingly heterogeneous Union, enhanced cooperation may offer the only hope of avoiding stagnation, while preserving key elements of the traditional framework. And yet opinions about the usefulness of enhanced cooperation vary widely.

An optimistic school of thought tends to focus attention on its presumed potential to regulate diversity in a principled way – in the sense that any uses of this possibility must adhere to the objectives of the Union. A more pessimistic school argues that, far from furthering the objectives of the Union, the various forms of voluntary cooperation among member states will in fact undermine the underlying assumption of the Community Method: that all countries should move together along the same integration path. True, the possibility of enhanced cooperation has never been used so far, presumably because of the strict conditions imposed by the treaties. But if these conditions are relaxed at the same time that national preferences become more varied as a consequence of enlargement, the temptation to form smaller, more homogeneous groupings may well become irresistible. This is because growing heterogeneity in the member states' socioeconomic and geopolitical conditions, hence in policy preferences, makes it increasingly difficult to enact rules that are both uniform and (Pareto-) efficient, i.e. such as to increase the welfare of at least one member state without decreasing that of some other member state. If one accepts this conclusion – to which we return in later chapters – then it follows that the large-scale enlargement of the Union, far from being the manifestation of an ongoing process of federalization, is likely to lead to *confederate* arrangements. That such arrangements are the only ones capable of coping with a great variety of conditions across member states was the important insight of the doctrine of Manifest Destiny.

Neo-Federalism

In spite of the recognized need to introduce more flexibility in the traditional approach to European integration, the idea of a one best way to the distant goal of political union is far from being dead – even the ill-fated Constitutional Treaty courted the favour of neo-federalists by formally abolishing the pillar structure introduced by the Maastricht Treaty. The same idea of a unidirectional integration process also under-lies several proposals made by neo-federalist leaders in the hope of overcoming the crisis of confidence in the European institutions follow-ing the French and Dutch rejections of the Constitutional Treaty. Thus the then French foreign minister Douste-Blazy, cited in an article pub-lished in *Le Monde* of 23 September 2005 (Vernet 2005: 2), argued that the *rélance* of European integration could only take place outside the framework of the present treaties, starting with the group of countries willing to move forwards. No member of the Union would be excluded a priori from the *avant-garde*, but the criteria of admission to this club of 'good Europeans' should be very selective. According to the former head of French diplomacy, his model of a 'small house within the large house' would go beyond the kind of enhanced cooperation envisaged by the treaties. It would include foreign policy, security, research, as well as fiscal, budgetary, and monetary policy. Douste-Blazy stressed the fact that his model differed from 'variable geometry' in that all inhabitants of the 'small house' would take part in all the common policies of the Union, so that the unitary approach would be, to this extent, preserved (cited in Vernet 2005: 2).

The Belgian prime minister Guy Verhofstadt in his *Manifesto for the United States of Europe* also spoke of an *avant-garde* or 'hard core', initially the countries of the euro-zone, which should push ahead in the direction of ever closer, social as well as economic and political, union (cited in Dohmen and Schlamp 2005). Verhofstadt acknowledged that after the latest enlargements the EU is no longer a homogeneous group, therefore those members unwilling or unable to join the hard-core club should form a loose 'Organization of European States'. In a style reminiscent of the apodictic federalism of the 1950s, the Belgian leader claimed that the Constitutional Treaty had been rejected not because it was too ambitious, but rather because it was not ambitious enough (Dohmen and Schlamp 2005). But the hope that a first meeting of the new Euro-group could take place in the first half of 2006 turned out to be too optimistic: the general reception of Verhofstadt's ideas was hardly enthusiastic.

Among neo-federalists the former German foreign minister Joschka Fischer occupies a distinct position. In a lecture given at Berlin's Humboldt University on 22 May 2000 – which stimulated a far-ranging debate, and is held by some to have been the catalyst that led to the calling of the Constitutional Convention two years later – Fischer was one of the first leaders to resurrect a proposal that had been advanced after the first enlargements of the European Community: namely that the member states wishing to deepen their political integration should sign a new treaty – the kernel of a federal constitution – in the hope that this pioneering group could eventually become a magnet capable of attracting the majority, if not the totality, of the other members of the Union. Fischer's analysis and proposals are not simply more detailed, but also more innovative than the projects mentioned above, or similar ideas advanced with increasing frequency since the constitutional debacle in 2005. Unlike many neo-federalists and federalists of the older generation like Spinelli, Fischer realized that the federalist project has a chance of becoming reality only if national institutions are not merely preserved, but in fact become active participants in the integration process; hence, he envisaged a division of sovereignty between the federation and the nation states. Divided sovereignty entails a bicameral federal parliament which would represent both the Europe of the nation states and the Europe of the citizens, thus bringing together the national political elites and the different national publics. In order to avoid potential conflicts, the lower house of the federal parliament would be composed of directly elected representatives who are at the same time members of the national parliaments. The upper house, representing the member states, could be organized either as a directly elected senate (the American model), or as a council whose members are appointed by the member states (the German model). For the federal executive Fischer again suggested two possible models. Either the European government evolves from the present European Council, meaning that the federal government would be constituted by the governments of the member states; or it is derived from the present European Commission, with a directly elected president enjoying wide executive powers.

All this presupposes a constitutional treaty establishing the matters to be regulated at the federal level and those regulated at the national level. The treaty would transfer to the federation the 'core sovereign powers' (including, presumably, the power to tax and spend), and competence over what must necessarily be regulated at European level; all other competences would remain with the member states. At this point

Fischer introduced the most original element of his analysis, which clearly differentiates his position not only from that of other federalists, old and new, but also from the position of those who advocate the generalization of the Community Method as the sole adequate answer to the increasing complexity of European governance. According to Fischer the crisis of the traditional methods of integration is evident. The federalist project could not possibly be realized by continuing to drive forward the integration process by means of policies designed by remote supranational institutions. The method itself, Fisher argued, is one of the problems confronting the Union today, since despite its past successes it has proved unable to achieve the political integration and democratization of the EU. This is the reason, according to the German leader, why member states prefer to operate outside the framework of the Community Method whenever they decide to deepen the integration process, as in the case of monetary union, or of the Schengen Agreement on the abolition of border controls. Following this model, the irrevocable commitment to a federal union should be preceded by a period of enhanced *intergovernmental* cooperation in such policy domains as environmental protection, crime control, immigration and asylum, and, of course, foreign affairs and security (Fischer 2000).

Supranational institutions appear to have no significant role in this pattern of enhanced cooperation, which would be primarily the responsibility of the national governments. At the same time – and this is one of the most attractive features of the proposal – the aim of the various forms of intergovernmental cooperation should be openly political: Euro-leaders should not rely on the Monnet approach of integration by stealth. In spite of its innovative features, however, the approach proposed by Joschka Fischer runs into some of the same difficulties as the traditional methods: there is no guarantee that enhanced cooperation would automatically lead to the final goal of a federal union. Like the cryptofederalist approach discussed in the next chapter, it could lead to the abandonment, in practice, of the ultimate goal. Fischer was aware of these problematic aspects of his proposal, but in the end he could do no more than appeal to an act of political will to produce a new constitution for a federal Europe.

Federalist Teleology

What is the ultimate purpose towards which the process of European integration is directed – its teleology or, in Euro-speak, its finality? For old and new federalists that purpose can only be, naturally enough, the full political integration of the continent. Only a federation, Joschka Fischer argued, can resolve all the problems and contradictions which have been accumulating in the course of half a century of piecemeal, mostly economic, integration. But what could a European federation concretely do, how would it resolve those problems and contradictions? Here the answers suggested by different federalist leaders become vague, sometimes contradictory. True, in his lecture at Humboldt University the former German foreign minister listed several areas of federal competence: environmental protection, crime control, immigration and asylum, and 'of course' foreign and security policy. But as already noted, it is not evident that the approach he advocated would avoid the mistakes of the past. More seriously still, Fischer provided no indications of how a future federation would get the material and normative resources needed to fulfil its basic functions, for example in the area of foreign and security policy. Other federalists are even less specific in their references to a possible federal agenda, perhaps assuming that a fully fledged European federal state would have more or less the same goals and tasks as the contemporary welfare state: a national welfare state writ large. However, the key problem in a supranational polity characterized by deep economic, political, social, and cultural cleavages is precisely how to reach agreement on what collective goods the central government should, and could, provide.

The difficulty of reaching agreement on concrete policy goals explains why federalists have always paid much more attention to issues of procedural and institutional design: ways of setting up a constitutional convention; composition and organization of the branches of the future federal government; relations between the European Parliament and the national parliaments, and between European and national courts; role of the European parties; division of competences; fiscal federalism; and so on. In contrast, one looks in vain for serious discussions of what a European federal state could actually do, and especially of what it could *not* do. Arguably the best illustration of the difficulties to be expected is provided by foreign and security/defence policy. It is of course unthinkable that a European federation, whatever the constitutional arrangements, would not assume full responsibility for what has always been considered the essential function of a state: the protection of its territory, and of the life and interests of the people residing in that territory. Yet a consistent foreign and security/defence policy presupposes a common understanding of what ought to be treated as vital European interests.

According to customary usage, our 'vital' interests are those for which we are ready to fight in order to preserve them. In other words, 'the importance of vital interests comes not necessarily from some intrinsic quality, but rather from what we are ready to do about some infringement of them, real or imagined' (Brodie 1973: 342). As the Yugoslav crises and the Iraq war have abundantly shown, however, the members of the EU are still far from a common understanding of what are the vital interests of the Union, if any. Without such a shared understanding an effective common policy is impossible – which is why the Euro-elites prefer to project the model of the EU as a 'soft' or civilian power (see chapter 7). In this connection, it is revealing that Joschka Fischer did not even attempt to suggest which countries might be prepared to have a truly common foreign policy. To become a magnet capable of attracting other members of the EU, a pioneering group of integrationist states must be able to provide some concrete proof of federalism in action. Unfortunately, the most recent developments – including the inability to reach a common EU position on the diplomatic recognition of secessionist Kosovo, or on the most appropriate response to Russian operations in Georgia – show that no such group of states yet exists.

The harsh truth is that no two member states of the Union – even among the founding members – hold compatible views on key aspects of foreign and defence issues. Just one week after Fischer's Humboldt University speech, for example, both French president Chirac and prime minister Jospin made it clear that they did not share the optimism of the German foreign minister. Directly addressing the German chancellor and his foreign minister in a meeting at Rambouillet Castle, the two French leaders emphasized the need to move by small steps, relying on the traditional integration methods, rather than by bold visions. More fundamentally France and Germany – the two countries that like to think of themselves as the 'motor' of European integration – disagree on such key elements as the appropriate relation between NATO and the EU's security policy. Where they do agree, the reasons of the agreement may be quite different, leading to different policy stances. So France and Germany share the conviction that authorization by the UN Security Council should normally be a precondition for military intervention. However, French insistence on seeking a Security Council mandate aims at imposing a procedural constraint on the 'overriding predominance' of the United States, whereas Germany has a much less instrumental position on the issue of a UN mandate, reflecting a greater faith in the UN potential for collective action on behalf of the international community

(Brenner 2002). Basic differences become even more obvious in the case of France and Britain – the two EU members with the greatest military capabilities. Britain strongly objects to France's view of the European Security and Defence Policy as part of a broader EU attempt to balance the preponderance of the US. The Treaty of Nice explicitly extended the possibility of 'enhanced cooperation' to the second pillar (Common Foreign and Security Policy), while military and defence matters were excluded, reportedly because of pressures during the Intergovernmental Conference coming from the British government. This exclusion was the consequence of deep disagreements concerning the independence of Europe's military capabilities with respect to NATO, with France favouring an independent European military capability, and the UK opposing it.

Aware of the many obstacles on the road to common foreign, security, and defence policies, a number of neo-federalists prefer to emphasize other justifications for a European federal state. They contend that a federal and 'social' Europe represents the only possibility of rescuing the national welfare state threatened by globalization and neo-liberalism. In addition, this vision of a supranational federation dedicated to the defence and propagation of a mythical 'European social model' overlooks the normative and political constraints under which the federation would have to operate – even assuming that in a moment of Euro-enthusiasm a majority of EU citizens express themselves in favour of full political integration. Under the assumption of a sufficiently broad popular support, the new federal entity would certainly be based on democratic principles, so that the democratic-deficit problem of the present EU would be resolved – at least initially. Yet the federation would be unable to provide the variety of public goods that Europeans are accustomed to expecting of their national welfare state, and hence could not retain for long the loyalty of its citizens. Since I discussed this point at some length in a previous publication (Majone 2005: chapters 9 and 10), here it will be sufficient to summarize the argument. A federation of sharply divided polities, lacking a sense of solidarity generated by historical heritage and a sense of national community, would find it extremely difficult to pursue redistributive and other policies with clearly identified winners and losers. Because of the opposition of the losers, such policies can only be enforced by majority rule, but the majority principle presupposes a fairly homogeneous polity, as Arend Lijphart (1984), Robert Dahl (1989), and other distinguished political scientists have shown. Hence, majoritarian policies would have to be largely excluded from the federal agenda as being too divisive. In the end, a modern state, whether unitary or federal, so restricted in its ability to provide the public goods citizens demand, could not attract and retain sufficient popular support to be politically viable.

Arguments about the intrinsic limits of a multinational federation are hardly new, although federalists prefer to ignore them. In a prescient essay originally published in 1939, Friedrich Hayek concluded that

> the central government in a federation composed of many different people will have to be restricted in scope if it is to avoid meeting an increasing resistance on the part of the various groups which it includes ... There seems to be little possible doubt that the scope for the regulation of economic life will be much narrower for the central government of [such] a federation than for national states.
>
> (Hayek 1948: 265)

Hayek was writing before the rise of the welfare state. However, his observation is even more apposite today as it implies that a European federation would be unable to pursue precisely those policies that characterize and legitimate the contemporary nation state: health, education, social policy, industrial policy, income redistribution, and more generally all policies favouring particular socioeconomic groups or jurisdictions at the expense of other identifiable groups or jurisdictions. To repeat, a European super-state unable to provide these and other public goods would lose whatever popular support it may have enjoyed initially. The nation states would remain, for their own citizens, the principal focus of collective loyalty and the real arena of democratic politics. Democratic life would continue to develop at the national level, while the federation, far from correcting the democratic deficit, in the long run would make it worse because of the disappointed expectations of those who had imagined something like a European welfare state (see chapter 5). In turn, this loss of legitimacy would prevent the federal government from acting energetically even in areas, such as foreign policy and defence, where the European national states do need to pool their sovereignty in order to play a more incisive international role.

That a political project like that of a federal Europe does not, at present, enjoy majority support is no compelling reason why it should be abandoned. Only a very crude positivistic philosophy would take prevailing preferences as the last word on the desirability of an outcome (Morgan 2005). A key function of political leadership is to try to influence peoples' preferences through argument and persuasion. European federalists who still believe in the demise of the nation state; advocates of a European welfare state; Euro-nationalists convinced that a Europe 'speaking with one voice' would be a superpower capable of shaping the new world order – these and other supporters of a politically united Europe are entitled to try and persuade as many people as possible of the soundness of their respective projects. Open advocacy of federalism, whatever the ultimate purpose, is intellectually more honest than the cryptofederalist strategy of integration by stealth to be discussed in the following chapter. Since the French and Dutch rejections of the draft Constitutional Treaty and the Irish No to the Lisbon Treaty, however, some federalists are beginning to think that the federal vision ought to be protected against the uncertainties inherent in the operation of the democratic process.

A 'Federalist Deficit'?

Somewhat paradoxically, the growing difficulty of treaty ratification by popular vote has tended to reinforce the elitist nature of the European project, to the point that integrationist elites increasingly perceive public opinion as the main obstacle to the progress of the federalization process. Actually, doubts about the wisdom of consulting public opinion on European matters had been voiced long before the French, Dutch and Irish referendums, for example by former Commission president Romano Prodi. In an interview given to the American journalist Alan Friedman, and published in the *Wall Street Journal* of 30 April 2000, Mr Prodi expressed deep scepticism about the usefulness of holding popular referendums on the European Constitution – especially, he said, at a moment when all opinion surveys indicate growing opposition to the EU. His scepticism was revealed even more forcefully when Prodi rebuked the Commissioner for Enlargement – that same Guenther Verheugen who had once admitted that the euro had been introduced 'behind the backs of the population' – for saying that Germany (Verheugen's own country) should hold a referendum on any future enlargement of the EU. In a similar spirit, some scholars and commentators are now beginning to speak of a 'referendum threat' (Trechsel 2005: 406), and of a 'federalist deficit' (Cohen 2008: 5) – i.e. a slowing down or reversal of the federalization process, caused by popular referendums: not only those on the Constitutional Treaty or the Lisbon Treaty, but also future referendums, for instance on Turkey's accession to the EU. The argument is that in an association of twenty-seven or more member states whose political, socioeconomic, religious, and cultural heterogeneity is probably greater than in any free association of states which ever came together, supposedly to form a new federation, the probability of a negative popular vote is high. The risks of deadlock, the argument continues, are not as high at the level of the EU's summit diplomacy, where Euro-elites are able to deliberate, bargain, trade votes, and coordinate their moves. The real threat to the federalist cause comes from the direct expression of voters' preferences.

In some countries, such as Ireland, referendums are mandatory for amendments to EU treaties; in other cases, it is the national government that takes an autonomous decision to hold a referendum – as has already been announced by both the French and German governments in the case of Turkey's accession to the EU. In either case, the risk that the popular vote may block the federalization process is high. Hence, 'Reducing or even fully overcoming the federalist deficit might ... become of the utmost importance to the future process of European integration' (Trechsel 2005: 410). To reduce this deficit, it is suggested, federalists should be prepared to accept even a worsening of the Union's democratic deficit. The idea of reducing the direct role of the voters in the ratification process is the exact opposite of what earlier federalists had been arguing. It will be recalled (see above) that after the collapse of the plans for a European Political Community, Altiero Spinelli and his followers had concluded that, instead of relying on cooperation with the national governments in the construction of a federal Europe, it was necessary to mobilize the peoples by means of an elected constituent assembly with the task of drafting a European Constitution. The draft Constitution was to be ratified not by the national parliaments, but by referendums in all the member states. Some thirty years later, the gulf separating elite from public opinion has become so wide that neo-federalists are looking for ways of neutralizing the 'referendum threat'. How, in practice? The answer suggested by a superficial analogy with a crucial moment in American history is: by eliminating the requirement that all member states must approve the constitution and its subsequent amendments.

A 'federalist deficit' of this kind was precisely the problem facing American federalists in the summer of 1787, when they were attempting to amend the Articles of Confederation in the direction of a more centralized federation – something which would have required the assent of all the thirteen former colonies, and now sovereign states. Unfortunately, some states opposed ratification of the text prepared by the federalists in the Constitutional Convention. The way to get around this obstacle was found by James Madison. The Preamble to the US Constitution of 1787 opens with the celebrated lines: 'We the People of the United States, in Order to form a more perfect Union ... do ordain and establish this *Constitution* for the United States of America.' At that time the vast majority of the inhabitants of the former British colonies considered themselves, first and foremost, Virginians, Pennsylvanians, New Yorkers, New Englanders, etc. As we saw in chapter 1, James Madison's 'invention' of an American People, distinct from, and superior to, the peoples of the thirteen separate states, was a conceptual innovation with far-reaching political consequences. The direct appeal to the sovereign people of America was meant to discredit the states' pretensions of sovereignty – and their insistence on the unanimity rule for all decisions affecting their sovereignty – but the fact remains that the practical implications of Madison's innovation violated an agreement that had been freely accepted by all the states. In the words of Yale's Bruce Ackerman:

> Modern lawyers are perfectly prepared to admit that the Constitutional Convention was acting illegally in proposing its new document in the name of We the People. The Founding Federalists, after all, were not prepared to follow the ratification procedures set out in the Articles of Confederation that had been solemnly accepted by all thirteen states only a few years before. The Articles required the unanimous consent of all thirteen state legislatures before any new amendment could come into effect. In contrast, the Federalists blandly excluded state legislatures from *any* role in ratification, and went on to assert that the approval of special constitutional conventions meeting in only nine of the thirteen states would suffice to validate the Convention's effort to speak for the People.
>
> (1991: 41, emphasis in the original)

To many of Madison's contemporaries, and also to later political leaders like John Calhoun, the idea of an American People to whom the constituent power belonged, appeared a myth contrived for political purposes. Nevertheless, the myth had some plausibility: a common language; legal systems derived from, and still very much influenced by, English common law; similar political and administrative systems at state level; a fairly homogeneous population, largely of English, Scottish, or Irish stock; above all, a war fought together for eight years against the former colonial power. The thirteen states 'were not forming an altogether unprecedented union, they were perpetuating and perfecting a union which had always existed since the plantation of the British colonies of North America' (Lippmann 1943: 73). None of these conditions is even remotely approached in contemporary Europe, so that the Madisonian remedy for the 'federalist deficit' is simply unavailable to the Euro-elites. The impossibility of applying the strategy of the American federalists to the present European context provides the most intuitive demonstration, *a contrario*, of the practical consequences entailed by the absence of a European demos. The very way in which the citizenship of the Union has been derived from the possession of nationality in one of the member states implicitly denies the existence of a 'European People'. Opinion surveys point to the same conclusion: Eurobarometer data reveal that there is no long-term growth in European identity among citizens of the EU (Commission 2001b). The crucial point, in any case, is that EU treaties are agreements between sovereign states, and sovereignty implies veto power over proposed changes to the agreements. Instead of advocating ratification by stealth, federalists should try to convince the national governments to overturn what has been an established principle since the founding treaties. Until there is more clarity about the final destination, it is useless to complain that in an EU with twenty-seven members unanimity makes further progress impossible.

Until that happens, the EU remains, to speak with Madison (*Federalist 20*, see Padover 1953: 79), a 'government over governments, a legislation for communities'. The democratic legitimacy of such a polity is necessarily limited, implying that the scope of its powers should be correspondingly narrow. True, the national leaders in the European Council are democratically legitimated, and so are the governments represented in the Council of Ministers, while European treaties must be ratified by all the national parliaments, and in some cases by referendum. Hence, the role of the national political executives and parliaments in the institutional architecture of the Union provides some derived legitimacy. According to many students of the EU, further legitimacy is provided by the directly elected European Parliament; though it is doubtful that the normative capital available to the EP itself is sufficient to legitimate the entire integration process. As will be seen in chapter 6, there are several reasons for questioning the legitimating power of the only directly elected European institution; here it suffices to remind the reader of the perfect correlation between the growth of the EP's powers and the steadily decreasing turnout percentages at EP elections since the first direct election in 1979.

The often expressed concerns about the EU's 'democratic deficit' do suggest that a serious legitimacy problem of some kind exists; but the problem could be due less to the absence of a vibrant democratic life at

EU level than to a growing perception that 'Brussels' can do little to help people solve their everyday economic and security problems, as will be argued in later chapters. Instead of economizing the limited legitimacy capital available to the European institutions, the Euro-elites have consistently followed the strategy of first expanding the powers of the Union, and only later trying to find the requisite normative resources. This is a particular application of the strategy of fait accompli so dear to 'European saints' like Jean Monnet and Paul-Henri Spaak, as will be seen in the next chapter. Such an approach is understandable in light of the elitist character of the federalist project, but in the long run it is unsustainable. The problem is that the EU's expanding policy commitments are, to use Walter Lippmann's language, insolvent, being unsupported by sufficient normative and material resources.

3

Cryptofederalism

Federalist Revisionism

After the collapse of the European Defence Community in 1954, and the consequent abortion of the pre-federal EPC, most federalists chose to continue the struggle, so to speak, underground. They pursued political integration under the guise of economic integration – the strategy that came to be known as the Monnet method, or, more descriptively, as the method of integration by stealth. I use the label 'cryptofederalism' to denote a type of federalist revisionism characterized by this roundabout approach to the political integration of Europe. The approach of the revisionists is obviously different from the strategy of the orthodox, or 'Hamiltonian', federalists, who openly worked for a constitution dividing the powers of government between a federal Europe and its member states, with democratic institutions at each level, and with federal powers in all fields of common interest, including foreign affairs, security, and defence.

In the decade following the end of World War II, federalism, although always an elite movement, had been a non-negligible factor in European politics, especially in Germany, Italy, and the Netherlands. Already by the mid-1950s, however, the federalist vision had lost its credibility and whatever popularity it had enjoyed for a few years after the end of World War II. The underlying reason for the loss of credibility and public support has been mentioned in the preceding chapter: all the analyses and predictions inspired by that vision had been refuted by history. The rise of cryptofederalism can only be understood against this background of wishful conjectures and factual refutations. In this respect there are some suggestive analogies between the federalist revisionism of the 1950s and the Marxist revisionism of the 1890s. A crucial factor in the former case was the realization that the nation state was not going to wither away; in the latter, the realization that Marx and Engels's predictions of an impending collapse of capitalism and the inevitability of the socialist revolution were based not on fact, but on wishful thinking. Marxist revisionists 'were not people who abandoned Marxism completely ... but those who sought to modify the traditional doctrine ... or who held that some of its essential features were no longer applicable in the present state of society' (Kolakowski 1978: 98). Similarly, cryptofederalists did not abandon orthodox federalism completely; on the contrary, they could legitimately claim that they were keeping alive its legacy and at least some of its intermediate aims in a hostile political environment. In both cases, however, the abandonment of the original vision had as a practical consequence a loss of interest in 'ultimate goals' and a concentration on means. Eduard Bernstein, the founder of nineteenth-century German revisionism, summed up his attitude in a formula which became famous as the target of orthodox attacks: 'What is generally called the ultimate goal of socialism is nothing to me; the movement is everything' (cited in Gay 1962: 74; Kolakowski 1978: 108).

Also for Paul-Henri Spaak and Jean Monnet, the first and best-known representatives of cryptofederalism, the finality of European integration became increasingly unimportant; what mattered was the movement, the process – especially the creation of European institutions. In June 1955 Monnet had left the High Authority of the ECSC to set up the Action Committee for the United States of Europe, and thus he is often considered to have been an orthodox, rather than a crypto-, federalist. But as Max Kohnstamm, one of his closest associates, later explained, Monnet used the expression 'United States of Europe' more as a tribute to the USA, a country he knew well and loved, than as a definite ideological commitment. In fact, the French leader and 'European saint' used several expressions more or less interchangeably: in addition to United States of Europe, 'European entity', 'union', 'federation', and 'confederation' (Kohnstamm 1989). Richard Mayne, a member of Monnet's personal staff when the latter was president of the High Authority, believed that the French leader favoured new forms of relationship between states rather than a fully fledged European federation (Mayne 1989).

Lack of a serious interest in the teleology of European integration, and fascination with the process of institution-building, were even more pronounced in the case of Spaak (cited in Milward 1992: 324). According to the Belgian statesman, 'everything which tends toward European organizations' was good. In 1949 he commended a proposal for common European postage stamps as having equal value with any other proposal. In the words of Alan Milward: 'Any form of integration, any form of common authority in Western Europe, had become the indispensable guarantee for post-war security, and he [Spaak] became increasingly indifferent to what that authority might be or do' (1992: 324). A striking demonstration of this bias in favour of institution-building, regardless of what a new European institution might actually accomplish, was the establishment of the European Atomic Energy Community – the now almost forgotten though still surviving Euratom, which came into existence simultaneously with the EEC on 1 January 1958. The EEC (Rome) Treaty covered in principle all sectors of the economy, hence there was no compelling reason why nuclear energy, being also an economic sector, required the institution of a separate Community. Nevertheless, the 1955 Spaak report proposed that the two goals of sectorial integration (atomic energy) and general economic integration (the common market) be pursued by separate organizations, with separate treaties. In fact, the motives leading to Euratom were exclusively political. Among these motives was a conviction which Jean Monnet – paraphrasing Lenin's dictum about communism as the conjunction of Soviet power and electricity – expressed in the following terms: 'The United States of Europe means: a federal power linked to the peaceful exploitation of Atomic Energy' (*Les Echos*, special end-of-the-year issue, 1955, cited in Lucas 1977: 11). We saw in the introduction that the French government had initially strongly sponsored Euratom, which seemed to offer an opportunity to share the enormous costs of atomic energy research and development while enjoying most of the benefits. However, when it became clear that the other member states, and especially Germany, disliked the idea of a common nuclear project, France was instrumental in placing Euratom in a permanent state of hibernation (Tsoukalis 1993).

The Monnet Method

The Monnet method of integration by stealth should be distinguished both from the Community Method, which is primarily a set of quasi-constitutional principles derived from the founding treaties, and from neofunctionalism. Monnet was keenly aware of the fact that the integration of only two industrial sectors, like coal and steel, was bound to upset the equilibrium of the rest of the economy. He did hope that the resulting disequilibrium would force the integration of other economic sectors, but even on this point his approach differed from that of neofunctionalists à la Ernst Haas. Unlike Monnet and his followers, the neofunctionalists were interested in 'final goals'; according to them, the integration process must move towards the establishment of a central political authority. This focus on central political institutions is close in spirit to orthodox federalism, as may be seen in Haas's definition: 'Political community ... is a condition in which specific groups and individuals show more loyalty to their central political institutions than to any other political authority' (cited in Eilstrup-Sangiovanni 2006: 107). With this definition, neofunctionalists – again like the federalists of the early postwar years – had effectively assumed away the nation state from the very start (Milward and Sørensen 1994). On the other hand, we know that Monnet had no definite finality in mind, much less a pluralist political community of the type envisaged by Haas. It is also to be excluded that he, the father of the French five-year plan of investment and modernization, was betting on the demise of the nation state. Finally, it seems that Monnet had little confidence in the neofunctionalist explanation of the dynamics of the integration process by means of the notion of 'spillovers', according to which initial steps towards integration trigger, more or less automatically, endogenous economic and political forces providing the impetus for further integration.

In any case, by the 1970s no automatic progression from a common market to economic union, and ultimately to political union, was any longer expected. While economic integration was moving forwards, political integration was blocked, not only by French president de Gaulle but, more fundamentally, by the persistent lack of popular support for the European idea. These developments contributed to the virtual abandonment of neofunctionalism as a unified approach to the study of European integration, but they hardly had any effect on the practitioners of the Monnet method precisely because the latter attached little importance to ultimate goals. The leading idea of the method was simple: to implement, wherever possible, the strategy of the fait accompli – the accomplished fact, which makes opposition or argument useless – especially by promoting institutions for tackling problems experienced by several countries (Marc 1989). Whether such institutions would eventually merge into a central political authority was not a question that particularly concerned either Monnet or his followers. It is true that the open-ended commitment to creating 'ever closer union among the peoples of Europe' has provided an ideological justification for the expansion of Community and Union competences. But as Edward Carr noted long ago: 'The conception of politics as an infinite process seems in the long run uncongenial or incomprehensible to the human mind' (1964: 89). Just as the development of a true European political identity has been made impossible by the absence of well-defined and stable geographical boundaries (see chapter 2), so the absence of a finite political goal has impeded the development of a coherent long-term strategy, facilitating instead the opportunistic tactics of the cryptofederalists.

Because the strategy of the fait accompli makes argument useless, the notion of a critical assessment of results, not to mention public debate, is foreign to the method of integration by stealth. Lacking a systematic evaluation of the effectiveness of the measures undertaken, it is always difficult to determine whether European policies are initiated in order to solve some concrete problem which could not be tackled at the national level, or mainly as a means of institution-building and expansion of supranational competences. People familiar with policy-making in Brussels tend to favour the second hypothesis. Thus N. J. D. Lucas, who analysed Community energy policy from the late 1950s to the mid-1970s, concluded that 'sectorial policies will not be designed simply to produce an optimal technical solution, but to some extent will be designed to promote the influence of the Commission and to forward the aim of European political unity ... technical soundness need not be a high priority in Commission work' (1977: 96–7).

Knowledgeable observers of the Brussels scene, as well as insiders, have paid tribute to the skill of the Commission in using all the ambiguities built into the European treaties in order to advance the integrationist cause by roundabout means, while at the same time expanding its own competences. As one of the first and most influential members of the college of commissioners recalled in the late 1980s: 'The Commission was determined to push ahead with the process of integration, not only in the economic field but also from the institutional and political aspects, and to this end to make use of all weapons and methods provided in the [Rome] Treaty and to employ all the opportunities for further development' (von der Groeben 1987: 31). No European leader, either then or later, appeared to be worried about the long-run implications of an approach which basically consists in trying to achieve several objectives using the same policy instrument.

Goal Displacement

When several objectives are pursued simultaneously it becomes easy to confuse means and ends, process and outcome. Such confusion – which may be quite convenient for those who control the decision agenda – is known to students of formal organizations under the name of *goal displacement*. This organizational distortion was first explored, almost

a century ago, by the German-born Italian political sociologist Robert
Michels. Bureaucratization, according to Michels, entails the danger that
the original objectives of the organization are lost sight of as the result of
preoccupation with institutional problems (Michels 1962). It will be
recalled that this was precisely the problem of socialist revisionism in
the late nineteenth century – and of the cryptofederalist approach to
European integration today. Michels observed that the radical programmes of socialist parties and trade unions in imperial Germany
became increasingly modified and conservative, once bureaucratic hier-
archies were developed. The leaders, interested in preserving and
furthering their organization's power, were willing to abandon radical
objectives in favour of more moderate ones that did not threaten the
organization's survival in a hostile society. Hence the dilemma facing the
leaders of any new movement: they must build a strong organization and
assure its survival in order to achieve the movement's goals, yet preoccupation with institutional problems leads to the surrender of those very
goals, or at least to a reversal of priorities: the means becomes a goal, and
the goal a means.

    Goal displacement has been so important in the practice of crypto-
federalism as to become a key feature of the political culture of the EU.
A good example of the systematic confusion of means and ends has
been mentioned in chapter 1, where we saw that the effective management of a seriously depleted resource is not the sole, or even the main,
objective of the conservation part of the CFP. Rather, the policy is used as
an instrument to pursue a variety of objectives such as the promotion
of the cause of European integration and of income redistribution across
member states – the latter by means of subsidies that actually encourage
overfishing. The tendency to confuse process and outcome is evident
in the practice of measuring success in procedural rather than substantive terms. Thus an agreement to proceed in a certain direction may
be advertised as an achievement of historic significance, though many
important issues might remain unresolved, and ultimate success is still
far from being certain. Agreement on EMU, for example, was celebrated
as a turning point in European integration. However, the Maastricht
Treaty, which introduced monetary union, although extremely detailed
on procedural matters, left a number of fundamental policy questions
unanswered. In order to make political agreement possible, the question
of measures to coordinate economic policies, or to provide compensa-
tory budgetary transfers, was sidestepped. Also issues of external monetary policy, unitary external representation of the monetary union,

exchange-rate policy, and political accountability were left unsettled. Even the basic question, whether it made economic sense to adopt a one-size-fits-all monetary policy for structurally different economies, was never properly discussed. As a result, EMU is a high-risk project with no easy exit option if things go wrong. The chosen strategy simply assumes an irrevocable commitment to the single currency, and accords no place to failure (Tsoukalis 1993).

The so-called Lisbon Strategy for Growth and Jobs, also mentioned in chapter 1, is another instructive example of the primacy of process over outcome. At the summit held in the Portuguese capital in March 2000 the EU Council announced extremely ambitious objectives, including the surpassing of the US economy by 2010. In order to achieve these objectives, it was assumed that the Union would grow at an annual average rate of 3 per cent, so as to create twenty million new jobs – while maintaining a commitment to solidarity and equality, and respect for the environment. Progress was to be evaluated yearly by the Commission with a report presented to the Spring European Council. Unfortunately, Commission data kept showing that, far from closing the gap and then overtaking the US economy, the EU as a whole continued to lag behind in terms of growth rates, employment, and especially productivity. In the report published in January 2003, for instance, the Commission concluded: 'The overall picture that emerges from this review is rather disappointing. The reaction to the slowdown in economic growth is characterized by policy inertia and backtracking' (Commission 2003: 17). The 2010 target had been set by the EU leaders in the heady days of 2000, when the European economy was booming – while its basic structural problems remained unresolved. The experts knew all along that the goal was in fact unfeasible: it would have required an annual growth rate of productivity of about 4 per cent. Instead, in recent years productivity in Europe has been growing at about 0.5 to 1 per cent, while in the US productivity growth has been about 2 per cent per annum. The disappointing results finally convinced EU leaders that it was wiser to drop the target date of 2010, which they did on the occasion of the 2005 Spring European Council. By then businesses and economists were pronouncing the Lisbon economic reform process comatose, if not quite dead. In particular, the three largest economies of the euro-zone – France, Germany, and Italy – had made little attempt to fulfil their Lisbon promises.

The European Union is generally considered unique among international regimes because of its high level of institutionalization. Only strong supranational institutions, the founding fathers thought, could match the power of the nation states. In important respects they were certainly right: without strong institutions such as the Court of Justice, the most important normative achievement of the integration process – the limitation of the discretionary powers of the national governments – would have been impossible. On the other hand, a high level of institutionalization entails a high level of bureaucratization, hence a greater scope for goal displacement. In the next section we examine another manifestation of this organizational pathology.

Perils of Eurocentricity

Eurocentricity – meaning an exclusive focus on the European dimension of issues, even where a broader (or, in some cases, a narrower) perspective would be more appropriate – may be considered a form of goal suboptimality. In its *Communication on the Precautionary Principle*, for instance, the European Commission maintained that, in considering the consequences of alternative strategies in international food-safety regulation, one should take into consideration '*the overall cost to the Community*, both in the long- and short-term' (Commission 2000: 19, emphasis added). Such a narrow conception of the Community interest could perhaps be justified if the cost of measures favoured by the EU authorities was felt by exporters in rich countries alone; but what if the cost is borne by very poor countries? Euro-leaders claim to be deeply committed to assist, financially and otherwise, developing countries, especially African ones; but World Bank economists showed that the precautionary standards proposed by the Commission in 1997 – standards significantly stricter than the international ones – would have a serious impact on some of the poorest African countries. According to these calculations, the EU standards would reduce African exports of cereals, dried fruits, and nuts to the EU by 64 per cent, relative to regulation by international standards. The projected total loss of export revenue for nine African countries amounted to US$400 million under EU standards, compared with a gain of US$670 million if international standards were adopted. The health benefits to EU citizens of the precautionary European standards, it should be added, were shown to be practically nil (Majone 2005: 136–8).

Speaking more generally, the failure of the European Commission to have the Precautionary Principle (PP) – an extremely conservative form of risk regulation – accepted as a 'full fledged and general principle' of international economic law is an excellent demonstration of the limits of

Eurocentricity in a globalizing world (Commission 2000: 3). The EU's commitment to, and application of, the principle has been repeatedly criticized by the World Trade Organization (WTO), by the United States, and by many other developed and developing countries. What international organizations and third countries fear is that something as poorly defined as the PP may be too easily misused for protectionist purposes. The Commission did not choose to advocate the PP internationally because of any demonstrated conceptual or technical superiority of the principle over other criteria of risk regulation – on the contrary the PP violates basic principles of decision-making under uncertainty – but simply in response to political pressures coming from the European Parliament and from the EU Council.

Eurocentricity may be dysfunctional not only for third countries, but for the member states of the EU as well. One of the reasons for the declining influence of the European level on national authorities is precisely the regional focus of many EU policies – a focus that is often irrelevant or counterproductive in an integrating world economy. To exemplify, recent telecommunications directives have been criticized for being insufficiently aware of the global dimensions of the industry, and for representing 'just attempts of the Commission to push Europeanization forward' (Engel 2002: 15). Already the Commission's 1990 Green Paper on *The Development of European Standardization: Action for Faster Technological Integration in Europe* (1990b) had been strongly criticized by some national standardization bodies because of its exclusive focus on EC-mandated standards, neglect of international standardization, and, in the words of the Dutch Interdepartmental Committee for Standardization, 'an almost cavalier disregard of all interests other than the Community's' (cited in Joerges *et al.* 1999: 19). The recurrence of such criticisms is hardly surprising: Eurocentricity and cryptofederalism are two faces of the same coin. As has been pointed out, under the integration-by-stealth approach policies are often initiated less to solve concrete problems in the most effective way than for their contribution to the cause of European integration and to the expansion of the powers of European institutions. Hence a narrow regional focus is an inherent feature of the Monnet method.

What the Brussels authorities forget, however, is that regulation has become an international activity, subject to peer review and scholarly criticism, and open to comparisons with best international practice. National regulators increasingly oppose Eurocentricity precisely for this reason. They are aware that their reputation depends on conceptual innovation and the ability to discover efficient solutions for concrete regulatory problems, rather than on their commitment to political objectives related to European integration. Membership of international networks, such as those operating under the umbrella of the Organisation for Economic Co-operation and Development (OECD), helps national regulators avoid the narrow regional focus which could lead to the isolation of the EU. A regulatory authority that sees itself as a member of an international network of agencies pursuing similar objectives and facing analogous problems is strongly motivated to defend its professional standards and policy commitments against external influences, and to cooperate with the other members of the network. This is because the agency executives have an incentive to maintain their reputation in the eyes of their colleagues. Unprofessional, self-seeking, or politically motivated behaviour would compromise this reputation and make cooperation more difficult to achieve in the future. The importance of the social mechanisms of reputation and trust is one reason why national regulators increasingly organize their voluntary transnational (European and extra-European) networks outside the EU framework.

Cryptofederalist Myths (1): 'Economic Prosperity'

The opening lines of the Commission's White Paper on *European Governance* read: 'European integration has delivered 50 years of economic prosperity, stability and peace. It has helped to raise standards of living, built an internal market and strengthened the Union's voice in the world. It has achieved results which would not have been possible by individual Member States acting on their own' (Commission 2001a: 9). As noted in chapter 1, the same optimistic message is spread by EU leaders on every possible occasion. In the Berlin Declaration issued on 25 March 2007 to celebrate the fiftieth anniversary of the signing of the Treaty of Rome, the German chancellor Angela Merkel repeated that 'European integration has given us peace and prosperity. It has created a sense of community and overcome hostilities' (Merkel 2007). In reality the accomplishments celebrated by the integrationist elites are more in the nature of legitimating myths than achievements of the integration process. This is not to deny that such cryptofederalist myths, like all myths, contain a grain of truth. It is certainly true that since the end of World War II Europe has experienced unprecedented prosperity. The doubts raised by careful observers of the European scene concern not the evidence of economic progress, which gives the myth the necessary plausibility, but the causal influence of the integration process on the economic development of the continent. If that causation cannot be clearly determined – and most accurate quantitative studies indicate that the gains from the common market were very small in relation to the increases in income that the member states enjoyed in the decades since the end of World War II – then it must be admitted that the myth of fifty years of prosperity made possible by European integration rests on the *post hoc, ergo propter hoc* fallacy: inferring a causal connection from a mere sequence in time. Let us review some of the evidence.

Already in the mid-1960s the distinguished economist Gottfried Haberler argued that the elimination of economic controls introduced in Germany during the depression and the war released energies that led to spectacular growth in output and consumer satisfaction, with spill-overs into world trade and finance. He further pointed out that lifting exchange controls, eliminating quotas, and reducing tariffs 'preceded and overlapped the regional reduction of trade barriers and regional integration in the European Common Market ... the quantitative effects on trade of worldwide integration and liberalization have been much greater than those of the ... much advertised regional scheme' (cited in Gillingham 2003: 41). To maintain the contrary, Haberler concluded, was to put the cart before the horse. Another well-known economist, Tibor Scitovsky, illustrated his own calculations of the benefits of the common market remarking that 'the most striking feature of these estimates is their smallness. The one that is really important [is] the gain from increased specialization ... which is less than one-twentieth of one per cent of the gross social product of the countries involved. This is ridiculously small' (cited in Leibenstein 1980: 29–30). Bela Balassa esti-mated that, taking into account economies of scale as well as other sources of gain from the common market, there was a 0.3 per cent rise in the ratio of the annual increment of trade to that of GNP, probably accompanied by a 0.1 per cent increase in the growth rate. Thus, by 1965 the cumulative effect of the common market's establishment on the GNP of the member states would have barely reached one-half of 1 per cent of GNP (Balassa 1967).

Again, economic historian Alan Milward has shown that the geo-graphical pattern of West European trade which became identified with the common market actually began before the creation of the EEC. According to Milward, studies showing that there was a significant increase in trade between the members of the EEC as a result of the tariff changes incorporated in the Treaty of Rome underestimate the remarkable increase in trade between those same countries over the three years before they signed the treaty (Milward 1992: 167–73). In sum, there is agreement that between 1950 and 1970 Europe was the fastest-growing region in the world, Japan excepted. During this period European GNP grew on average by about 5.5 per cent per annum, and industrial production by 7.1 per cent (compared to a world rate of 5.9 per cent), so that by the end of the period output per head in Europe was almost two and a half times greater than in 1950. After reporting these and other equally striking statistics Paul Kennedy noted, however, that 'this growth was shared in all parts of the continent – in northwestern Europe's industrial core, in the Mediterranean lands, in eastern Europe; even the sluggish British economy grew faster during this period than it had for decades' (1987: 421). It follows that the earliest stages of economic integration of the six original members of the EEC (which first reached the stage of a full customs union in 1968) could not have played a relevant causal role in the impressive development of Europe during the first two decades after the end of World War II. Furthermore, the British economist E. J. Mishan, writing in the late 1960s, warned against the pitfall of misinterpreting 'the recent economic expansion in Germany, France and Italy, each of which enjoyed a more rapid economic growth before they formed a customs union than after' (1969: 179).

What is undisputed, at any rate, is that growth has stagnated, or even regressed, since the launch of the two most important economic projects: the Single Market Programme and EMU. After the phase of very rapid catch up with the United States after the war, convergence in the levels of per capita income stopped at the beginning of the 1980s. Since then per capita income in the EU has remained, as noted, at around 70 per cent of the US level. In other words, a common trade policy, the customs union, a supranational competition (antitrust) policy, extensive harmonization of national laws and regulations, the Single Market, and finally a centralized monetary policy, apparently made no difference as far as the economic performance of the EC/EU, relative to its major competitors, was concerned. During the 1990s, growth of EU GDP was disappointing both in absolute terms and with regard to the US: 'Overall growth slowed from the 1980s, which itself had slowed from the 1970s, in spite of the implementation of far-reaching reforms in both the macro-environment (consolidation of public finances and lower inflation, EMU) and micro-environment (Single Market Programme, Uruguay Round and to a certain extent labour market reform)' (Sapir et al. 2004: 25).

The will to improve poor economic performance has driven EU policy over the last thirty years: from the Single Market Programme, meant to be a response to perceived 'Euro-sclerosis' in the mid-1980s, to EMU in the 1990s, and the 'Lisbon Strategy' in the following decade. To remind the reader, at the summit held in the Portuguese capital in March 2000, the European Council announced two extremely ambitious objectives: by 2010 the EU should become the most competitive, knowledge-based economy in the world; in the same period it should grow at an annual average rate of 3 per cent, so as to create twenty million new jobs. In fact, the data show that, far from closing the gap, and then overtaking the US economy, the EU as a whole continues to lag behind in terms of employment and productivity, and in most years also in terms of growth rates. Despite the cyclical upswing in 2006 and 2007, per capita GDP is still about 70 per cent of the American level, while the growth rate of productivity in Europe has continued to decline since the mid-1990s. As already mentioned, in recent years this rate has been about 0.5 to 1 per cent, while US productivity growth has been about 2 per cent per annum. In 2005, in particular, figures produced by the Conference Board (and reported by the *Financial Times* of 18 January 2006) show productivity growth in the fifteen old members of the EU of only 0.5 per cent, compared with 1.8 per cent in the US, and 1.9 per cent in Japan. Annual growth in national output per hour worked in the EU-15 averaged 1.4 per cent between 1995 and 2005, compared with 2.4 per cent in the US. According to some experts, the fact that the productivity gap with the US has persisted for the entire decade 1995–2005, i.e. over a full business cycle, indicates that the erosion of European productivity levels is by now a structural problem – the result of insufficient technological innovation, and of labour markets not competitive enough to force companies to drive productivity higher. Far from being able to catch up with, and then surpass, the American economy, the EU will find it increasingly difficult to keep up its present, unsatisfactory, performance.

It could be objected that the contribution of European integration to aggregate welfare should not be measured exclusively in terms of GDP, productivity, or allocative efficiency. According to some economists, this contribution would have to be assessed instead in terms of the reduction of so-called X-inefficiency. An economic system is X-inefficient when it is not on its theoretical production-possibility frontier because of informational or motivational constraints (Leibenstein 1980). The argument is that regional integration may significantly reduce this type of inefficiency, while the search for static efficiency along the actual frontier is liable to secure modest gains – less than 1 per cent in the case of European economic integration, as indicated above. That regional integration could reduce X-inefficiency by favouring learning, imitation of best practice, and competition among firms and countries is an attractive hypothesis. Unfortunately, it is not supported by the experience of the EC/EU, where centralized, top-down harmonization has been practised much more than inter-jurisdictional competition. As the Canadian economist Albert Breton wrote in his ground-breaking study of competitive governments:

> I believe that the European Union is quite stable but that the stability has been acquired by the virtual suppression of intercountry competition through excessive policy harmonization ... To prevent the occurrence of instability, competition is minimized through the excessive harmonization of a substantial fraction of social, economic, and other policies ... If one compares the degree of harmonization in Europe with that in Canada, the United States, and other federations, one is impressed by the extent to which it is greater in Europe than in the federations.

> (Breton 1996: 275–6)

The principle of mutual recognition – first enunciated by the European Court of Justice in the Cassis de Dijon judgment of 1979 – was indeed supposed to reduce the need for ex ante, bureaucratic harmonization, and to facilitate regulatory competition among the member states. A cornerstone of the Single Market Programme, this principle requires member states to recognize regulations drawn by other EU members as being essentially equivalent to their own, allowing activities that are lawful in one member state to be freely pursued throughout the Union. In this way, a virtuous circle of regulatory competition would be stimulated, which should raise the quality of all regulation, and drive out rules offering protection that consumers do not, in fact, require. The end result would be ex post harmonization, achieved through market processes rather than by administrative measures. However, the high hopes raised by the Cassis de Dijon judgment and by what appeared to be the Commission's enthusiastic endorsement of the Court's doctrine were largely disappointed. For political, ideological, and bureaucratic reasons, ex post, market-driven harmonization was never allowed to seriously challenge the dominant position of the centralized, top-down version. While the Cassis de Dijon doctrine was greeted enthusiastically at a time when the priority was to meet the deadlines of the Single Market ('Europe '92') project, institutional and political interests militate against wholehearted support of mutual recognition and regulatory competition.

The most obvious example of this failure concerns the all-important services sector: as will be seen in the next chapter, the prospect of an integrated European market for services is arguably dimmer today, after the big bang enlargement of the years 2004–7, than it was two decades ago.

In sum, the claim of the Commission's White Book that European integration has delivered fifty years of economic prosperity is largely based on a logical pitfall – the *post hoc, ergo propter hoc* fallacy (Commission 2001a). As we saw in chapter 1, this fallacy remains a favourite rhetorical device of Euro-elites. It will be remembered that at the spring 2007 meeting of the European Council the heads of state and government of all twenty-seven member states proclaimed that the Lisbon Strategy for Growth and Jobs was successful, after all. This success, the EU leaders claimed, was demonstrated by the faster growth and falling unemployment figures that had recently been experienced by the member states. Now, it is common knowledge that after years of stagnation – and an unusually long economic downturn between 2001 and the end of 2003 – in 2006 the European economy started to grow again. A number of factors explain this good performance, including a favourable international environment, the export-led upturn of the German economy after the disappointing results of 2005, and, not least, a trend towards longer working hours without extra pay in the major economies of the euro-zone. According to a number of economists and politicians, the demand for shorter working hours – which had led to the French law on the 35-hour week and to analogous demands in other European countries – was one of the reasons why large parts of the euro-zone have been experiencing sluggish economic performances. As Wolfgang Muenchau of the *Financial Times* pointed out, the trend towards longer working hours demonstrated that the largest companies, in Germany and elsewhere, were now prepared to take matters into their own hands – never mind the 'social dimension of the Lisbon Strategy' to which the heads of state and government of the EU made their ritual genuflection at the Brussels summit of 8 and 9 March 2007 (Muenchau and Atkins 2004: 11).

The question is, again, about the causal role of the Lisbon Strategy in these developments, and specifically in the cyclical upturn of 2006. If the strategy means anything today, it is as an attempt to coordinate, in a flexible, non-binding way, the economic policies of the member states. But policy coordination is precisely what has *not* happened. That governments of the euro-zone do not coordinate their fiscal policies has been candidly admitted by Jean-Pierre Jouyet, the French minister for Europe, in an interview with the German newspaper *Handelsblatt* (Berschens 2007: 6). Since the launch of the Lisbon Strategy, the governments of the major continental economies have each attempted to solve their structural problems in a different way. The economic policies of these countries, and specifically of France and Germany, still diverged widely in 2007, leading to large differences in key economic indicators. In sum, the so-called Lisbon Strategy seems to be irrelevant to economic policy-making in the EU. At best, it is a reminder of the structural problems that reduce the efficiency of the European economy – and of the reluctance of the member states to work out a collective solution to such problems.

Cryptofederalist Myths (2): 'Stability, Peace, and a Stronger Voice in the World'

What about the claim that European integration delivered fifty years of peace and stability, and strengthened the Union's voice in the world? Peace in Europe as the greatest achievement of the integration process is the most common of all commonplaces of Euro-rhetoric, but largely a fiction nevertheless – in fact, another instance of the *post hoc, ergo propter hoc* fallacy. It is certainly true that since the end of World War II Western Europe has enjoyed over half a century of uninterrupted peace. Doubts concern, once more, the causal role of the integration process in the preservation of international peace in the old continent. A moment's reflection suggests that it is hardly believable that after the disastrous results of two world wars in fifty years, West European states had either the resources or the will to again use military means to resolve their conflicts. This is precisely the conclusion Albert Hirschman had reached almost thirty years ago: 'the European Community arrived a bit late in history for its widely proclaimed mission, which was to avert further wars *between* the major Western European nations; even without the Community the time for such wars was past after the two exhausting world wars of the first half of the twentieth century' (1981: 281, emphasis in the original). Several additional pieces of evidence may be quoted in support of Hirschman's contention. What has been said to explain Winston Churchill's defeat at the 1945 elections, namely that he lost because of his reputation as a 'man of war', applies not only to Britain but to all European countries, especially to those which lost the war: winners and losers were all seeking an enduring peace (Sked and Cook 1979). The present strength of the European peace movement proves that the public mood has not changed much in this respect. Aspirations to enduring peace and the 'repudiation of war' expressed in the post-1945 constitutions of countries like Germany and Italy explain the reluctance of the members of the EU to engage in military actions – not only in distant theatres, but even in Europe's backyard. When the Yugoslav crisis broke out in June 1991, Jacques Poos, the Luxembourg foreign minister and president of the European Council for the first six months of that year, declared: 'This is the hour of Europe, not the hour of the Americans' (cited in Gordon and Shapiro 2004: 33; see also W. Wallace 2005: 437). Unfortunately, the EU proved unable to enforce stability and peaceful coexistence among the peoples of the former federation, and had to appeal to the United States for help. The civil war in Bosnia was ended by the intervention of the American superpower, which then mediated and guaranteed the Dayton Agreement of November 1995 between Serbs, Croatians, and Moslems.

The United States' help was again sought in 1999, this time in Kosovo. President Clinton was willing to provide military assistance only on condition that the war be conducted exclusively from the air, on targets selected by the US military – with the well-known disastrous consequences for the population and the civilian infrastructure of Serbia. The Union's ability to determine the modalities of the air-strike campaign was restricted by its relatively small contribution to Operation Allied Force (Brenner 2002: 5). On a number of other occasions the EU – 'one of the most formidable machines for managing differences peacefully ever invented' according to some academic commentators (see chapter 7) – proved incapable of taking at least adequate diplomatic and economic sanctions (Menon *et al.* 2004: 11). Thus, it failed to impose sanctions on Uzbekistan when in May 2005 the armed forces of that country opened fire on peaceful demonstrators in the city of Andijan, killing probably several hundreds. The EU expressed horror at the worst massacre of demonstrators since Tiananmen Square, but in practice it displayed, in the words of the editor of the *Economist* of 27 August 2005, a 'spinelessness worthy of a sea full of jellyfish'. The United States also took no concrete steps in this episode, yet the Americans had a point when they said they were awaiting Europe's lead. As a former member of the Soviet Union Uzbekistan is part of Europe's 'near abroad'. It is a member of the European Bank for Reconstruction and Development, and has a partnership and cooperation agreement with the EU. In short, the political responsibility of the Europeans was a good deal greater than that of the Americans. Still, in this case as before in Bosnia and Kosovo, the Union displayed its inability to ensure peace and respect of basic human rights even in areas of clear European interest.

In the above-mentioned essay, Hirschman advanced the 'ironic conjecture' that although the EC had arrived too late to claim to have averted further wars between European countries, it could nevertheless have as one of its important missions 'the avoidance of civil wars or wars of secession *within* some of the Western European countries, as it provides the newly secession-prone regions with novel channels for voice' (1981: 281, emphasis in the original). It is doubtful, however, that the EU has either the moral or the material resources necessary to intervene in conflicts of this type. Surely its failures in the former Yugoslavia do not justify any optimism in this respect. Apart from such an extreme case, we may observe that being one of the founding members of the European Community, and actually hosting the EU headquarters, has not helped the people of Belgium to bridge the deep division between the Flemish and the Walloons which undermines the foundations of their federation. Several months after the 2007 political elections, disagreements on federalism still prevented the formation of a national government, forcing the king to postpone further consultations indefinitely. The expectation that the Belgian federation will eventually break up seems to be rather widespread especially among Flemish-speaking people. Neither is it the case that Spain's membership of the Union has helped terminate four decades of violence in the Basque region that have claimed more than 800 lives. Northern Ireland seems to have finally found peace, but the EU as such hardly played a role in the peace process. In chapter 7 we will come back to the issue of secessionism in Europe, and the very limited ability of the EU to play a role in settling such conflicts.

The Commission's White Paper on Governance (2001a) also claims that European integration has strengthened the Union's voice in the world, achieving results which would not have been possible for individual member states acting on their own. One can accept this assessment as far as international trade policy is concerned – up to a point, and always keeping in mind that member states do not equally benefit from being forced to share their external-trade powers with others (Meunier 2005). In fact, the behaviour of a single member state can create serious problems for the credibility of the other members of the EU, and for the Union itself. A good example is provided by the French rejection of the Blair House Agreement reached in November 1992 – an EU–US deal and 'peace clause' supported by the large majority of member states. The rejection of the agreement one year later forced the Commission to reopen the negotiations, at the cost of a serious loss of credibility of the European negotiators. Certainly the EU, as the major power, with the US, in international trade, can play a role in the WTO and other international economic forums which no individual European country could match. Even in this area, however, actual results are less impressive than one would assume from the Commission's statement.

It suffices to recall the international problems created by the protectionist measures of the Common Agricultural Policy – e.g. the failure of the Seattle and Cancún Rounds, and the general expectation of failure of the Doha Round. Nor are these the only problems. The EU has been accused of using, besides the CAP, food-safety regulations – in particular those based on the PP – as protectionist devices (see above). As a result, the EU has often clashed with its major trading partners and with the WTO, while its reputation has been seriously damaged among developing countries. An important cause of the international isolation of the EU in trade-related matters is the insistence of the WTO that departures from international standards be justified by scientific studies and formal risk analysis. A well-known example is the Beef Hormones case. In 1997 the United States and Canada filed complaints with the WTO against the European ban of meat products containing growth hormones. According to these two important trade partners, the EU ban violated the WTO's Sanitary and Phytosanitary (SPS) Agreement. The SPS Agreement does allow WTO members to adopt health standards stricter than international standards, provided the stricter standards are supported by risk assessment. In the specific case the risk assessment conducted by the Community's scientific experts had not established any significant health risks connected with the use of growth hormones. Hence the Commission was forced to defend its position with the political argument that a ban on beef containing growth hormones was necessary to restore consumer confidence. In the end the WTO decided against the EC, proving that Eurocentric regulations, such as those based on the PP, can lead to international isolation. As already mentioned, the trading partners of the EU view this principle largely as a protectionist device. From their perspective it must appear odd that the Union is accused by some European intellectuals and neo-federalist leaders of being too 'neo-liberal' (see the following section).

A Neo-Liberal EU?

Arguments about the alleged conservative and 'neo-liberal' character of the present EU have been voiced with increasing frequency since the constitutional debacle of 2005. Such arguments are best understood as attempts to redefine the 'finality' of the integration process along lines which should make it easier to attract popular support. A small but influential body of elite opinion proposes a strong social dimension as the only way to legitimate the integration process. This is the position, for instance, of the Belgian political leader and convinced federalist Guy Verhofstadt, and of members of the European intelligentsia, including a luminary like Juergen Habermas. Like Verhofstadt, the German philosopher interpreted the rejection of the Constitutional Treaty as a rejection of the EU's neo-liberal stance, and the expression of a widespread demand for a more welfare-orientated Union. In an article in the *Sueddeutsche Zeitung* (2005) Habermas wrote that with the achievement of the basic economic freedoms, the common market, monetary union, and the Stability and Growth Pact for the euro-zone, neo-liberals had attained all their objectives. Now, he warned, the time has come to deepen the social dimension of integration, and in particular to soften the impact of monetary union by means of the progressive harmonization of the fiscal, social, and economic policies of the member states. The entire integration process, according to Habermas, is distorted by the neo-liberal philosophy pervading the European treaties: this is the original sin which Social Europe is supposed to redeem.

Even casual acquaintance with the recent history of Europe, however, is sufficient to cast serious doubts on the plausibility of this analysis. In the 1950s, liberalism, as a political and economic doctrine, was at its nadir in Western Europe, with the partial exception of Germany. Central planning, industrial policy, and public ownership as the main mode of economic regulation were advocated by practically all political parties, including most liberal groups. The nationalization of key industries, in particular, was seen as the most effective solution to every sort of problem: not only to eliminate the political power and economic inefficiency of private monopolies, but also to stimulate regional development, redistribute resources in favour of targeted social groups, protect consumers, foster 'industrial democracy', and, not least, ensure national security. These, or very similar, views were held by political leaders of the right and of the left; they were essential ingredients of the contemporary Zeitgeist. Those same years also witnessed the rise of the European welfare state, hence the puzzle: how could the authors of the Treaty of Rome – who at home accepted and practised interventionism and *dirigisme* in all sectors of economy and society – espouse economic liberalism at the European level? A sudden ideological conversion is to be excluded since the same political leaders and their followers continued to support interventionist policies domestically – at least until the 1980s.

The thesis of a general neo-liberal bias of the process of European integration is also contradicted by more recent events. Thus, it is misleading to consider monetary union a 'neo-liberal objective', as Habermas does in the above-mentioned newspaper article – quite the opposite. No other cryptofederalist project has been as politically motivated, and as consistently pursued, by integrationist leaders – from the 1970 Werner Report to the Delors Committee Report of 1989 – as the adoption of a single currency for an economic area characterized by deep structural differences, and in the absence of serious coordination of economic and fiscal policies at national level. The political motivation of EMU has been emphasized by competent observers from the very beginning. A few years after the project was fully implemented, two well-known political economists wrote:

> Uncertainty about the empirical magnitude [of the various benefits and costs of monetary union] suggests the absence of a clear economic case in favour of EMU. Given the risks and uncertainties that pervade the process, there would have to be a clear margin of benefits over costs for economic considerations, narrowly defined, to provide a justification for such a radical departure in policy. The absence of such a margin implies that the momentum for monetary union must therefore derive from other, primarily political, factors.
>
> (Eichengreen and Frieden 1995: 274)

Many other experts have pointed out that the EU is far from being an optimal currency area, in the sense of being able to make easy domestic adjustments to external shocks. Areas within which factors of production can move readily may establish a common currency with a reasonable chance of success because the effects of external shocks will be corrected by shifting resources between industries according to conditions of international demand. In the EU there are no adequate adjustment mechanisms, such as labour flexibility and large budget transfers, to act as effective substitutes for the exchange rates. The EU budget remains very small, with no provisions for a stabilization function, and there is no indication that the member states are willing to expand it. In sum, all the evidence points to the conclusion that, far from having been planned as a neo-liberal ploy to impose discipline on spendthrift welfare states, EMU must be considered a risky cryptofederalist strategy to make the integration process, hopefully, irreversible. Monetary union was also a political deal between some of the larger member states, notably France and

Germany; and a means for other countries, such as Italy, to postpone much-needed structural reforms.

The underlying political rationale of EMU explains why a number of distinguished economic liberals, both economists and policy-makers, in Europe and in the US, have questioned its wisdom. Before the final decision on EMU was taken, the president of the Bundesbank reminded European leaders that 'More than a single currency, the emerging single European market needs converging policies, which are still not in place in all participating countries. The repeated references to alleged huge savings in transaction costs for the countries of a single currency area are not in the least convincing' (Poehl 1990: 36). Given economic realities, Poehl concluded, the willingness of the German government to transfer responsibility for monetary policy to the European level 'can be accounted for only in a broader political perspective, with the long-term objective of creating a political union' (1990: 37).

Shortly after the signing of the Maastricht Treaty, Martin Feldstein, one of America's most distinguished economists and former chairman of the president's Council of Economic Advisers, argued that the EU should abandon its plans for monetary union. In an *Economist* article entitled 'The Case against EMU', he expressed his judgement that a single currency for Europe would be an economic liability. The question, he wrote, is not: 'Are the economic benefits great enough to outweigh the political disadvantages of the federal structure for Europe that would follow the adoption of a single currency?' Rather, the proper question is: 'Would the political advantages of adopting a single currency outweigh the economic disadvantages?' (Feldstein 1992: 19). Contrary to the European Commission's slogan 'One Market, One Money', Feldstein argued that monetary union is not needed to achieve the advantages of a common market. Actually, an artificially contrived monetary union might reduce the volume of trade among the member states, and would almost certainly increase the average level of unemployment over time. His conclusion: 'Those who most fervently advocate monetary union do so ... because they see it as a means to a political union, and a particular type of political union, at that' (1992: 22). Feldstein – an 'enthusiastic supporter' of a single European market for goods and services – adds that he can understand those who are willing to accept the adverse economic effects of monetary union in order to achieve a federalist political union that they favour for non-economic reasons. What he cannot understand 'are those who advocate monetary union but reject any movement towards a federalist political structure for

Europe. That is a formula for economic costs without any of the supposed political benefits' (1992: 22).

In 2006, Kenneth Rogoff, economics professor at Harvard and former
chief economist of the International Monetary Fund, was still warning
about the fragility of EMU. As reported by the German journalist Henrik
Mueller, Rogoff predicted that in the next five to ten years countries with
a large public debt may have to abandon the euro. In addition, Germany
would be better off going back to its own currency: without being tied to
the Mediterranean countries with their traditional financial weaknesses
Germany could have lower interest rates. Rogoff pointed out that the end
of monetary union would not have the dramatic consequences often
assumed, the reason being that the euro was always 'a political project',
while the 'economic logic behind it [was never] too convincing' (Mueller
2006). It is also noteworthy that the UK, the most 'neo-liberal' member of
the EU, has not joined the euro-zone, and gives no indication of wishing
to do so in the foreseeable future. On several occasions, Gordon Brown,
when Chancellor of the Exchequer, warned that monetary union
deprives the members of the euro-zone of the flexibility necessary to
adapt to globalization.

The other supposedly neo-liberal objectives mentioned by Habermas
are hardly more convincing, as such, than monetary union. The Stability
and Growth Pact, meant to impose some fiscal discipline on the members
of the euro-zone, never worked as intended. The reform of the pact in
June 2005 eliminated the elements of automatism in the original agreement and introduced considerable room for intergovernmental margins
of manoeuvre. Increased uncertainty surrounding the determination of
acceptable intermediate budget balances makes it more problematic for
the Council of Ministers of the EU to trigger sanctions against errant
member states. Underlying political motivations are revealed by the fact
that the fiscally virtuous member states defended the original pact, while
most of those states exceeding, or at risk of exceeding, the deficit threshold sought reform.

Further, it is difficult to subscribe to Habermas's view that with the
Treaty of Nice the other major neo-liberal goals – the implementation of
basic economic freedoms and the common market – have been achieved.
In November 2005, after two years of studies, discussions, and consultations, the European Commission decided to withdraw its draft directive
for the liberalization of port services. Initially acclaimed as the most
important liberalization measure in the area of transportation, the draft
proposed to eliminate cargo-handling monopolies by allowing shipping

companies to use their own staff to unload cargo, to set limits to permissible state aid in this sector, and generally to stimulate competition among the ports of the EU. Faced by the opposition of the European Parliament and the trade unions, the Barroso Commission progressively softened many of the draft measures, to the point of making the revised text, in the opinion of some analysts, practically useless. In the end, in one of its worst defeats in recent years, the Commission decided to withdraw the watered-down version of the directive, implicitly admitting that it considered itself too feeble politically to face the combined opposition of the EP and of the port workers, one of Europe's most protected labour forces. Again, the Directive on Services in the Internal Market, at last approved by the European Parliament and the Council in December 2006, has been so weakened, with respect to the original draft of Commissioner Bolkestein, as to be largely irrelevant to the liberalization of labour markets. As a result, the most significant part of the European economy – the services sector, contributing 70 per cent of the GNP and more than 50 per cent of the employment of the EU – is still largely segmented along national lines (see chapter 4). Furthermore the strategically important energy policy is still mostly decided at the national level. This was made clear at the meeting of the Council of Energy Ministers of 14 March 2006, when the national policy-makers flatly rejected the Commission strategy paper on a Community energy policy. Add to all this several recent indications of a resurgent economic nationalism, and it becomes rather hard to believe that the neo-liberals, in Brussels and in the national capitals, have achieved their main objectives in Europe.

What about the more general contention of Habermas and a number of other writers, namely the alleged neo-liberal bias of the European treaties themselves? The truth is that different economic and social philosophies coexist in the founding treaties, and also the subsequent amendments are all characterized by socioeconomic syncretism. The critics fail to see, or prefer to ignore, that those elements of a liberal economic constitution to be found in the treaties have mere instrumental value – they serve integrationist objectives and do not express any ideological commitment. As mentioned above, the founders of communitarian Europe came from countries where public ownership of key industries, national planning, aggregate-demand management, and redistributive policies of various types were considered perfectly legitimate forms of state intervention in the economy. This ideological background is evident in the 1951 Treaty of Paris establishing the European

Coal and Steel Community. Although the declared objective of the treaty was the elimination of trade barriers and the encouragement of 'normal' competition (rather than competition per se) in the coal and steel industries, many provisions were hardly compatible with economic liberalism. The High Authority, the supranational executive of the ECSC, was given extensive powers of intervention, including the right to levy taxes, to influence investment decisions, and in some cases even to impose minimum prices and production quotas. Because of the particular focus of the Coal and Steel Community and of Euratom, the corresponding treaties could largely avoid questions of general economic philosophy. Such questions played a much greater role in the preparatory work for the establishment of the EEC, when it was realized that the integration of highly regulated national markets would have been impossible without a serious effort to deregulate and liberalize the economies of the member states.

Thus, the fact that monopolies and cartels have an inherent tendency to carve up markets was the main motivation for introducing fairly strict competition rules. It would be futile to bring down trade barriers between the member states if the national governments or private industry remained free to use subsidies or cartel-like arrangements to divide up markets and to reserve them for home producers. Even a customs union, let alone a common market, must worry about the effects of cartels and concentrations: as tariff barriers go down, firms might resort to various non-competitive practices in order to offset the effects of the removal of protection. On the other hand, a customs union – which is what the EEC was initially – represents a preferential trade agreement among a subset of countries, and as such it is considered with suspicion by economic liberals, who much prefer the multilateralism (freer trade for all countries) and the most-favoured-nation principle of the General Agreement on Tariffs and Trade (GATT) and WTO charters. For this reason the distinguished German economist Wilhelm Roepke was opposed to the establishment of the EEC. According to the first commissioner responsible for the competition policy of the European Community, 'Roepke was not prepared to acknowledge that the EEC Treaty was based upon the market economy philosophy and that the rules of competition in particular were in accordance with neo-liberal ideas and were now being extended to international trade within the Community' (von der Groeben 1987: 48). Also the father of the German 'economic miracle', the Minister of Economic Affairs, Erhard, was sceptical about preferential trade agreements, favouring a multilateral, rather than a regional, approach to free trade. A number of German academics of the *Ordo*-liberal school took the same position, and also opposed early projects of monetary union, supporting instead the idea, popularized by F. A. Hayek, of competing national currencies.

We may conclude that the influence of neo-liberalism on the European treaties and on European policies is much more limited than the critics claim. To the extent that such an influence can be traced, as in the case of competition rules, the reason is not ideological, but strictly functional: the impossibility of integrating a group of heavily regulated economies without some limitations on the interventionist tendencies of national governments, and on the cartelization tendencies of private and public enterprises. Scholars who, like Fritz Scharpf (1999), believe that competition policy should not be given a higher, quasi-constitutional, status than all other legitimate purposes of public policy do not seem to be aware of this constitutive role of competition policy in market integration. The special role of the rules on competition and state aid is further demonstrated by the fact that, within the EU, such rules take the place of WTO-authorized countervailing duties to compensate for the damage caused by national measures to the industries of other WTO members. The possibility of taking countervailing measures is the reason why multilateral trade integration has proceeded so far without any domestic policy harmonization: members of the WTO enjoy domestic policy autonomy and must respect the exercise of that autonomy by other WTO members (Roessler 1996: 50–51). EU members, on the other hand, have surrendered their policy autonomy in matters relating to intra-EU trade, and this delegation of powers to the supranational level is the true explanation of a strong European competition policy.

Be that as it may, even the Treaty of Rome, though more 'neo-liberal' than the ECSC and Euratom treaties, contains several interventionist features, most striking in the articles dealing with the Common Agricultural Policy. The objectives of the CAP, as defined by the treaty, are complex and in part contradictory, but the European Court of Justice has realistically interpreted them as giving priority to supporting farmers' incomes over increasing agricultural productivity or ensuring reasonable prices for consumers. Thus the Court has recognized the essentially redistributive character of a policy which still absorbs about 40 per cent of all budget expenditures of the EU (down from about 75 per cent in 1980). These redistributive objectives – aimed at building what has been called a 'welfare state for farmers' – are pursued with a variety of interventionist and protectionist means. The operational core of the CAP is the common organization of markets for specific products, based on the instruments of politically determined prices, Community preferences, and financial transfers. To appreciate the importance attached to the CAP by the Treaty of Rome one has to keep in mind that in post-war Europe 'agriculture became the equivalent of a large nationalized industry, managed by interventionist policies which sought to impose macroeconomic objectives in return for exemptions from the forces of open economic competition' (Milward 1992: 229). Short of leaving agriculture outside the scope of the European common market – an option favoured by some countries but categorically refused by France – the only solution was to move from state intervention to supranational intervention. Hence the paradox that to neofunctionalist students of European integration the most inefficient and socially perverse common policy – the top 20 per cent of farmers and agribusiness receive about 80 per cent of CAP support – represented a working model of the federal union of the future: the symbol of the inevitable transfer of governmental responsibility from the national to the European level. Today the CAP remains a crumbling relic of the federalist visions of the past.

The CAP is the most obvious, but certainly not the only, sign of the influence of interventionist philosophies on the Rome Treaty. One can find evident traces of such philosophies even in the 'neo-liberal' core of the treaty. Thus, Article 85 deemed inconsistent with the common market 'all agreements between firms ... and all concerted practices likely to affect practices between Member States'. As an American specialist of antitrust policy, F. M. Scherer, observed, the reference to 'all agreements' has the ring of the per se prohibition embodied in judicial interpretations of America's Sherman (Anti-Trust) Act. However, Scherer continues, Article 85 goes on to permit exceptions for agreements and concerted practices that contribute 'towards improving the production or distribution of goods or promoting technical or economic progress while reserving the users a fair share in the [resulting] profit ... Thus a complex balancing process – what U.S. jurists call a "rule of reason" approach – was instituted' (Scherer 1994: 35). This is a more realistic assessment of the way competition rules are used in the EU than is conveyed by phrases such as 'singleminded maximization of free market competition', or 'zealots of undistorted competition' (Scharpf 1999: 167).

Of course, interventionism became more pronounced in later treaties, which introduced specific Community competences in such areas as industrial policy and regional policy. Walter Hallstein, the first president of the European Commission, is supposed to have once said that 'the Communities are in politics, not in business' (see von der Groeben 1987: 31). Whether or not the dictum is true, it expresses well the cryptofederalist tenet that economics is the handmaid of politics. To cryptofederalists all socioeconomic ideologies – neo-liberalism as well as *dirigisme*, neo-corporatism or regionalism – are acceptable as long as they can be used to advance the integration process, and to expand the competences of the supranational institutions.

4

Unintended Consequences of Cryptofederalism

Purposive Action and Unintended Consequences

Intended and anticipated outcomes of purposive action are always, in the nature of the case, relatively desirable to the actor, though they may seem objectively negative to an outside observer. In any case, they pose few questions to social theory. In contrast, unintended consequences, being unplanned, unexpected results of action orientated towards some goal, become a phenomenon demanding a social-scientific explanation. In fact, this phenomenon has attracted the attention of outstanding political and social thinkers from Machiavelli and Vico to Marx, Pareto, Max Weber, and, more recently, Hayek, and Popper. As Robert Merton (1949) has pointed out, however, the diversity of context and variety of terms by which this phenomenon has been known in the past have tended to obscure its generality. In the eighteenth century Adam Smith and other Scottish thinkers such as David Hume, Adam Ferguson, and Dugald Stewart succeeded in building up a social theory that made unintended, or unforeseen, consequences of purposive human action its central object (Schneider 1967). The theory was used to analyse the existence and functioning of institutions, such as governments, and of social aggregates, such as states or social classes. Adam Smith's 'invisible hand', by which 'man is led to promote an end which was no part of his intention', is the best-known application of the Scottish approach.

The social-scientific relevance of unintended consequences of purposive action has been further demonstrated by such twentieth-century theorists as Friedrich Hayek and Karl Popper. Hayek used the insights of the Scottish philosophers to reject the claim of legal positivism that law is only what a legislator has willed: 'law is never wholly the product of design but is judged and tested within a framework of rules of justice which nobody has invented' (1969: 103). Popper, for his part, has always insisted that the main task of the theoretical social sciences is precisely to trace the unintended, and more especially the unwanted, consequences of purposive action. The development of institutions and social aggregates, he suggests, should be analysed not only in terms of intended consequences, but also (or especially) of the unintended consequences of individual decisions and actions. Such an approach brings the social sciences close to natural science and science-based technology in that both lead to the formulation of operational rules – constraints – stating what cannot be done, in principle or in practice. For Popper, the violation of some constraint is the major cause of unwanted consequences (see especially Popper 1969: 124–5 and 342–3).

The distinguished sociologist Philip Selznick attaches considerable weight to unanticipated consequences in organized action: 'it is a primary function of sociological inquiry to uncover systematically the sources of unanticipated consequence in purposive action … the notion of unanticipated consequence is a key analytical tool: where unintended effects occur, there is a presumption, though no assurance, that sociologically identifiable forces are at work' (Selznick 1966: 254, footnote omitted). A question of great theoretical interest concerns the sources of unintended consequences, i.e. the conditions defining an inherent predisposition for unanticipated consequences to occur. The tendency to disregard cognitive, institutional, or resource constraints, whether out of ignorance or hubris, is certainly a significant reason why apparently rational choices may produce unwanted results.

Thus, the fragmentation of bargaining and policy-making processes, the tendency to make commitments not backed by adequate resources, and a political culture of total optimism which induces European leaders to underestimate, or even ignore, the risks inherent in large-scale projects, are all factors explaining the predisposition for unintended consequences to occur in the EU. The fact that the aim of action limits perception of its ramified consequences is specifically mentioned by Selznick as an important cause of unanticipated consequences. On the one hand, the limitation imposed by the means–end chain is unavoidable since not all consequences are relevant to the end-in-view. On the other hand, the very necessity of concentrating on the aim 'will restrain the actor from taking account of those consequences which indirectly shape the means and ends of policy … [hence] there will always be a minimum residue of unanticipated consequences' (Selznick 1966: 255). This dilemma is particularly acute in the EU, where all important decisions are the collective choice of leaders pursuing different, even conflicting, aims. A related source of unintended consequences has been emphasized in the preceding chapter. This is the habit of pursuing several objectives with the same policy instrument – a procedure that actually defines the modus operandi of cryptofederalism. Trying to achieve several objectives simultaneously – some declared, others more or less hidden – implies not only that outcomes will generally be sub-optimal in terms of the stated objectives, but also that it will be more difficult to perceive the ramified consequences and synergies of the different courses of action.

As Adam Smith's numerous references to the socially beneficial effects of self-interested behaviour suggest, the members of the Scottish school generally contended that something eminently advantageous for society as a whole grows out of individual activities that do not foresee or intend it. Typical of their optimism is Stewart's claim that 'In every society … which, in consequence of the general spirit of the government, enjoys the blessings of tranquillity and liberty, a great part of the political order which we are apt to ascribe to legislative sagacity is the natural result of the selfish pursuits of individuals' (cited in Schneider 1967: 112). Modern scholars like Popper and Selznick, on the other hand, recognize that the unanticipated consequences of human decisions need not be always, or even usually, beneficial; on the contrary history shows that they can be quite negative.

A vivid illustration of the significance of unanticipated consequences in the EU context may be briefly given here (for a fuller discussion see sections on 'Unintended Consequences of Monetary Union' and 'Synergistic Effects' below). Like most EU projects, monetary union was meant to achieve several objectives, not all openly stated. The Commission adver-tised EMU as being necessary for completing the work initiated with the Single Market project. At the 1991 Intergovernmental Conference on EMU, Commission president Delors was particularly insistent on the need to complete the single market with a single currency. Monetary union was also supposed to provide, in the words of former Dutch prime minister Wim Kok, 'the foundation for Europe's increased power in the world' (cited in Zimmermann 2004: 244). We already noted that different member states supported, or at least accepted, monetary union for different domestic reasons, while to integrationist leaders monetary union was, above everything else, the point of no return on the road to the full political integration of Europe. The first and most obvious consequence of EMU, however, has been to split, perhaps permanently, the EU into two, or even three, camps: the members of the euro-zone, the de jure and de facto opt-outs, and possible future dropouts (see chapter 3). In particular the UK – home to the greatest financial centre in Europe – chose to remain outside the euro-zone, and, as previously noted, shows no intention of wanting to adopt the European currency in the foreseeable future.

Furthermore, the optimistic expectations that the single currency would be not only the tangible symbol of political union, but the basis of Europe's increased power in the world, have been largely disappointed: the political cohesion of the EU, always fragile, has never been as wanting as in the years following the introduction of the single currency. Moreover the budgetary restrictions imposed by the EMU Stability Pact are one of the reasons why the member states were unable to develop that capacity for independent military action which, after the sobering experience of the war in Kosovo, everybody had agreed was necessary (see chapter 7). In particular, the creation of the Rapid Reaction Force of up to sixty thousand troops – with the necessary command, control, and intelligence capabilities, logistics, and other combat-support services – supposed to be in place by 2003, had to be postponed to 2010 – and it is seems unlikely that the new deadline will be met. The same budgetary restrictions also forced the governments of the euro-zone to reduce their financial support of R & D, even though a higher rate of technological innovation is one of the main aims of the Lisbon Strategy.

As these examples show, unintended consequences are sufficiently important and visible in the EU that they should have attracted the attention of students of European integration. In fact, EU scholars have hardly paid attention to this phenomenon, let alone to its possible causes. Neofunctionalist scholars are an exception in this respect: not unlike the philosophers of the Scottish school, they assumed that something advantageous for European integration would grow out of the self-interested activities of national leaders who do not foresee or intend any such aim. Because of their assumption of a more or less automatic progress towards political unity, however, neofunctionalists failed to consider the possibility that the choices of some leaders may interact with the choices of other leaders, and of supranational policy entrepreneurs, to produce unwanted, rather than beneficial, results.

The Invisible Hand of Neofunctionalism

Let us examine more closely the role of unintended consequences in neofunctionalist accounts of the dynamics of integration by stealth. According to Haas and his school, member states set the terms of an initial agreement and try to control subsequent events, but they do not

totally determine the direction and extent of change. Rather, supranational policy entrepreneurs like the European Commission, assisted
by various interest groups and by some of the more integrationist
governments, try to exploit the inevitable unintended consequences
that occur when states agree to delegate powers to independent institutions for accomplishing a limited task, and then discover that accomplishing the task has effects upon other of their interdependent activities.
Ernst Haas tried to capture the nature of these dynamics with his concept
of spillover. In his own words, 'neo-functionalists rely on the primacy of
incremental decision-making over grand designs, arguing that most
political actors are incapable of long-range purposive behaviour because
they stumble from one set of decisions into the next as a result of not
having been able to foresee many of the implications and consequences
of the earlier decisions ... A new central authority may emerge as an
unintended consequence of incremental earlier steps'. Hence, integration
is 'the unexpected outcome of initial decisions whose long-term consequences have not been adequately understood by the parties involved'
(Haas 1971: 23).

As we saw in chapter 1, and as is now frankly admitted by members of
the school (e.g. Schmitter 2005), for all their attention to unintended
consequences, neofunctionalists proved unable to anticipate a number of
important developments. In his *The Uniting of Europe*, published in
1958, Haas had stated categorically: 'The progression from a politically
inspired common market to an economic union and finally to a political
union among states is automatic ... The inherent logic of the functional
process in a setting such as Western Europe can push no other way'
(cited in Moravcsik 2005: 353). After the collapse of the plans for a
European Defence Community in the mid-1950s, however, many observers realized that the political integration of the continent, if at all
possible, was far from being an automatic, unidirectional process. As it
turned out Haas and his followers had considerably overestimated
the effectiveness of the supranational institutions relative to the
problem-solving capacity of the national governments. Their mistake
was to assume, without empirical evidence or theoretical reasons, that
the supranational institutions enjoyed a comparative advantage with
respect to their national counterparts. In fact, it was suggested in chapter
1, the advantages of national policy-makers in terms of financial, institutional, cognitive, and, not least, normative resources were, and remain,
overwhelming. This situation explains why in fields as varied as telecommunications, environment, and consumer protection, some national

policies are by now significantly more advanced than the corresponding European policies, which often cannot go beyond least-common-denominator solutions. Even in the area of competition policy, where important powers have been delegated to the European level, the EU no longer sets the pace – today many national regulators are at least as competent as their supranational colleagues.

Confidence in the superiority of the supranational institutions may have been inspired by the belief that the nation state was doomed, at least in Europe. Like the federalists of the immediate post-war period, the first students of European integration greatly underestimated the resilience of the traditional state institutions. Whatever the cause, this belief in the effectiveness of the supranational institutions had serious implications for neofunctionalist theory, since the progressive transfer of loyalties and political demands from the national to the European level was predicted precisely on the basis of the superior problem-solving capacity of the higher level. These implications are of course much more obvious today than they were in the 1950s, or even later. In pre-EMU days, for example, complaints about the disappointing economic performance of the EU could be answered by reminding the critics that Community competences did not include macroeconomic policy-making. Also in policy areas of Community competence it was difficult for ordinary citizens, and sometimes even for the experts, to allocate responsibility for unsatisfactory outcomes as between 'Brussels' and the national governments. The centralization of monetary policy, the constraints on the fiscal autonomy of the national governments imposed by the Stability Pact, and, not least, the 'big bang' enlargement of the Union, have changed popular perceptions dramatically. Nowadays, the decisions taken by the European Central Bank in Frankfurt, unlike most decisions taken in Brussels, are widely reported by the media, and have a direct impact on millions of people since they affect the interest rate of residential mortgages, the conditions of consumer credit, and also (via the budgetary constraints set by the pact) the provision of social services. To many Europeans, the social consequences of enlargement – unemployment, wage competition, and petty and organized crime linked to deregulated immigration – appear to be even more obvious. As a result, the EU is increasingly perceived less as a potential source of solutions than as a cause of some of the problems which most concern the average citizen.

Neofunctionalists failed to anticipate another consequence of the continuous growth of European competences. Because of their belief that all important decisions are made by elites, they underestimated the importance of popular support for the long-term viability of the integration process; they could not conceive that the limited normative resources available to the supranational institutions would one day become a serious constraint on further task expansion. It has already been noted that as long as the tasks delegated to the supranational level were largely confined to negative integration, no more legitimacy was needed than what non-majoritarian institutions, such as independent courts and regulatory authorities, typically enjoy at the national level. However, serious legitimacy problems arose after the Single European Act greatly extended Community powers, and measures of positive integration also began to proliferate in areas remote from market integration.

The third, and methodologically most significant, consequence which neofunctionalists failed to foresee is inherent in the very strategy they were trying to theorize and rationalize. Jean Monnet's idea of pursuing political integration by stealth, i.e. under the guise of economic integration, was bound to produce suboptimal results – both economically and politically. As every competent economist knows, it is a mistake to pursue two or more objectives using the same policy instrument. Precisely this methodological pitfall, however, is the key idea behind the Monnet strategy. When goals are multiple, one of these should be assumed as the objective to be optimized, while the remaining ones are to be treated as constraints, but such clear choices are seldom made by EU policy-makers. In chapter 1 we saw the results of this method of policy-making in the case of the conservation part of the Common Fisheries Policy – one of the few exclusive competences of the Union! The examples could be multiplied. Also, the Sapir Report noticed that 'Quite often in the EU economic system, policy instruments are assigned two objectives at the same time: for example, fostering growth and improving cohesion' (Sapir et al. 2004: 4). Unfortunately, this is not a feature of economic policy-making alone, but a methodological flaw built into the entire EU policy-making machinery. Hence the recommendation of the report to assign one objective to each policy instrument should be extended to all decisions taken at European level: political objectives should be pursued by political means, economic objectives by the economically most effective instrument. The gain to be expected from a direct, rather than roundabout, approach to integration would be not only greater intellectual honesty, but also greater decision-making efficiency (Majone 2005).

Unintended Consequences of Monetary Union

Superficially, monetary union and the near-doubling of the membership of the EU in the space of a few years – the big bang enlargement which created a market of almost half a billion consumers, as a former president of the European Commission liked to boast – may appear to be the crowning achievements of cryptofederalism. Closer analysis discloses that the two projects have so far failed to deliver the promised benefits; and some of their unintended consequences might jeopardize a third 'historic enterprise', the Single Market Programme. This programme was supposed to eliminate all barriers to the free movement of goods, services, capital, and people among the member states. Launched in 1985, it was due to be concluded by the end of 1992 – hence the 'Europe '92' slogan. Almost two decades later, the objectives are far from having been fully attained. In fact, the dramatic expansion of both the services sector and the geographical boundaries of the EU has created conditions that make the goal of a single market seem more remote today than twenty years ago. The interaction between enlargement and the Single Market project will be examined in the following sections. Some of the unwanted consequences of monetary union are the topic of the immediately following pages.

Plans for monetary union were almost contemporary with the establishment of the EEC. One could assume, therefore, that the consequences – both intended and unintended – of such a far-reaching integrationist move would have been reasonably well understood by the time the European Council meeting in Maastricht in December 1991 reached agreement on the completion of EMU and the introduction of the single currency by 1999. As we shall see, such was not the case; rather, monetary union provides striking evidence of the phenomenon discussed in this chapter. As soon as the Treaty of Rome was signed in 1957, Jean Monnet asked one of his closest associates, Pierre Uri, and the Belgian monetary economist Robert Triffin to draft a plan for a European monetary system (Uri 1989). The main focus of the Rome Treaty was of course on creating a common market, but in its text one also finds some recognition of the importance of macroeconomic policies, and of monetary policy in particular. The CAP itself, being based on common prices for agricultural products, by implication made it necessary to pay attention to exchange rates, and indeed the treaty referred to the exchange rates between the currencies of the member states as a matter of Community interest.

A monetary committee consisting of senior officials from the finance ministries was set up as early as 1958; it was followed in 1964 by a committee of governors of the national banks, established to minimize the risk of conflicting monetary policies by the member states, but also to co-opt the central bankers. During the 1960s, however, the usefulness of something like a regional monetary union was not at all obvious since the Bretton Woods system of fixed exchange rates, which was based on the free convertibility of the US dollar, provided the international frame-work. Only when the United States proved unable, or unwilling, to ensure monetary stability, did plans for EMU revive. Monetary stability was still considered important for the smooth functioning of the com-mon market, and especially for the viability of the CAP, but by now everybody understood that beyond the technical objectives there was a much more important political aim: as the French liked to put it, monetary union was 'la voie royale vers l'union politique' (Tsoukalis 1993: 178). For all these reasons, in the 1970s EMU was to replace the customs union as the main goal of the European Community. However, the combination of stagflation, severe energy problems, and monetary disorder that charac-terized the decade ensured the quick death of the first plans for EMU. Still, attention for the issue never disappeared, and in the late 1980s EMU came back with a vengeance on the European agenda, quickly reaching top rank. The European Commission, under Jacques Delors, and the French gov-ernment were the main driving forces behind this comeback.

EMU, it will be recalled, was presented as the necessary complement to the Single Market project. In 1990 the European Commission pub-lished *One Market, One Money* – the study mentioned by Martin Feldstein in his 'The Case against EMU' (1992; see above). The conclu-sion of the study was that the direct benefits – linked to the elimination of the costs of foreign-exchange transactions and of the uncertainty asso-ciated with exchange-rate fluctuations – would be relatively small, but the dynamic gains were expected to be much larger. A single currency, the Commission argued, would enhance the credibility of the internal market programme and the gains associated with its completion: 'one market', 'one legal system', and now 'one money'. The adoption of the euro (at that time still called ECU, European Currency Unit) as a new international currency was supposed to bring seigniorage gains as well, resulting from the willingness of foreigners to hold it. Finally, a common monetary policy vis-à-vis the rest of the world would produce gains in prestige and political power; many proponents of monetary union saw the single currency as a political project to liberate Europe from its dependence on the dollar. This was the idea of a 'European monetary personality', as it was called, and of a currency able to rival the US dollar on world markets. In this sense Dutch prime minister Wim Kok had spoken of EMU as 'the foundation for Europe's increased power in the world' (cited in Zimmerman 2004: 244).

The Maastricht Treaty provided a legal framework for monetary union, but left many basic institutional questions unresolved, especially in the design of the external monetary policy-making machinery. These and all remaining open questions were left to be settled in the future, however; the priority of the Delors Commission was to make the integration process irreversible, and France's, to eliminate the dominating position of the Bundesbank in Europe. Finally, on 1 January 2002 the euro was introduced among enthusiastic predictions of faster economic growth, far-reaching structural reforms by the governments of the eurozone, greater productivity, further intensification of intra-EU trade, and price stability. Today it is generally acknowledged that those forecasts, like so many other ones, were too optimistic. Even a 'good European' like Mario Monti, for eight years Single Market and then Competition Commissioner in Brussels, in an interview published by the Italian financial newspaper *Sole-24 Ore* of 24 November 2005, admitted that monetary union had so far failed to accomplish all the positive results that had been promised. The euro, according to Professor Monti, a respected monetary economist, is a currency in search of a single market – a single market which does not yet exist because of the protectionism still practised by the national governments, and their reluctance to undertake the necessary structural reforms. Note the circularity of these arguments: during the debate on EMU people were told that monetary union was needed to complete the single European market, and also to force the national governments to undertake structural reforms; now people are told that the single currency cannot produce the hoped-for benefits unless a fully fledged single market is established, and the requisite structural reforms are carried out. As already mentioned, among the hoped-for benefits was the intensification of intra-EU trade. Actually, the volume of such trade has been decreasing for the last ten years: the euro has not inverted, but rather accelerated (because of the overvaluation of the single currency) a trend favouring imports from the United States, China, and from other third countries, and diverting trade from within the EU.

Official expectations were particularly unrealistic concerning the international role of the European currency. The dollar remains the global monetary standard and, despite occasional signs to the contrary, the euro's share in international foreign-exchange reserves comes nowhere close to suggesting a displacement of the American currency. Experts like Kenneth Rogoff do not expect the international role of the euro to grow significantly, because of the uncertainty surrounding the future of EMU. This uncertainty is partly due to Europe's failure to actively manage an external monetary policy – an inertia caused not only by structural features of the European economy, but also by gaps and institutional flaws in the governance structure of the euro-zone. Most European central bankers seem to be convinced that a more assertive role for Europe in the international monetary system would have to be based on far-reaching internal market reforms, in particular labour-market liberalization, so as to gradually reduce the competitive advantage of the US as an optimal currency area (Zimmermann 2004: 235). It is also true that the institutional mechanisms of the euro-zone are not yet sufficiently developed to support even modest activism in external monetary policy. An American political economist observed some years ago that

> Prudence might have counseled that the European Union take certain steps well before the creation of the euro area: namely, fill in the holes in external policymaking machinery ... Further development in policymaking institutions at the European level would be necessary for the EU presidency or chair of the euro-11 Council to articulate a common external monetary policy and negotiate in these matters with the G-7 partners. If the EU fails to develop these institutions and policy processes, the Council might well effectively cede its prerogatives in the external monetary arena to the ECB, in which case the euro area would lack coherent political authority to serve as the counterpart to the US Treasury in addressing an important range of international monetary and financial contingencies that contain a political dimension.
>
> (Randall Henning 2000: 41–2)

No significant innovation in external policy-making machinery has taken place since these lines were written, and the recent enlargements of the Union further complicate the situation. Thus, a first unwanted consequence of EMU is to have made evident both the difficulty of reaching agreement on key questions of economic governance, and the temerity of proceeding with full monetary union before such questions were settled. The similarity with the tendency of EU leaders to take part in important international negotiations without having first reached agreement on the Union's vital interests in the matter suggests that we are dealing here with a general feature of the political culture of the Union, akin to total optimism but perhaps better labelled as hubris.

Another important, but apparently unanticipated, consequence of EMU has already been mentioned: unlike most policy decisions taken in Brussels, the decisions taken in Frankfurt by the ECB are widely advertised, and their consequences, e.g. on the cost of home mortgages, have a direct impact on the welfare of all the citizens of the euro area, indeed of the entire EU. For the first time, the practical implications of a European policy are immediately perceived not just by experts or special-interest groups, but by the average citizen. In turn, this new salience of supranational decisions is likely to stimulate popular demand for greater effectiveness, not just in the monetary field, but of EU policies generally; hence a demand for better enforcement of accountability by results. By the same token, poor economic performance will pose more of a threat to the credibility and legitimacy of EU institutions. It is not by chance that the reasons given by French and Dutch voters for their rejection of the Constitutional Treaty were mostly of a socioeconomic nature: a stagnating standard of living, unemployment, price increases allegedly caused by the introduction of the euro, and fears of immigration from the new, and much poorer, member states. Such fears are quite wide-spread: in a 2006 survey by Eurobarometer on 'The Future of Europe', 63 per cent of respondents in the EU-15 (70 per cent in Austria and France) believed that enlargement would create unemployment, up from 43 per cent in 2003 (Commission 2006: 56).

It is difficult to overemphasize both the novelty and the political significance of growing popular demand for concrete results. Until recently it did not matter greatly whether or not public opinion sup-ported, or even knew much about, decisions taken at EU level. The elaborate compromises reached in Brussels were usually pushed through national parliaments, where the governments that had signed the deal dominated the agenda. This situation produced another distinctive fea-ture of the political culture of the EU: the primacy assigned to process and procedures over actual results. However, the permissive consensus of the past (see chapter 1) was possible only as long as the Euro-elites managed to keep European issues out of the political debate. EMU, eastern enlargement, and, not least, the negative results of the French, Dutch, and Irish referendums, have contributed to the politicization of 'Europe' even in traditionally pro-integration countries. Today European leaders are becoming aware that their voters are no longer willing to take the benefits of integration on faith. This explains why, at the European summit of June 2005, EU leaders conceded that 'the citizens remain committed to the European project ... [but] ... expect the Union to prove its added value' (European Council 2005). One year later, the same European Council promised again that it would try to improve the delivery of concrete results from Union policies.

As already mentioned, the most evident, but also the most paradoxical, of the unintended consequences of monetary union is the resulting segmentation of the EU. While the euro was supposed to be the visible symbol of the irresistible advance towards a politically united Europe, EMU has split the EU into different 'clubs' – perhaps permanently. Rather than 'One Market, One Money' we now have a Union divided into two groups: the members of the euro-zone, and the de jure (UK, Denmark) and de facto (Sweden) opt-outs. But a third group may emerge in the not too distant future: as we saw in chapter 3, a well-known American economist, Kenneth Rogoff, in 2006 predicted that in the next five to ten years the Union may actually be split into three camps with the addition of the future dropouts of the euro-zone – countries with a large public debt, like Italy and Portugal (cited in Mueller 2006). According to Rogoff these two countries, and possibly others as well, may be forced to abandon the common currency because rigorous implementation of the Maastricht parameters could entail social and economic costs too high for their voters to accept. But also other member states could decide that in an increasingly heterogeneous Union the costs of a centralized monetary policy exceed the benefits (see the next section). If such a segmentation of the Union into two, or more, groups were permanent, the future implications would be as far-reaching as they are ill-understood (or deliberately ignored) today. These implications are part of the general issue of diversified integration to be discussed in chapter 8. In the following pages we continue our discussion of causes of unintended consequences, starting with the interactions between large-scale integrationist projects. One instructive example of the possible consequences of such interactions is the contradiction between the centralization of monetary policy and the mutation of the old, fairly homogeneous EU into a heterogeneous Union with twenty-seven (and in the future more than thirty) members at quite different levels of socio-economic development.

Synergistic Effects: Enlargement, EMU, and the Single Market Programme

Risk regulators speak of synergistic effects when the (positive or negative) health effects of a substance are compounded by the presence of other substances, or of particular environmental conditions. Similarly, interactions between large-scale economic or political projects are likely to produce synergistic effects. Such compounded effects turn out to be another significant cause of unanticipated consequences: the very scale of operations makes it difficult or impossible to trace all the ramified consequences of the interacting projects. In this section we explore some important synergistic effects between the three 'historic enterprises' of the EU.

To start with the latest enterprise, it seems intuitively clear that the big bang enlargement of the Union should bear consequences for monetary union. In this connection one has to keep in mind that the new member states *must* accept EMU as part of the body of laws and practices known as *acquis communautaire* – they are not allowed to opt out as some of the older member states did. Of course, in addition the new members have to satisfy the Maastricht limits on budget deficits, public debt, and inflation; but these criteria are purely financial and thus only indirectly linked to the real economy and to general socioeconomic conditions. For example, the per capita income of the poorest member of the group of states admitted in 2004, Latvia, was only 37 per cent of the EU-15 average in 2001. But the same country had a modest budget deficit of 1.6 per cent of GDP, and a public debt of only 15.9 per cent, and hence amply satisfied two key Maastricht criteria. Bulgaria, admitted to the Union in 2007, in 2006 had a public debt of 32 per cent of GDP and a budget *surplus* of 2.3 per cent. Like Latvia, it would have easily satisfied the Maastricht limits for the budget deficit (3 per cent), and for public debt (60 per cent). However, its population had decreased by more than a million since 1992, and infant mortality is almost three times the EU-15 average. In comparison with previous enlargements, one sees that income disparities between the new member states from Central and Eastern Europe and the EU-15 are considerably larger than those of the three Mediterranean countries (Greece, Spain, and Portugal) whose income levels, when they joined the Union in the 1980s, were around 65 per cent of the old EU-10 average. The average income of the new eastern members is only around 40 per cent of the EU-15 average. This is about the same difference as that between Western Europe and the United States in 1945, when the old continent was in ruins while the economy of a physically intact America was booming.

In spite of their poverty, the new member states view the inflation rate as the only problematic parameter as far as their admission to the euro-zone is concerned. But they also wonder why so much importance should be attached to the level of inflation when their public finances are sound, while in 2006 five of the (then) twelve members of the euro-zone were the object of procedures for excessive deficit. Actually, the new members of the EU argue that the inflationary pressures they experience only prove the dynamism of their economies, and they are asking that the Maastricht criteria be changed – a demand supported by a number of Western economists who deem these criteria neither necessary nor sufficient to determine the capacity of a country to join EMU.

In reality, the recent enlargements of the EU are likely to raise more serious problems for the current than for the future members of the euro-zone. An obvious problem is the difficulty of achieving consensus about the stance of monetary policy among twenty-four (or more) countries, rather than the dozen or so currently represented in the Governing Council of the European Central Bank. In the present situation the ECB Executive Board – formed by the president, the vice-president, and four other members appointed from among persons of recognized standing and professional experience in monetary or banking matters – has a strategic position within the Governing Council, which comprises, in addition to the members of the board, the governors of the national central banks. This advantage is maintained even when the distribution of desired interest rates is different among large and small countries. But according to a well-known European monetary expert, Paul De Grauwe (2004), things could be very different in the enlarged euro-zone, where the ECB Board will lose its strategic advantage. For instance, a coalition of mostly small countries in the Governing Council could defeat a board's proposal concerning the appropriate interest rate. The outcome would be a decision that suits this coalition which, though numerically large, represents a relatively small fraction of the euro-zone's GDP. Such an outcome would be bound to lead to serious conflicts within the monetary union. The essence of the problem, De Grauwe explains, is that at present the small countries are overrepresented in the Governing Council, and this overrepresentation will be all the more serious in the enlarged euro-zone (De Grauwe 2004). To minimize the risk of decisions that no longer correspond to the needs of the entire system it would be necessary to streamline the voting rules of the Governing Council so as to reduce the weight of the small countries in the decision-making process. Such a reform might be politically rather difficult to implement, however.

Again, if the old EU-15 was not an optimal currency area, this will be even more true of an EU with twenty-seven or more members at vastly different levels of economic development. Hence, in the enlarged euro-zone the shocks will be more asymmetric than in the original one, so that some of the initial members will more frequently be outliers – in terms of inflation and output – compared with the average economy on which the ECB will have to focus. As a consequence, these members will perceive the policies of the Central Bank to be less responsive to shocks than they were before the enlargement. The constraints imposed by a one-size-fits-all monetary policy may thus entail costs too high to make monetary union acceptable in terms of an economic calculus: countries that today consider the economic benefits of monetary union greater than the costs could very well think otherwise in the enlarged Union. The only way to meet the challenge posed by enlargement is to make sure individual member states have the instruments to deal with asymmetric shocks, and in this respect particular importance attaches to reform of the labour markets to make them more flexible. But experience has shown how politically difficult such structural reforms are; hence the conclusion that enlargement is the greatest challenge facing EMU today (De Grauwe 2004).

Another important consequence of enlargement, to be discussed in chapter 5, is that the model of a 'social Europe' strongly committed to furthering socioeconomic equality, or at least some degree of interstate cohesion through income transfers, is no longer credible. The financial resources of the Union are simply insufficient for the task on the scale the new situation would require, while the rich member states refuse to increase the EU budget – if anything, they wish to decrease it as a percentage of Union GDP. Moreover, despite significant economic growth in the new member states, the present level of heterogeneity in the EU-27 is likely to persist for decades. According to the semi-official Sapir Report 'neither theory nor the experience of earlier enlargements convincingly supports a hypothesis of automatic convergence' (Sapir et al. 2004: 102). It has been calculated that despite the growing share of the regional funds in the EU budget, the rate of convergence is so slow that it would take forty years to reduce by one-half the difference in the level of income of the poor and rich regions of the old EU-15. A similar lesson can also be derived from the attempts of some older members of the EU to deal with internal regional differences: Italy, with the north–south divide, Germany with the west–east gap. In Italy, after half a century of regional policies and financial transfers on a massive scale, the 'southern problem' still figures prominently on the national agenda. Indeed, this 'southern problem' has generated a 'northern problem', in the sense of a growing resistance of northern taxpayers to finance inter-regional redistribution on anything like the present scale. In Germany, the per capita GDP of the eastern *Länder* is expected to barely increase between 2007 and 2009: from 68.0 to 68.2 per cent of the western level, in spite of a continuing loss of population in the eastern part of the country, and massive transfers from Berlin. At this pace convergence in per capita income between East and West Germany would take 320 years(!), according to recent calculations made by the Halle Institute of Economic Research (Beyerle 2008).

Eastern enlargement, in combination with far-reaching structural changes in the European and world economy, is a serious challenge for the Single Market project as well. In all modern economies the services sector accounts for at least 70 per cent of GDP and 50 per cent of employment. In the EU, between the years 1980 and 2000, the share of services in the economy increased by 13 percentage points, to 72 per cent. Hence the free movement of goods, which has been more or less achieved, is no longer sufficient to ensure market integration: no common market may be said to exist without a reasonably integrated services sector. Most services are still regulated at the national level, however, while socioeconomic conditions vary so much across the Union – income inequality, as measured by the Gini concentration coefficient (a statistical index measuring inequality in the distribution of income in a population), is more pronounced in the enlarged Union than in arch-capitalist USA – that ex ante (centralized) harmonization of national laws and regulations is bound to reduce aggregate welfare, while ex post harmonization (via mutual recognition and regulatory competition) has become politically unfeasible. Centralized harmonization is bound to reduce aggregate welfare under the conditions prevailing in the present Union because when countries differ significantly in terms of resources – hence also of preferences and policy priorities – the regulations that maximize aggregate welfare have to be different rather than harmonized. This is true even in the case of minimum harmonization – unless the minimum standard is so low as to be exceeded by all national standards, in which case it is simply irrelevant. On the other hand, the major alternative to ex ante harmonization, i.e. mutual recognition, presupposes more homogeneity (and more trust) between countries than can be assumed in the present Union, as will be seen in the following pages.

The growing resistance to both centralized harmonization and mutual recognition is the reason why the integration of the national markets for services has proved to be so problematic. 'Is Europe still capable of moving forward?' asked the editorial of the French newspaper

Le Monde of 16 February 2006. The topic was the draft Services Directive then being considered by the European Parliament. The editor of the influential French newspaper stated very clearly the dilemma facing the EU today. On the one hand, integration of the market for services is simply indispensable: with agriculture and industry no longer creating new jobs, only the services sector could contribute decisively to a reduction of the high level of unemployment in the euro-zone. On the other hand, in a socially and economically highly differentiated Union, such integration implies serious social problems, especially with respect to wages (*Le Monde* 2006). In fact the Services Directive 2006/123/EC seeking to facilitate the exercise of the freedom to provide services – a freedom enshrined in the Rome and all subsequent European treaties – became the most controversial piece of EU legislation in recent history. Previous directives liberalizing particular services, such as banking, had relied on the principle of mutual recognition, and the original draft of the Services Directive proposed to proceed in the same way. This proved to be politically impossible. To understand why the application of the same principle became so controversial after eastern enlargement, it is first necessary to examine in some detail how mutual recognition has been applied in the old EC/EU.

The Theory and Practice of Mutual Recognition

In its famous Cassis de Dijon judgment of 1979, the European Court of Justice ruled that a member state may not prohibit the sale in its territory of a good lawfully produced and marketed in another member state, even if such good is produced according to technical and quality requirements not conforming to those imposed on domestic products – except when the prohibition is justified by the need to ensure fiscal supervision, to protect public health or the environment, or to ensure the fairness of financial transactions. The European Commission's 1985 White Paper on *Completing the Internal Market* extended the Cassis de Dijon doctrine to the free movement of people and of services, and attempted to clarify the distinction between matters where harmonization is essential and those where it is sufficient that there be mutual recognition of the equivalence of the various requirements laid down under the respective national laws. The key word here is 'equivalence'. According to the White Paper, 'the objectives of national legislation, such as the protection of human health and life and of the environment, are more often than not identical' (Commission 1985: 17). Thus, the principle of mutual recognition rests on an empirical assumption of equivalence of certain basic rules enacted at the national level. Only if this assumption is factually correct does it follow that 'the rules and controls developed to achieve those objectives, although they may take different forms, essentially come down to the same thing, and so should normally be accorded recognition in all Member States' (1985: 17).

But the essential equivalence of the health, safety, or other social standards enacted by the member states cannot be taken for granted – even when the policy objectives may be assumed to be the same. This was shown, for example, by the judgment of the ECJ in the 'wood-working machines' case decided in 1986. In this case the Court was confronted with two different national approaches to occupational safety: the German regulation was less strict and relied more on an adequate training of the users of this type of machinery, while the French regulation required additional protective devices on the machines. The Court ruled against the Commission, which had held that both regulations were equivalent, and found that in the absence of harmonization at Community level, a member state could insist on the full respect of its national safety rules, and hence restrict the importation of certain goods.

In addition to the hypothesis of essential equivalence, the Commission's White Paper also attached great importance to mutual trust among the member states. For instance, it mentioned mutual trust as the first element of the new approach to the mutual recognition of university diplomas. Trust among the member states was to replace the impossible task of harmonizing vastly different national systems of professional training and licensing. Each state is to trust other member states' courses of study as being generally equivalent to its own, and a competent national authority must accept the evidence offered by another member state. Thus, the principle of mutual recognition is very demanding in terms of loyal cooperation as well. An American scholar has observed that the principle presupposes a higher degree of comity among the members of the EU than the Commerce Clause of the US Constitution requires among individual states. As this scholar points out, the Commerce Clause has been interpreted by the US Supreme Court to allow each state to insist on its own quality standards for goods and services, unless the subject matter has been pre-empted by federal legislation, or unless the state standards would unduly burden interstate commerce (Hufbauer 1990: 11).

It is therefore quite remarkable that in the past it has been possible to pass important pieces of legislation based on mutual recognition, such as

Directive 89/48 on 'a general system for the recognition of higher education diplomas awarded on completion of vocational courses of at least
three years' duration'. The system introduced by this directive is general
in the sense that it applies to all regulated professions and to employed
professionals as well as to the self-employed, and that it deals with both
entry into and exercise of a profession. Unlike the older, sectorial directives dealing with individual professions, this one does not attempt to
harmonize the length and subject matters of professional education, or
even the range of activities in which professionals can engage. Instead, it
introduces a system by which the states can compensate for eventual
differences in the length of the training or in the contents of the professional curriculum without restricting the freedom of movement. In the
latter case, for example, the host country can demand that the applicant
take a test or alternatively acquire practical experience for a period not
exceeding three years. The applicant is free to choose between these two
'compensation methods', while the competent authority of the host
country bears the burden of showing in detail the deficiencies in the
requirements for the diploma submitted by the said applicant. The
procedure is to be concluded within four months, ending with a reasoned
decision that may be appealed in the courts of the host member state. In
sum, Directive 89/48 created, for the first time in Europe, a single market
for the regulated professions. A member state can no longer deny access
to, or the exercise of, a regulated profession on its territory to EU citizens
who already exercise, or could legitimately exercise, the same profession
in another member state.

Another impressive application of the philosophy of mutual recognition is Directive 89/646 on credit institutions, often referred to as the
'Second Banking Directive'. The basic regulatory framework for
European banks is represented by this directive and by three more
narrowly focused directives concerned with the definition of a bank's
capital, the solvency ratios banks should adopt, and with procedures for
winding up credit institutions. These last three technical directives aim at
harmonizing basic prudential standards, thus establishing a foundation
on which mutual recognition can take place; all other conditions are
defined and controlled by the authorities of the country where the credit
institution is licensed, and must be accepted by the other member states
(home-country principle). Within this basic regulatory framework, a
European bank needs a single licence from its home country to be
allowed to establish branches or market directly financial services in
any other member state without further authorizations or controls:

disregarding the very few exceptions, the host country in which the bank provides its services has no power to seek further authorization or exercise supervision. The question we are concerned with in the following section is why an approach that was used without serious problems in the late 1980s should become so controversial some fifteen years later.

Mutual Recognition after Enlargement

Like the Second Banking Directive and other liberalizing measures based on mutual recognition, the draft Services Directive presented in early 2004 by Commissioner Bolkestein – who at the time was responsible for the internal market – was also based on the home-country principle. The draft aimed to go beyond past sector-specific attempts at building a single market for services, by adopting a horizontal approach which covered services of general interest, including health and social services not directly provided by the state, while non-profit services (e.g. in educational and cultural activities) were left out. Moreover, the draft did not address sectors already covered by European regulations, such as the directives dealing with the professions, or with 'posted workers' working for no more than twelve months in another EU country; it only aimed to complement such measures. Bolkestein was convinced that there was only one way to dismantle the many regulatory and bureaucratic obstacles still remaining at the national level: to make access to the market for services as automatic as possible by resorting to mutual recognition through the home-country (also called 'country-of-origin') approach. The most controversial aspects of the draft directive had to do with the conditions applicable to workers providing cross-border services (for example construction workers). In principle such movement falls under the 1996 Directive on the Posting of Workers, by which *host-country* conditions are always imposed on posted workers, except for social-security dues when the period of posting abroad does not exceed twelve months. Thus, a French firm hiring a Polish construction worker must apply French standards and regulations, and offer a French wage and French working hours. Under these conditions the firm obviously has no incentive to hire Polish or other East European workers; as a result, labour mobility across Europe is severely restricted.

Despite the 1996 directive, and despite restrictive arrangements limiting freedom of movement for labour coming from the new member states (excluding Cyprus and Malta), after the 2004 enlargement Germany experienced a large influx of temporary workers from the east. The explanation for this apparent anomaly is the fact that Germany (like Sweden and Denmark) has no general minimum wage, so that German companies do not have to pay workers from Eastern Europe at the same rate as German workers. Hence, despite the host-country provisions of the Posted Workers Directive, workers from the east could be paid the wages of their home country – in many cases €2 to €3 an hour, a miserable wage by German standards, but presumably better than being unemployed at home. In some sectors the consequence has been a significant lay-off of German workers as firms brought in personnel from the east. For instance, the trade union of slaughterhouse workers spoke of 26,000 lost jobs, or one-third of all employees in the sector, being replaced by East Europeans (Nicolaïdis and Schmidt 2007). Germany (and the two Nordic countries) could have solved the problem by legislating a national minimum wage, but this apparently obvious solution was rejected for domestic political reasons.

It should be kept in mind that the 2004 Bolkestein draft explicitly stated that the directive on posted workers would not only remain in force, but in case of conflicting rules it would prevail over the new directive. The proposed regulation focused instead on the temporary provision of services rendered by self-employed individuals in another EU country. Article 16 of the Bolkestein draft stated: 'Member States shall ensure that [service] providers are subject only to the national provisions of their Member State of origin'. According to economist Kostoris Padoa Schioppa (2007: 741), 'This sentence by itself, if adopted, would have implied a true revolution. That was so well understood by trade unions, by protected employees and by their parties in continental Western Europe that they aimed only at its cancellation, after massive demonstrations where they pretended to represent social Europe.' The Services Directive finally approved in December 2006 – against the strong opposition of East European governments – made no reference to the home-country principle, so that the host-country rule now applies to self-employed and to employee workers. As a matter of fact, the new directive does little more than restate the principles that have evolved in the case law concerning the freedom to provide services, and the freedom of self-employed professionals and companies to set up the base of their operations anywhere in the EU ('freedom of establishment'). The elements of novelty are few and relatively unimportant: the obligation for all authorities involved to communicate with applicants through a single point of contact, and to offer the possibility to complete all procedures electronically; the duty of the member states to supply information on their regulatory systems, such as the regulation of the professions and the means of redress available against service providers, should things go wrong; and the ban on the prohibition of advertising.

At the Lisbon summit of March 2000 all member states had agreed on the necessity of a deeper and wider internal market for services as a crucial element of a general strategy to make the EU the most advanced economy in the world by 2010 (see chapter 3). In 2002 the Council urged the Commission to come up with a horizontal proposal to tackle all the many, costly, and sometimes prohibitive obstacles to a truly integrated market for services. With its horizontal approach based on home-country control, the Bolkestein draft moved precisely in the direction indicated by the Council. Its rejection will have serious consequences not only for the Lisbon Strategy, but also for the entire European economy. Given the importance of the services sector, even a satisfactory development of agriculture and industry would have only a limited impact on growth and employment in the EU because of the decreasing share of these two sectors in overall activity (Pelkmans 2007). In sum, the same EU leaders who in March 2000 had acknowledged the importance of the services sector for achieving the ambitious goals of the Lisbon Strategy, failed to consider the broad implications of socioeconomic heterogeneity when, at the Laeken Council of December 2001, they decided to proceed with the big bang enlargement of the Union: a classic example of unanticipated consequences.

A recent reconstruction of the history of the Services Directive from the initial draft to the approval by the EP and the Council of the final, watered-down, text in December 2006 comes to the conclusion that 'There is little doubt that the EU's biggest enlargement since its inception conditioned the reactions to the services proposals ... the level of differences in national regulatory and legal settings was becoming too great to sustain the permissive consensus on liberalization that had (more or less) prevailed until then' (Nicolaïdis and Schmidt 2007: 724). In addition, other students of this significant episode in the history of EU policy-making agree that the campaign against the 'Frankenstein Directive' – as the Bolkestein draft had been renamed by its opponents – could elicit popular support because diffuse fears of 'social dumping' and wage competition, previously associated with globalization, now had a specific (East) European focus. Whereas in the old EU such fears had not prevented fairly extensive use of mutual recognition and the home-country approach, after eastern enlargement public opinion could be fed concrete images such as that of the 'Polish plumber' taking away jobs from French workers – an intentionally deceptive symbol since France has a minimum-wage law, but one which played a role in the rejection of the Constitutional Treaty, as well as in the fate of the Bolkestein draft.

After passage of the watered-down Services Directive, some economists predicted that it would take a decade, or more, to have an internal market for services. The OECD *Economic Survey of the European Union 2007* was moderately optimistic on this score (OECD 2007). However, such forecasts are based on the assumption of rapid economic convergence between the new member states and the old EU-15 – a rather doubtful assumption, not only because growth figures can be misleading in the case of poorer countries, whose backwardness provides greater scope for faster economic growth; but especially because the process of eastern enlargement of the EU is far from being concluded. Thus Nicolaïdis and Schmidt (2007) report that in Poland Solidarność justified its opposition to the Bolkestein draft by pointing to the risk that Polish workers would soon suffer from wage differentials with Ukrainian workers. In Western Europe, on the other hand, opposition to the Bolkestein draft was also supported with the argument that a host-country regime would benefit workers from the new member states by offering them Western wages rather than the much lower wages they would get under the home-country regime. This disingenuous argument attempts to conceal the fact that while the host-country regime offers better conditions to the few eastern workers who are lucky enough to be offered a job in the west, it effectively denies access to western labour markets to most of their compatriots. Nevertheless, the argument is politically convenient. It has also been accepted by some labour leaders from the new member states – partly out of deference to their western colleagues – and could evidently be repeated with each new enlargement bringing in countries whose GNP is below the EU average, for example the Balkan countries or Turkey.

Many of the same people who opposed the 'neo-liberal' philosophy of the Bolkestein draft also maintain that the EU should be much more than a free-trade area: it should have a strong social and political dimension. Paradoxically, with the services sector still largely regulated at the national level, it can no longer be ruled out that the enlarged EU may regress, if not to the stage of a free-trade area, then to that of a customs union, with elements of a common market, mostly for goods: in 2001 intra-EU export of services represented only 20 per cent of trade in the internal market, compared with a share of the services sector in Union GDP of more than 70 per cent. It is indeed ironic that after the introduction of the common currency, the near-doubling of EU membership in the span of a few years, and the setting of overly ambitious goals at the Lisbon summit of March 2000, one has to face the prospect of a true single European market receding into the indefinite future.

Cryptofederalist Hubris

One of the most striking manifestations of the EU's political culture of total optimism is the willingness of European leaders not only to accept, without any serious analysis, the risks inherent in any major political project, but even to increase those risks by expanding the scale of the project. As already noted, the original plans for EMU envisaged no more than a handful of countries – essentially the D-mark bloc plus France. The final decision to start with eleven, soon to become twelve, countries was made possible by an elastic interpretation of the Maastricht parameters, and by unrealistic assumptions about the willingness of the future members of the euro-zone to engage in far-reaching structural reforms of their economies and welfare systems. On this, as on so many other occasions, integrationist aspirations, short-term political advantages, and institutional self-interest carried more weight than the declared policy objectives. Similarly, the original plan to open accession negotiations with no more than five Central and Eastern Europe countries was soon superseded by the decision to go ahead with the big bang enlargement, opening formal negotiations with all ten CEEC candidates, plus Malta and Cyprus. Each incumbent member state was pushing for its own favoured candidate(s), while the Commission was doing its best to minimize the burdens imposed by the more ambitious plan. Eastern enlargement gave the Brussels bureaucracy an extraordinary opportunity to play for the first time a role of political leadership, and through the direct grants, also the role of the patron vis-à-vis the CEEC countries. Its assurances that there would be no additional financial burdens for the old members of the Union implied overly optimistic assumptions about real growth of the budget through annual growth in EU GDP. As we know, the politically important message the Commission intended to convey was that the reforms needed for enlargement were feasible at no cost to the older members of the EU.

As in the case of monetary union, so in the case of enlargement; EU leaders carefully avoided any public discussion of potential problems. Hence it is impossible to know precisely how many leaders anticipated (or even cared) that enlargement of the Union on the scale finally decided would make the search for a common European interest even more elusive than in the old EU. The radical diversity of positions within the enlarged Union was soon demonstrated by the war in Iraq, which started shortly after the negotiations for the accessions of the ten new members were concluded in December 2002. The strong Atlanticist stance of the new CEEC members was quite predictable: countries feeling threatened by a resurgent Russia look to the United States, not to the EU, for protection. The importance of American protection becomes clear when one notes that in some regions of Estonia and Latvia, for example, up to 50 per cent of the local population is composed of ethnic Russians, who complain of being treated as second-class citizens because of their national origin. More difficult to understand were the outbursts of former French president Chirac who, having initially supported the big bang enlargement, now went as far as to suggest blocking the accession process in retaliation for the alignment of 'new Europe' with the American position. As the American journalist Elisabeth Pond wrote at the time, 'The recriminations over foreign policy threatened to erode even the hard-won commonality in economic and other domestic issues as well. Certainly they dashed Blair's hopes of bringing Britain into the European Monetary Union any time soon' (2004: 69). Despite the repeated professions by Euro-leaders of their commitment to a common foreign policy, the would-be world power had never appeared so divided within itself. The absence of a common position on international issues again became evident on the occasions of Kosovo's unilateral declaration of independence from Serbia, and of the Russian–Georgian conflict over the independence of Abkhazia and Ossetia in August 2008. While Britain, Poland, and the Baltic republics accused Russia of 'open aggression' against Georgia, and insisted, *inter alia*, that plans for a new EU–Russia partnership agreement should again be put on ice, EU (rotating) president Sarkozy expressed the opinion prevalent in 'old Europe' that it was 'wholly normal' for Russia to 'wish to defend its own interests' (cited in Schlamp 2008).

The failure of the EU–Russia summit held in Helsinki in November 2006 had already given a foretaste of future problems. At this summit, Poland, supported by Lithuania, refused to approve a mandate to the European Commission to negotiate a new cooperation and partnership agreement between the EU and Moscow – an agreement the older members of the Union strongly supported. The immediate reason for opposing the EU–Russia agreement was Moscow's embargo on Polish pork and beef imposed in 2005 over alleged health concerns, but also Polish, Lithuanian, and Estonian plans to remove Communist-era memorials played a role. When the Estonians tried to relocate a bronze statue commemorating Red Army soldiers who died fighting Nazi Germany, they provoked strong protests by young ethnic Russians, and in the ensuing public disturbances one person was stabbed to death. It is to be expected that in the future enlargement will continue to affect the international position of the EU in a number of ways.

At the Helsinki EU–Russia summit, shrewd commentators observed, then president Putin seemed to be almost amused by the opposition of the new EU members from Eastern Europe. Apparently the Russian leader realized that the recent enlargement had weakened, not strengthened, the EU's international status, compounding the difficulty of the Union speaking with one voice. He must have also been aware that another newcomer, Cyprus, had been using its veto power in matters relating to Turkey's accession, and that such examples are likely to be followed by other member states in the future. Russia's new assertiveness was demonstrated as well by Putin's rejection of any intimation that the Russian energy market should be liberalized along the lines of EU competition rules. The Russian leader was all too aware of the fact that energy questions are not dealt with between Russia and the EU, but bilaterally with individual member states.

As already mentioned in chapter 2, the broader geopolitical implications of enlargement were considered with alarm by several informed observers, including the distinguished German historian Heinrich August Winkler who saw the continuous geographical expansion of the EU as an expression of 'European Bonapartism' (Winkler 2005: 15). Professor Winkler, it will be recalled, was particularly critical of the wish of some integrationist leaders to push the domain of the EU to the borders of Syria, Iraq, and Iran 'so that Europe may finally become a world power'. In light of the growing list of applicants from Europe's periphery, including Turkey, such concerns do not appear to be completely unfounded. In September 2005, the president of the Transcaucasian Republic of Georgia expressed the belief that his country would be invited to join the EU (and NATO) by 2008; and a few months before the French and Dutch voters rejected the Constitutional Treaty to express their dissatisfaction with enlargement, as well as with other EU policies, Ukraine's president Viktor Yushchenko had told the European Parliament that his country was ready to open EU entry talks by 2007. It is reasonable to assume that these leaders based their hopes, at least in part, on the encouragement given by some key figures of the European Commission to the big bang enlargement. At the time of the first eastern enlargement, policy entrepreneurs from within the Commission – especially officials in the Directorate General for Enlargement then headed by Guenther Verheugen – kept moving towards a commitment to expand the borders of the Union, despite initial resistance from other parts of the Commission, and from most incumbent member states. As befits the political culture of the EU, 'the difficulty of devising a coherent strategic policy was not reflected in open controversies, but rather in the striking absence of thorough debate. Policy-makers were busy with other issues, but they were also nervous about opening up a divisive debate about the future of the EU integration model' (Sedelmeier 2005: 409).

Optimism bordering on self-deception, indifference towards long-term consequences, institutional self-interest, and, not least, the absence of genuine public debate: all explain why the temptation to overreach has found so little resistance in the EU. Hubris, which in earlier Greek authors signified illegal action, eventually came to mean excessive aggrandizement, transcending the limits of human nature and tempting the gods; hence it was thought to bring nemesis upon the overly ambitious (Jaeger 1976). With reference to the cases considered in this chapter, many of the unanticipated consequences of the most ambitious integrationist projects of the 1990s may be seen as the punishment for transcending the normative and material limits of the Union. Recent statements by the European Council suggest a new realization of the stringency of those limits. As already mentioned, the EU Council, still reeling from the shock of the constitutional debacle of May–June 2005, admitted that 'citizens ... expect the Union to prove its added value', and promised that it would try to improve the 'delivery of concrete results' from EU policies. It also acknowledged that 'the pace of enlargement must take the Union's absorption capacity into account', and asked the Commission 'to provide a special report on all aspects pertaining to the Union's absorption capacity', notably including 'the perception of enlargement by citizens ... and the need to explain the enlargement process to the public' (cited in Micossi and Gros 2006: 2).

5

The Mirage of Social Europe

Misleading Analogies and Conceptual Ambiguities

As already mentioned, a small but influential body of elite opinion sees not only economic, but also political integration as steps towards the ultimate goal of a 'Social Europe' – just as the national market and the liberal state of the nineteenth century are thought to have prepared the ground for the modern welfare state. Only a strong social dimension, it is held, can legitimate the process of European integration, and at the same time rescue the national welfare state threatened by globalization. The addition of an enveloping social dimension to the integration process, the champions of Social Europe assert, would enjoy widespread popular support. After the rejection of the Constitutional Treaty, for example, Belgian prime minister Guy Verhofstadt claimed that the French and Dutch voters had opposed the treaty, not because it was too ambitious, but rather because it was not sufficiently ambitious: it did not go far enough in the direction of a supranational welfare state. Members of the intelligentsia such as Juergen Habermas explained the failure of the draft Constitution primarily as an indication of the opposition of the voters to the neo-liberal bias of the document, and an expression of popular demand for a more welfare-orientated Union (see chapter 3). Habermas wrote: 'If something can be deduced with certainty from the [French and Dutch] vote, it is this: that not all western nations are willing to accept the social and cultural costs of welfare inequality, costs which the neo-liberals would like to impose on them in the name of accelerated economic growth' (2005: 3). Now that the neo-liberals have achieved all their objectives, he continued, it is time to deepen the social dimension, and in particular to soften the impact of monetary integration by means of the gradual harmonization of fiscal, social, and economic policies. As has already been shown, however, the alleged neo-liberal bias of the European treaties is largely a myth. On the one hand, the founding treaties authorized some highly interventionist policies, e.g. in agriculture and in the coal and steel industries – and interventionism became even more pronounced in later documents. On the other hand, those free-market principles that can be found in the treaties were introduced primarily in order to make possible the integration of heavily regulated national markets. It was the *dirigisme* of the national governments that forced the founding fathers to accept, however reluctantly, certain principles of a liberal economic order. Again, in listing EMU among the neo-liberal measures calling for social compensation, the German philosopher seems to be unaware of the fact that the motivation behind monetary union was political, not economic. Integrationists saw EMU as a decisive step towards European unification, while different national leaders had different, but in each case largely political, reasons for supporting it. In contrast, we saw that most 'neo-liberal' economists opposed the idea of a centralized monetary policy for structurally diverse economies. Even after the introduction of the common currency, a number of distinguished economists continue to remain sceptical about the long-term success of the project.

In sum, the ideological inspiration of the founding treaties, and of such 'historic enterprises' as EMU and the Single Market, is not neo-liberalism. Rather, I argue, free-market principles were relied upon only to the extent that they seemed to be useful to the cause of European integration, or to particular national interests. It is hard to understand, therefore, for what reason or in which sense this opportunistic philosophy ought to be balanced by developing a fully fledged social policy at European level. In any case, the available empirical evidence, briefly reviewed below, in no way suggests widespread support for delegating to Brussels relevant competences in the social field. On the contrary, the data indicate that, to paraphrase the German philosopher, very few, if any, West European nations are willing to accept the social, economic, and political costs of an ambitious, and necessarily centralized, European social policy. *Pace* Habermas, market integration remains the main, and for many people the only, justification for the European project. If this is true then it follows that to rid the economic constitution of the EU of its alleged neo-liberal features, or even to weaken them, would undermine the only generally acknowledged *raison d'être* of European integration. As we saw, it is precisely those features that make economic integration possible. In particular, weakening the EU competition policy – as was suggested by Nicolas Sarkozy when, shortly after his election to the French presidency, he proposed to eliminate competition as one of the primary objectives of the Union – would also throw the door wide open to economic nationalism at a time when the socioeconomic heterogeneity caused by large-scale enlargement already creates serious problems for the Single Market project.

Without economic integration and a growing economy, the very idea of Social Europe becomes meaningless; but an efficient integration of national markets is impossible without those 'neo-liberal' economic principles which the critics would like to reform, if not to repeal: this is the dilemma the champions of a European welfare state are unwilling to face, let alone resolve. Karl-Heinz Ladeur recently made a similar point in stronger language. Referring to those scholars, especially in the larger member states, who regard the EU as a 'federation of welfare states' which ought to be strong enough to stem the tide of globalization, he writes: 'The [European] social state without a common economic, cultural, political project is a nightmare of decline' (Ladeur 2008: 158, footnote omitted). Indeed, the view of the EU as a federation of welfare states – the European analogue of the Habermasian notion of a 'world welfare policy without a world government' (Habermas 2000) – is only a futile attempt to avoid hard political problems. One cannot oppose the rising tide of scepticism about an integration process with no clear finality and no obvious limits with the argument that it is unnecessary to invent something new like a fully fledged European federal state: all that is needed, according to Habermas, is to rescue the European model of the welfare state by projecting it beyond the national borders, in a different, supranational, format. A supranational welfare state decoupled from a common political project would indeed be a bureaucratic nightmare – and given popular resistance to large-scale transnational redistribution, an authoritarian nightmare as well. The level of centralized harmonization of social standards required by a 'federation of welfare states' would have been politically difficult to enforce even in the old EU; in the enlarged Union it is simply politically infeasible (see chapter 4).

Confusion about the foundations and limits of Social Europe is fed in large part by misleading analogies with the development of the national welfare states. The English sociologist T. H. Marshall, reflecting on the development of the British welfare state in the post-war decades, concluded that 'social policy uses political power to supersede, supplement or modify operations of the economic system in order to achieve results which the economic system would not achieve on its own, and ... in so doing it is guided by values other than those determined by open market forces' (Marshall 1975: 15). Even if sufficient political power and legitimacy were available to the European institutions, it would be hardly possible to use the available resources to 'supersede, supplement or modify' the operations of a fragile and still incomplete European market in order to carve out an autonomous sphere for a true social policy at European level, as will be seen below.

Different, apparently more pragmatic, justifications have also been used to endorse the view that the European 'economic space' should be supplemented by a 'social space', based on the harmonization of national social policies – a thesis espoused by the European Commission since the 1970s, and obviously founded on the analogy with the harmonization of the different economic regulations of the member states. Of these other justifications three seem to be the most popular ones: the fear of 'social dumping', or of a 'race to the bottom', in the definition of social standards; the desire to overcome the 'institutional asymmetry' between policies promoting market efficiency (negative integration) and policies implementing social protection and equality (positive integration); and the hope that a more ambitious social policy could finally give the EU a legitimacy which so far has eluded all efforts to attain it by such devices as the steady expansion of the powers of the European Parliament, constitution-drafting by the Convention method, a Charter of Fundamental Rights, and a liberal use of the rhetoric of openness, transparency, and citizen participation. These three justifications will be critically examined in the following sections. Before doing this, however, it may be useful to call attention to the ambiguity of expressions like 'social space', 'social dimension', and even 'European social policy'. Because of such ambiguity, opinions about the present state and future prospects of Social Europe range from uncertain hope to outright pessimism.

The Treaty of Rome itself is far from being clear about what is to be understood by the expression 'European social policy'. The section on social policy – Title III of Part Three of the Treaty – enumerates a number of 'social fields' (employment; labour law and working conditions; vocational training; social security; occupational health and safety; collective bargaining and right of association) where member states should cooperate closely (Article 118 EEC Treaty). In the following article member states are urged to 'maintain the application of the principle that men and women should receive equal pay for equal work'. The same Title III also establishes the European Social Fund with the goal of improving employment opportunities and facilitating the geographical and occupational mobility of workers. What is arguably the most significant social-policy provision in the EEC (Rome) Treaty – the social-security regime for migrant workers – appears not in the section on social policy but in that on the free movement of persons, services, and capital. Finally, one of the objectives of the CAP is, according to Art. 39(b) of the Treaty, 'to ensure a fair standard of living for the agricultural community, in particular by increasing the individual earnings of persons engaged in agriculture'. So under the label 'social policy' the framers of the treaty included not only social security and interpersonal income redistribution, at least for certain groups such as farmers, but also inter-regional redistribution, elements of industrial and labour-market policy (vocational training, measures to improve labour mobility), and social regulation (primarily occupational health and safety, and equal treatment for male and female workers). Still, the enumeration of matters relating to the social field in Article 118 and the limited role attributed to the European Commission in this area – mainly restricted to promoting coordination of national policies, conducting studies, delivering opinions and arranging consultations – indicate that the social-policy domain, with the said exceptions, was originally considered to be outside the competence of the supranational institutions.

The Treaty of Rome rejected the view, fairly common even then, that differences in social conditions between member states could represent a form of 'unfair' competition, so that harmonization would be needed in order to prevent 'social dumping'. Apart from the condition of equal pay for male and female workers, introduced under French pressure, the treaty nowhere prescribes that national social policies be harmonized prior to, or concurrently with, trade liberalization within the common market. Rather, until the mid-1970s European policy-makers generally assumed that harmonization should be regarded as a corollary of, not a requirement for, market integration – ex post harmonization. After a decade of hesitation, a definite shift in the direction of ex ante, centralized, harmonization of social standards occurred in the mid-1980s. Several factors contributed to this shift: the enlargement of the Community, creating for the first time significant differentials in labour costs between member states; high unemployment and stagnating real wages; and, not least, the social activism of the Delors Commission (Sapir 1996). It should be noted that differentials in labour costs in the present EU-27 are much larger than they were after the accession of Spain, Portugal, and Greece in the 1980s (see section 'Negative and Positive Integration' below and chapter 4). Because differences in socioeconomic conditions are so great in today's Union, even the gradual harmonization of the social policies of the member states proposed by the advocates of

Social Europe would very probably reduce aggregate welfare, as shown in the following section.

The Single European Act (SEA) gave the Community a number of new competences in the social field. The main lines of development of supranational activities in this field are beginning to emerge clearly: they are regional development (new Title V, Economic and Social Cohesion), and social regulation (Art. 100A, Art. 118A, and the new Title VII, Environment). Previously, as noted above, both social policy and social regulation belonged, with very few exceptions, to the competence of the member states, with the Commission's power of initiative essentially limited to promoting collaboration and non-binding coordination among the national governments. In particular, Art. 118 of the Rome Treaty gave the Community no power to regulate occupational health and safety. The first directives in this area had to be based on Art. 100 (dealing with the approximation of laws directly affecting the operation of the common market), and thus required unanimity in the Council of Ministers. Under the new Art. 118A introduced by the SEA, directives in the field of occupational health and safety could be adopted by the Council by qualified majority, and with no proof needed that they are essential for the completion of the internal market. Another innovation introduced by Art. 118A was the concept of 'working environment', which makes regulatory intervention possible beyond the traditional limits of health and safety in the workplace (Majone 1996).

To complete this picture of Community expansion into the area of social regulation, we should also mention Art. 100A(3), which enjoins the Commission to start from 'a high level of protection' in matters relating to health, safety, and environmental and consumer protection. This means that the reference to 'minimum requirements' in Art. 118A ('the Council ... shall adopt, by means of directives, minimum requirements for gradual implementation, having regard to the conditions and technical rules obtaining in each of the Member States') does not imply that European standards should reflect the lowest level prevailing in the member states. Rather, in the opinion of the majority of the members of the Council of Ministers, such standards should represent a lower threshold for national regulators, who are free to maintain or adopt standards incorporating higher levels of safety (Majone 1993: 155; see also the following section). The 1992 Maastricht Treaty contained a new section on consumer protection, and introduced qualified majority voting for most environmental protection measures, as well as innovations in the regulation of occupational health and safety, broadened to include all conditions that may affect the health and safety of workers: organization of the labour market; length of work, its organization and nature, and ergonomic factors. It remained silent on most areas of traditional (redistributive) social policy.

The 1997 Treaty of Amsterdam conferred quasi-constitutional status to the Social Charter setting out twelve types of social rights, including rights for persons not in the workforce, such as the elderly, and rights for the employed. More controversially, it included rights pertaining to industrial democracy and collective bargaining at European level. Since the 1990s, however, efforts to reduce stubbornly high levels of unemployment have moved centre stage. The EU Council meeting in Madrid in December 1995 declared that 'job creation is the principal social, economic and political objective of the EU and its Member States' (EU Council 2005); similar concerns inspired the Lisbon Strategy launched at the beginning of the subsequent decade. In sum, EU policies in the social field have evolved along quite separate lines from those followed by the member states. The historical conditions prevailing at national level have created a dense web of welfare institutions covering most citizens 'from cradle to grave', while the EU – for reasons ranging from budgetary limitations to the reluctance of the member states to lose control over a policy area of great political salience – is a 'welfare laggard' in terms of traditional social policy. This is not to say that the aspiration to move beyond social regulation, in the direction of something recognizably similar to a European welfare state, has been given up – witness the Commission's intensive soul-searching concerning its, and the EU's, proper role in social policy (Leibfried 2005).

Social Dumping, Race to the Bottom, and Social Harmonization

One of the standard arguments in favour of the centralized harmonization of national social policies and regulations is the need to prevent the possibility that the member states take advantage of the single European market to engage in 'social dumping', or in a competitive lowering of social standards, in order to attract foreign investments. Indeed, many, perhaps most, measures of positive integration in the areas of health, safety, and environmental regulation have been justified by the argument that without EU-level harmonization member states would engage in a socially undesirable 'race to the bottom'. The notion of social dumping is notoriously vague. In a report entitled *The Social Dimension of the Internal Market*, published in 1988, the European Commission defined social dumping in the following terms: 'the fear that national social progress will be blocked or, worse, that there will be downward pressure on social conditions (wages, level of social protection, fringe benefits, etc.) in the most advanced countries [of the EEC], simply because of the competition ... from certain countries, where average labour costs are significantly lower' (cited in Sapir 1996: 559).

A vivid demonstration that this fear was well founded seemed to be provided in 1993, when the US-owned domestic appliances group Hoover Europe, faced with the need to close either its factory in Scotland or one in the Dijon region of France, decided to transfer the production of the French plant to Scotland. One of the reasons for the company's decision was a new collective agreement at the Scottish plant, where unions approved a wage freeze, greater flexibility, and a ban on strikes. The French workers and their government reacted angrily, protesting that what was involved was a British attempt to compete on low labour costs and lax social standards – 'social dumping', as the French prime minister denounced Hoover's decision the day after it became known. Intervention by the European Commission, headed at the time by the formidable Jacques Delors, himself a Frenchman, was demanded. But Delors could do little more than express sympathy when, at the peak of the crisis, he received a delegation of workers from Hoover France. The truth, he pointed out, was that differentials in labour costs between member states could not be eliminated, or even mitigated, by existing EU social legislation. Neither the Social Charter nor the Protocol and Agreement on Social Policy annexed to the Treaty of Maastricht, even if they had been ratified by the United Kingdom at the time, could have prevented Hoover from relocating from France to the United Kingdom in order to lower its labour costs. Only EU-wide minimum wages could have helped to reduce differentials across member states, but the Union has no competence to legislate on such matters. Besides, the process of relocation is a normal, and desirable, phenomenon in an integrated market. The objective of the single European market project – Jacques Delors's main, if partial, achievement – was precisely to facilitate the mobility of the factors of production. Ironically, at the same time as the Hoover decision to transfer production to Scotland, the Swiss multinational Nestlé announced that it planned to transfer part of its operations from Scotland to France!

An argument which is often used to justify centralized harmonization of social standards, not only in the EU but in most federal states, is that harmonization is needed to prevent member states from competing for industry by offering social standards that are too lax relative to the preferences of their citizens. Such competition is said to lower the level of social protection that states would pursue if they did not face international or inter-jurisdictional competition. It is not difficult to show, however, that the race-to-the-bottom argument is theoretically unsound. Following Revesz (1992) we may take the simplest case of two states that are identical in all relevant aspects, including (say) the level of environmental quality desired by their citizens. State 1 initially sets its standard of pollution control at the level that would be optimal if it were a completely independent country rather than a member of a federation. State 2 decides to set a less stringent standard, and we assume that industrial migration from State 1 to State 2 will ensue. To recover some of the lost jobs and tax revenues, the first state in turn considers competing on its own standard, and lowers it accordingly. The process of adjustment continues until an equilibrium is reached. The equilibrium outcome will be that the two states will not have experienced any net inflow or outflow of industry, but will have adopted suboptimal standards that do not correspond to the preferences of their citizens. In this sense a 'race to the bottom' may be considered a case of the 'prisoners' dilemma', in which both players will find it convenient to defect in every round of the (finitely repeated) game, even though both would gain by honouring their commitments. If the two states in our example could enter into a cooperative agreement to adopt the optimally stringent standard, they could maximize social welfare without engaging in 'unfair' competition for industry – assuming that the agreement is enforceable, and that preferences for environmental quality are exactly the same in the two jurisdictions. If the agreement is enforceable, for example because the two jurisdictions are part of the same federation, the suboptimal outcome could be avoided if the environmental standards were harmonized at the higher level, *provided* the harmonized standard were equal to the level the two jurisdictions would find independently optimal. Article 95(3) of the EC Treaty (ex Art. 100A(3) TEU) attempts to offer such a solution, at least for the richer members of the Union, stating that in proposing harmonization measures concerning health, safety, environmental protection, and consumer protection, the Commission 'will take as a base a high level of protection … Within their respective powers, the European Parliament and the Council will also seek to achieve this objective.'

The proviso about the harmonized standards corresponding to the actual preferences of the member states is crucial. If states have different preferences for environmental or other social standards, as is to be expected in a highly heterogeneous Union, then standards that maximize aggregate welfare will have to be different. A uniform European rule, even one that sets a minimum standard and allows the member states to adopt more stringent national standards, will not be optimal – unless the minimum standard is low enough to be exceeded by all the national standards, in which instance it is practically irrelevant. So it is quite possible that even if there is a race to the bottom, a European standard might still reduce aggregate social welfare. As a matter of fact, there is no convincing empirical evidence of a race to the bottom in social standards, even at the international level. For example, econometric analyses of trade patterns failed to find evidence of industrial migration to countries with lower environmental standards. Several possible reasons for this have been offered: corporations doing business in a variety of jurisdictions find it more cost-effective to operate according to the most stringent regulations rather than designing different production processes for each location; environmental compliance costs are too small, relative to other costs, and too similar across countries to weigh heavily in location decisions; multinational corporations believe that most countries are just a few years (less than the lifetime of a factory) behind the most advanced countries in environmental-standards stringency, so that it is better to invest now than be forced to retrofit later (Majone 2005: 153–4).

Especially the last reason – the fact that environmental quality is a 'superior' good, the demand for which grows as incomes increase – makes the race-to-the-bottom argument highly implausible within the EU. Thus, a detailed study on the future of the European 'Social Model' in the global economy found that 'So far, there are few signs that [a] race to the bottom is occurring; rather the race has been in the other direction, with the southern countries (in particular, Portugal) upgrading to northern European levels of [social] expenditure' (Ferrera et al. 2001: 174). Moreover, the race-to-the-bottom argument is not only theoretically weak and empirically unsupported, but also, as Revesz points out, incomplete. That is because the argument fails to consider the existence of alternative means of attracting foreign direct investments, other than lowering social standards. The 'race model' implicitly assumes that states compete over one variable only, e.g. environmental quality or labour costs. But it seems more reasonable to assume that if harmonization prevents competition on the social dimension, then states would try to compete over other variables, e.g. lower taxation of corporate profits. To avoid the possibility of any form of interstate competition, the central regulators would have to harmonize all forms of national rules. This would amount to eliminating any trace of national autonomy: the race to the bottom becomes, in the end, an argument for centralization and against subsidiarity.

Naturally, the fear of social dumping or, generally, of a race to the bottom is not the sole rationale for harmonization. A more plausible argument for EU-wide harmonization of social standards is the need to dismantle non-tariff barriers to trade within the Single Market. Even in this respect, however, ex ante, top-down harmonization probably has been pushed too far. A number of case studies have shown that the costs imposed by social standards are only a minor consideration in the location decisions of large multinational firms: quality of infrastructure, education of the labour force, or political stability are much more important influencing factors. Today it is also recognized that an initial difference in health, safety, or environmental standards need not distort international trade; rather, trade should lead to their eventual convergence. The reason is that, as already noted, social standards are positively correlated with the standard of living. Hence, as wealth grows as a result of trade, the endogenous demand for higher social standards grows as well. It deserves to be repeated that the Treaty of Rome rejected the view that differences in social conditions between the member states would represent a form of 'unfair' competition, so that to prevent 'social dumping' policies should have been harmonized prior to, or at least concurrently with, trade liberalization within the common market. The founding fathers believed that social harmonization was to be regarded as a corollary of, not a requirement for, market integration.

Negative and Positive Integration

This sequence of free trade first, followed by a more or less spontaneous harmonization of social standards, was normally accepted by European policy-makers until the mid-1970s. According to economist André Sapir, the absence of social harmonization for the original common market can be explained by two factors (Sapir 1996: 553). One factor has just been mentioned: the prevailing view, at the time of the negotiation of the Treaty of Rome, that social harmonization was simply not needed. France was the only country really demanding social harmonization, for fear that its advanced social protection system – legacy of the Popular Front period – would put its industries at a disadvantage. The other factor was the very favourable socioeconomic environment during the period 1958–73: the unemployment rate remained below 4 per cent throughout the Community, while the real earnings of industrial workers rose steadily at an annual rate of nearly 5 per cent; at the same time, differences between member states in labour costs in industry were never very significant. Data presented by Sapir (1996: 567) show that if we set the cost in the country with the highest level equal to 100, then in 1958 labour costs in industry were 100 for Luxembourg, 76 for Belgium, 70 for Germany, 68 for France, 60 for the Netherlands, and 58 for Italy. In 1972 the costs were 100 for Germany, 95 for the Netherlands, 92 for Belgium and Luxembourg, 78 for Italy, and 70 for France. By comparison, labour costs in the EU-27 differ by a factor of ten or more. In 2003, for example, the direct hourly labour costs were €20.63 in Denmark, €15.13 in (West) Germany, about €13.50 in Finland and Sweden, about €12.85 in the United Kingdom and in Ireland, €10.48 in France, about €8.60 in Italy and Spain, etc. In the more affluent new member states from Central and Eastern Europe these costs were €2.35 in the Czech Republic, €2.28 in Hungary, €2.06 in Poland, and €1.88 in Slovakia.

A decided shift in the direction of social harmonization occurred only in the mid-1980s, when after ten years of slow growth the Community was allegedly suffering from severe 'Euro-sclerosis'. The third enlargement in 1986 had divided the Community into a North and a South, the latter comprising Spain, Portugal, and Greece, and differences in labour costs across member states – even though much smaller than in today's EU – were for the first time significant. Wage differentials, high unemployment, stagnating real wages, and the policy entrepreneurship of Commission president Delors, are all factors explaining the shift towards social harmonization. Delors was looking forward to the day when 80 per cent of all regulations affecting the member states would come from Brussels. It seemed a realistic expectation then, based as it was on the more than eighty thousand pages of European legislation already on the statute book. Today it looks much likelier that the growing heterogeneity of the Union, coupled with the poor record for economic growth in the euro-zone, will have as a consequence not more top-down harmonization, but on the contrary increasing resistance to liberalization and European regulations in crucially important areas such as energy and the services sector (see chapter 4). At the same time, the insistence of those member states which are net contributors that the EU budget should not exceed 1 per cent of Union GDP suggests that in the future it may be impossible to preserve even those rather modest elements of a European welfare policy developed in half a century, starting with welfare for farmers and social security for migrant workers.

With this scenario in mind, one should reconsider the traditional distinction between negative and positive integration. Some scholars have written about an 'institutional asymmetry' built into the treaties – an asymmetry which they believe a common social policy would help overcome. The contention is that while negative integration and competition policy, being primary (i.e. treaty-based) European law, are directly enforceable by the European Commission and Courts, policies endorsing social protection and equality – positive integration – usually require intergovernmental agreement (in some cases unanimous agreement) and are therefore designed and implemented with much greater difficulty. These critics are right when they recognize the asymmetry between primary and secondary rules; they are wrong in maintaining that it should be corrected, or at least compensated. Indeed, the reader will recall the basic reason for this asymmetry: heavily regulated national markets could not have been integrated without primary rules restricting the interventionist tendencies of national governments, and the protectionist devices of both publicly owned and private firms. Further, since the method envisaged by the treaties makes the integration of national markets the starting point of a long march towards 'ever closer union of the peoples of Europe', it follows that negative integration is a *constituent*, as opposed to a contingent, element of the grand strategy of the founders of the EEC. Actually, the Treaty of Rome did not attach any normative connotation to the distinction between positive and negative integration: the common market was to be established using both methods, albeit with greater reliance on negative integration for the reason just outlined. The integrationist bias of many students of the EU explains why over the years the superiority of positive over negative integration has come to be taken for granted. Positive integration has been identified with positive values like social and environmental protection, equality, market-failure correction, and 'deep' integration and negative integration with deregulation, narrow economic interests, and 'shallow' integration. As it turns out, economic and other special interests often find it expedient to support measures of positive integration, such as harmonization, while fundamental rights under European law are often better protected by means of negative integration.

The best-known example of negative integration in the area of individual rights is Article 119 of the Treaty of Rome (now Article 141 EC), which requires application of the principle of equal pay, for male and female workers, for equal work or work of equal value. The article itself conferred no positive regulatory powers, until it was amended by the Treaty of Amsterdam. The new paragraph (3) inserted by that treaty extends the scope of the article to positive measures ensuring equality of opportunity and is thus not restricted to measures simply outlawing discrimination. So far, however, the most dramatic results have been achieved by Article 119 in its original, 'negative', formulation. In the landmark *Defrenne II* case (*Defrenne v. Sabena*, Case 43/75) the European Court of Justice held that the article is directly enforceable and grants rights to an individual if remedies do not exist under national law. It decided that the policy of the Belgian airline Sabena – forcing stewardesses to change jobs within the company (at a loss in wages) at the age of 40, but imposing no such requirement on cabin stewards doing the same work – was discriminatory, and required Sabena to compensate Ms Defrenne's loss of income. According to Evelyn Ellis (1998), the dramatic ruling of the *Defrenne II* case reveals the Court's frustration over non-compliance with Article 119 by the member states and over the weak-willed attitude towards this non-compliance demonstrated by the Commission. In the *Bilka* case of 1986 the Court indicated its willingness to strike down national measures excluding, in the absence of a clear justification, women from any employer-provided benefits, such as pensions. In a later case, the ECJ held that all elements of pay are due to all employees in a particular activity, without regard to the hours worked. In Germany, at that time, employees who worked less than ten hours a week for a commercial cleaning company did not receive statutory sick-pay. This regulation affected mostly women, thus the Court saw it as an indirect discrimination against women, hence as a violation of Article 119. Since the discriminatory impact on women of the hours requirement lacked an objective justification – or, at least, one was not provided by the German government – the plaintiff won her case.

The *Barber* case (1990), in which the Court extended the meaning of Article 119 to cover age thresholds for pension eligibility, demonstrates the symmetric effect of this norm. Mr Barber, having been made redundant at age fifty-two, was denied a pension that would have been available immediately to female employees. Instead he received a lump-sum payment. The Court held that this treatment was illegal since pensions are pay and therefore within the scope of Article 119. The decision, which required massive restructuring of pension schemes, caused a 'Barber Protocol' to be appended to the Maastricht Treaty, to the effect that *Barber* was not to be applied retroactively. Nonetheless, the implications for future pension plans were considerable (Ostner and Lewis 1995). These and other ECJ rulings show the impact 'negative law' can have on national legislation and legal practice by outlawing direct and indirect discrimination both in individual and in collective agreements. It is instructive to compare this direct impact with the uncertain, and often suboptimal, outcomes of many measures of positive integration.

Consider, for example, the difference between the judicial enforcement of the right not to be discriminated against on the grounds of, say, gender or nationality, and the promotion of substantive equality, or even of equality of opportunity. The latter objectives are much broader than the simple prohibition of discriminatory practices, and normally require positive interventions. The costs of such interventions will fall on the citizens of the member states affected by the measures, without having been authorized through the normal democratic process (in its financial implications, the *Barber* case was rather unique among measures of negative integration). Again, we saw that positive integration in the form of harmonized regulations, for instance in the area of environmental protection, imposes costs which may not adequately reflect national preferences and policy priorities. The welfare losses resulting from these potential distortions should be taken into account in calculating the benefits and costs of interventionist measures – a point generally ignored by the supporters of positive integration. These difficulties explain, at least in part, the reluctance of the founding fathers to endorse positive rights, and their preference for measures of negative integration (Majone 2005: 159–61). As noted, positive measures aimed at equality of opportunity only became possible after the Treaty of Amsterdam added a new paragraph (3) to Article 141 EC (former Article 119), empowering the Council to 'adopt measures to ensure the application of the principle of equal opportunities and equal treatment of men and women in matters of employment and occupation, including the principle of equal pay for equal work or work of equal value'.

At issue here is not the merit of the objectives of various positive measures, but whether, or to what extent, they can be legitimately pursued at European level. Supporters of a stronger role for the Union in most areas of social policy deem the concept of non-discrimination and the resultant negative law insufficient because they do not tackle the roots of inequality but, on the contrary, they are premised on the existing cultural and social divides to be found in the member states. One example of the static nature of the concept of non-discrimination cited is the comment of the ECJ – in *Hofmann* v. *Barmer Ersatzkasse* – that the

1976 Equal Treatment Directive was 'not designed to settle questions concerned with the organization of the family, or to alter the division of responsibility between parents' (cited in Ellis 1998: 323). This is taken to be too timid an attitude. What is required if real equality of opportunity is to be achieved, social-rights activists argue, is 'law and policy which encourage a degree of social engineering and transform some of the ways in which our lives are presently organized' (Ellis 1998: 324).

Of course, such sweeping legal and policy changes are incompatible with the nature of a system like the EU, based on the principles of subsidiarity, proportionality, and enumerated powers, and where national sovereignty in the crucial areas of taxation and social security is still preserved. Activists hope that the EU may evolve into a political union with the legal and financial resources needed to enforce all kinds of positive social rights – and in this sense able to overcome the 'institutional asymmetry' between the two modes of integration. But such a vision does not seem to be shared by a majority, or at least a significant minority, of EU citizens. As long as federalist aspirations continue to enjoy only elite support, the legitimacy of the integration process, such as it presently is, will continue to depend largely on negative integration. The principle of non-discrimination may not tackle the roots of inequality, yet its enforcement by the ECJ has contributed to a considerable improvement in the quality of the democratic process in the member states. In contrast, the following section will argue, an activist social policy at European level would actually aggravate the EU's legitimacy problem: instead of generating a sense of transnational solidarity it would reinforce the popular image of an ever expanding and highly bureaucratized Union. This image, for all its populistic overtones, is not altogether erroneous. The historical experience of both the American New Deal and the European welfare states shows that the expansion of redistributive social policies has been one of the main causes of political and administrative centralization in the twentieth century.

Legitimacy through Welfare?

According to its advocates, a fully fledged social policy at European level would not only prevent such undesirable phenomena as regime-shopping, social dumping and far-reaching deregulation of labour markets; it would also increase the legitimacy of the EU. Historically, social policy has made a crucially important contribution to the process of nation-building by bridging the gap between the state and civil

society. National insurance, health and welfare services, public education, housing policy, regional transfers were, and by and large remain,
powerful symbols of national solidarity. A comprehensive European
social policy, it is claimed, will do the same for the process of European
unification by providing a concrete demonstration of Europe-wide
solidarity. Unfortunately, this historical analogy is seriously misleading.
The obstacles – legal, political, financial, and administrative – to even a
small-scale reproduction of the national welfare states at European level
are so formidable as to justify the use of the term 'mirage' for such
visions. To begin with, the very modest role of traditional social policy
in the process of European integration is, to repeat, largely due to the
reluctance of the member states to surrender control of a politically
salient and popular area of public policy, and to transfer the necessary
competences and resources to the supranational level. In other words,
the social-policy domain has been effectively pre-empted by the member
states.

A second problem is the variety of welfare-state models coexisting in
Europe, each model and each of the numerous national variants being
rooted in historical and political traditions, and deeply embedded in
different socioeconomic contexts. Even in the old EU-15 at least
four main regional types were recognizable: a Scandinavian model; an
Anglo-Saxon model; the model of the 'Bismarck countries' of Central
Europe; and the welfare systems of the southern rim of the Union. In the
enlarged Union the situation, besides being more complex, is in a state
of flux. If the probability was always small of a European welfare state
somehow emerging as a transnational synthesis (or 'federation') of
national welfare systems, today that probability is close to zero. Under
present conditions, Habermas's apparently modest proposal to deepen
the social dimension by means of the 'gradual harmonization' of fiscal
and social policies (see above) in fact verges on the utopian. As Obinger
and co-authors write: 'With the benefit of hindsight, we may conclude
that the window of opportunity for the supersession of national social
programmes by European schemes has diminished with each enlargement, because each increase in membership has multiplied the number
of constituent units and thereby increased the number of possible veto
players potentially opposed to greater uniformity of provision' (Obinger
et al. 2005: 556).

The main obstacle to a European welfare state, however, is public
opinion. It is not only the national governments that refuse to surrender

control over social policy. One of the major strengths of the welfare state is the broad electoral base for core social programmes, as shown by the unpopularity of cutbacks. Naturally enough, the same voters who strongly support the national welfare state also resist any significant transfer of social-policy competences to the European level. Eurobarometer data mapping the responses of citizens in the EU-15 with regard to their preferred level of government for social policy-making, indicate that merely one-third of the population is favourable to a shift of social-policy competence to the Union (Obinger *et al.* 2005: 556). The only countries where a majority of citizens support social-policy integration are the net receivers of European transfers. If such countries are excluded, then the data show that support for a European social policy has declined among the wealthier member states – precisely the ones which would be the net contributors to the EU budget – at least since the late 1980s. In fact, the historical series of Eurobarometer data shows that opposition to involving the Union in policies dealing with the personal distribution of income is long-standing.

Precisely the impossibility of transferring to the supranational level even a 'light' version of the existing welfare states, and the commitment of voters to their own welfare model, demonstrate the political unfeasibility of a European federal state. A fully fledged European federation would face a highly constrained public agenda, being barred from pursuing policies subsidizing particular socioeconomic groups or jurisdictions at the expense of other identifiable groups or jurisdictions. To repeat a point already made, a European federation could not pursue precisely those redistributive policies that characterize and legitimate the national welfare state, and being unable to provide the variety of public and 'merit' goods citizens of modern welfare states take for granted, it could not attract sufficient popular support – or retain it in the long run. The nation state would remain, for its own people, the principal focus of collective loyalty and the real arena of democratic politics. Democratic life would continue to develop in this framework, while the federation, far from being able to correct the legitimacy deficit of the present EU, would actually make it worse because of the disappointment of those who had expected something like a European welfare state. In turn this loss of legitimacy would prevent the federal government from acting energetically even in those areas, such as foreign policy and defence, where the member states must pool their sovereignty if they wish to play a more incisive role on the international scene (Majone 2005: 207–9).

A Social Europe of Bits and Pieces?

Some champions of Social Europe argue that if a fully fledged European welfare state is politically and economically unfeasible at present, it should at least be possible to develop further certain of its present elements. At a later stage these elements could be fitted together to achieve a comprehensive regime. Thus, the CAP effects a considerable transfer of money from consumers and taxpayers to farmers, and for this reason it has been considered by students of EU social policy to form the core of a 'welfare state for farmers'. However, the CAP is not only an inefficient, but also a perverse type of social policy since financial transfers go disproportionately to well-to-do farmers and rich landowners. In 1992 the European Commission reported that the richest 20 per cent of European landowners and agribusiness companies received 80 per cent of EU farm aid, and it seems that the situation has not changed significantly since then. What is perhaps even worse is that the names of the recipients of EU agricultural subsidies have remained undisclosed for such a long time. Only in 2005, for instance, a Dutch minister of agriculture was called before the country's parliament to answer questions about pay-outs to his own farms. Knowing that his subsidies would soon be made public, the minister disclosed that his farms in the Netherlands and France received at least €185,000 in 2004, but denied that those funds in any way influenced his political decisions.

More shocking still – because so contrary to the spirit, if not the letter, of the treaty mandate 'to ensure a fair standard of living for the agricultural community, in particular by increasing the individual earnings of persons engaged in agriculture', Article 33 EC – is the fact that among the largest receivers of CAP transfers are some of the most prestigious aristocratic families of Britain, and the present owners of the large collective farms privatized after the fall of East Germany's Communist regime. According to a study by Professor Richard Baldwin of the Graduate Institute of International Studies in Geneva (reported by the *International Herald Tribune*, see Castle 2007: 1, 8) in the 2003–4 farming year the Queen of England and the Prince of Wales received €360,000 in EU farm subsidies, the Duke of Westminster, €260,000, and the Duke of Marlborough, €300,000. Despite the damage to the credibility of the European agricultural policy caused by subsidies to the wealthy, national governments are tepid about reform plans advanced by the Commission to make the system less unfair. In 2002 a plan to cap farm subsidies at €300,000 was blocked by Germany and Britain. While British leaders, from Mrs Thatcher to Tony Blair, have repeatedly called for reform of the CAP, this particular proposal was opposed, presumably because of the large share of the receipts from the agriculture budget going to the biggest landowners. The main losers under any plan to limit CAP subsidies would be precisely Britain and Germany, the two countries where many of the largest farms are concentrated. The capture of what was supposed to be the core of a 'welfare state for farmers' by powerful national interests exemplifies some of the problems that a European welfare state, necessarily dependent on the good will of the national governments, would have to face.

Regional policy is another potential candidate as building block of a future Social Europe. EU regional policy, which aims to complement, rather than replace, the regional policies of the member states, is the most conspicuous component of the so-called cohesion policy – the second largest item in the EU budget, after agriculture, making up about 35 per cent of total expenditure. Cohesion policy uses two main financial instruments – the Structural Funds and the Cohesion Fund – with the former accounting for about 90 per cent, and the latter for 10 per cent of the total. Structural Funds allocate money to regions on the basis of certain 'objectives', such as supporting the development and structural adjustment of regions lagging behind the average level across Europe's geographical units, or funding plans for border regions and regions in industrial decline. The Cohesion Fund – established in 1993 in preparation for monetary union – has a national rather than a regional focus, and targets those member states whose per capita GDP is lower than 90 per cent of the EU average, and that are following a programme of economic convergence. It is reserved for environment and transportation infrastructure. It should be noted that all members of the EU-15 except Luxembourg and Denmark (and Belgium and the Netherlands since 2007) have at least one region receiving financial aid, while only four countries (Greece, Spain, Portugal, and Ireland – the last country until 2003) have been receiving money from the Cohesion Fund. An odd feature of the system, caused by the predominant regional focus of cohesion policy, is that countries with a similar level of national GDP may be allocated very different levels of funding.

There is of course an important distinction between reducing inequality among individuals and reducing disparities across regions. The difficulty of targeting regions to achieve a better distribution of individual incomes is well known. Since most regions contain a mix of poor and rich individuals, a programme aimed at redistributing resources to a region whose average income is low may result, for example, in a lower tax rate. The main beneficiaries of the programme would then be rich individuals in poor regions. Thus, regional policy is an inefficient instrument of social policy, but in federal or quasi-federal systems it is quite difficult for the central government to aim redistribution directly at individuals. Even in the United States, where the federal government pays three-quarters of the cost of welfare assistance, the states set the benefit levels. States differ in their assessment of what a family needs to achieve a reasonable standard of living, and in the amount they are willing to contribute to help families meet that standard. States also differ in the requirements an applicant must satisfy to be eligible for welfare assistance. As a consequence of these differences, the level of welfare assistance among the American states varies widely (Peterson and Rom 1990). The fact that, in Europe as in America, the member states insist on non-individualized transfers of centrally allocated funds provides additional evidence of the inefficiency of regional policy as an instrument of social policy.

As a matter of fact, EU regional policy does not transfer resources to low-income regions as such, in the manner of an explicitly redistributive policy. Article 158 of the EC Treaty refers to a reduction in 'disparities between the levels of development', not of income levels. This is under-standable: as mentioned above, a policy of unconditional transfers to low-income regions would create identifiable winners and losers, and thus would be politically unfeasible in the EU. There is nevertheless a negative correlation between GDP levels and funds received under the EU cohesion policy: poorer member states and regions do get more funds than wealthier ones. However, the inverse relationship between transfers and GDP levels largely disappears once the CAP and other internal programmes are added to cohesion policy (Sapir *et al.* 2004). Such a result should not be puzzling: as we saw, the CAP, still representing 40 per cent of the EU budget, is *positively*, and strongly, correlated with income, so that well-to-do farmers, not to mention rich landowners, get much more than poor farmers.

In sum, cohesion policy is hardly more entitled than the CAP to be considered a potential candidate as building block of a future Social Europe. Leaving aside issues of interpersonal redistribution of income, what can be said about the effectiveness of the current EU cohesion policy in terms of economic convergence? As in the case of most European policies, and arguably more so in this case, the question of effectiveness is a difficult one to answer. According to the 2004 semi-official Sapir Report, in the period 1980–2000 a tendency of per capita

GDP to converge can be observed at the level of the member states, while within each country GDP levels and employment rates tended to diverge across regions, thus increasing inequality. It could be said, of course, that regional divergence would have been even more pronounced in the absence of the EU cohesion policy. The truth, according to Sapir and co-authors, is that, without more detailed information than is generally available about regional characteristics such as initial income, human capital, local industrial structures, and quality of local administration, one cannot disentangle the effect of cohesion policy from that of other programmes. Hence, 'it is not possible to establish conclusively what the relative performance of these regions would have been in the absence of EU cohesion policy and other policies' (Sapir *et al.* 2004: 60).

In any case, the debate about the effectiveness, and political implications, of the EU regional policy is becoming irrelevant. In the 1990s a number of scholars had enthusiastically greeted the call for greater regional equality, and the significant increase of the funds made available for regional policy after the Single European Act. The hope was that the new emphasis on regional policy would mark a fundamental shift in European integration. The outline of a new political order seemed to be emerging: a 'Europe of the Regions', in which the national governments would be outflanked by regional and local governments dealing directly with the European Commission. Experience has shown that these were cryptofederalist fantasies: the central governments soon demonstrated their ability to control the implementation of the EU regional policy (Allen 2005). But this is yesterday's snow. In the enlarged Union, reducing income disparities among the member states (rather than among regions in different countries) is, for the reasons discussed in previous chapters, a matter of absolute urgency and priority. But EU convergence policy cannot be a real factor in bringing about the requisite economic convergence as long as it is dispersed among small sub-national jurisdictions in different countries to care for different needs. The Sapir Report points out what should have been obvious all along, namely that EU policy 'can become an efficient tool of economic convergence only when accompanied by a set of financial and non-financial elements (labour market situation, investment opportunities, business climate, etc.) which are the result of national policies' (Sapir *et al.* 2004: 146). In line with this analysis, the report suggests that the new convergence policy should focus on low-income countries rather than low-income regions, using national per capita GDP (measured in Purchasing Power Parity) as an eligibility criterion. It acknowledges that during the catch-up process, increasing regional disparities within these poorer countries could emerge. However, this phenomenon could be mitigated by national growth, and should anyhow be eased by national, rather than EU, policies.

The re-nationalization of EU regional policy and of the CAP – both events could occur in the course of the next decade – would provide definitive proof of the impossibility of building up a comprehensive EU social policy out of bits and pieces of national welfare systems. In the present chapter I submitted that the vision of a Social Europe incorporating the core features of the national welfare systems – especially a basic social-security coverage for all citizens, and a more equal wage and income structure than in many other parts of the world – was and remains a mirage vainly pursued by integrationist elites. At the European Council of Hanover in June 1988 – when the Community consisted of twelve member states – Commission president Delors tried to convince sceptical national leaders that 'the social dimension is an integral part, even a precondition for the successful construction of Europe' (Delors 1989: 21). Twenty years later, when the EU has more than twice that number of (highly heterogeneous) members, we are forced to conclude that social policy is most unlikely to be the royal road to European unification – even less likely than monetary union, which also failed to represent the point of no return on the road to political integration which President Delors had envisaged.

6

The Democratic Deficit and All That

The Question of Standards

Everybody familiar with the European treaties will readily admit that the processes of collective decision-making in the EU do not satisfy democratic principles – even basic principles taken for granted at the national level. As argued in chapter 1, the Community Method – not the sole method of decision-making in the EU, but the most important one for economic integration – is the classic example of the sacrifice of democracy on the altar of integration, and as such it will also be referred to repeatedly in the following pages. However, agreement ends with the acknowledgement of a serious, possibly irredeemable, 'democratic deficit' of the EU and its policy-making institutions. One reason for the absence of agreement about the nature and possible remedies of the EU's democratic deficit is that different critics generally rely on different evaluative standards. The conceptual confusion is compounded by the failure to distinguish between standard-setting and standard-using: between defining new norms, and searching for solutions satisfying current norms (Majone 1998). Standard-using is the relatively straight-forward process of assessing various dimensions of performance against given benchmarks; whereas standard-setting is a process of deliberation where it is open to anyone to put forward a proposal as to what the standards should be, and to use persuasion to influence others to accept the proposal (Urmson 1968). In examining an argument about the EU's 'democratic deficit' it is therefore important to see whether the author is applying existing standards – usually derived from the theory and practice of representative democracy at national level – or whether (s)he is advocating new norms, presumably tailored to the special features of the Union. In the former case one must be aware of the analogical fallacy (arguing erroneously from an apparently similar case, see the following section); in the latter, the key issue is whether the proposed norms are compatible with the nature of the EU as we know it, or whether in fact they presuppose a radically different approach to European integration – a going back to the drawing board, so to speak (see section on 'The Big Trade-Off').

A survey of the recent literature identifies four main arguments, or clusters of arguments, concerning the democratic deficit (Majone 2005: 28–32). The oldest, and still most widespread, critical argument asserts that European integration has meant an expansion of executive power at the supranational level, a decrease in national parliamentary control, and no compensating executive accountability to the European Parliament. Some members of this school simply define the democratic deficit as the gap between the powers transferred to the Union and the efficacy of parliamentary oversight and control at European level. That policy-making at this level is dominated by executives – the national ministers in the Council and the non-elected members of the European Commission – who largely escape parliamentary control, is deemed to be unacceptable by the standards of parliamentary democracy. Indeed, in classical parliamentary systems the government is viewed as a sort of 'executive committee' of parliament, and can remain in office only as long as it enjoys the support of a parliamentary majority. Under the Community Method, on the other hand, no such relationship between the legislative and the executive power exists.

According to a second group of critics, the main cause of the democratic deficit is not so much executive dominance per se – which in one form or another can be observed in most contemporary parliamentary democracies – as the weak political accountability of EU policy-makers. Thus, not only is the EP not allowed to initiate legislation; even its right of censuring the Commission on questions of policy is severely restricted because of the procedural constraints on the exercise of this right. For a motion of censure to be adopted a double majority is required: at least half of the total number of members of the EP (MEPs) have to vote, and two-thirds of voting MEPs have to cast their vote in favour. And although the EP can dismiss the Commission, at least in theory, it has no power over the other policy-making body, the Council of Ministers. Again, although the EP can now veto the governments' choice for Commission president, and the team of commissioners, still the national governments are the agenda-setters in the appointment process. This second cluster of critical arguments, like the first one, applies normative standards derived from the theory and practice of parliamentary government at national level to reach the conclusion that a necessary (and perhaps sufficient) condition to correct the democratic deficit is to expand the powers of the EP. These critics considered the direct election of the EP as a first, crucial step in the direction of something close to a bicameral federal legislature. Direct election of the EP was supposed to bestow new legitimacy on the entire integration process.

Evidence from all the European elections held since 1979 shows that these expectations were ill-founded. What we find, rather, is a perfect correlation between the steady increase of powers of the EP and the constant *decrease* of the turnout in European elections. As we saw in chapter 1, in 1979 – when the only significant competences of the EP were the right to reject the budget, to amend it within certain limits, and to approve (or not) the annual accounts – the turnout was 63 per cent. At the 1989 elections the turnout was 58.5 per cent. By then a legislative 'cooperation' procedure had been introduced into various policy fields, with an enhanced consultative role for the Parliament. The EP was also assigned veto power over the accession of new member states and over the conclusion of agreements with associate states. The Maastricht Treaty gave the EP the right to vote on the Commission before it took office; empowered it to appoint a European Ombudsman and to establish committees of enquiry; and made formal provision for the Parliament to invite the Commission to present legislative proposals, thus giving it a sort of indirect legislative initiative. Most important, Maastricht introduced the co-decision procedure, under which the EP and the Council became equal co-legislators in the fifteen areas to which the procedure then applied. Also, majority voting replaced unanimity in a large number of treaty areas, and advocates of stronger EP powers, while admitting that with majority voting the position of national parliaments was further weakened, contended that a greater role for the EP would improve the democratic legitimacy of EU legislation. But at the 1994 European elections the turnout dropped to 56.8 per cent. New prerogatives for the EP were again added by the Amsterdam and Nice treaties. In particular, Amsterdam extended the power of co-decision from fifteen to thirty-eight treaty areas; however, voter participation further declined below the 50 per cent mark: to 49.4 at the elections of 1999, and to 45.7 per cent at the 2004 elections. Before the 1999 elections it was widely anticipated that the EP-induced resignation of the Santer Commission would raise the profile of the EP among European voters and stimulate increased turnout at the June election (Judge and Earnshaw 2002: 358–9). In the event, voter participation declined for the first time below 50 per cent, as just noted.

A third group of critics use these data to conclude that the root cause of the democratic deficit is the absence of truly European elections.

Because of the absence of real contestation on European issues, the preferences of EU citizens are reflected indirectly, if at all, in the policy choices made by integrationist elites. What is even more serious, EU citizens are in no position to hold any of the law-making and policy-making institutions – Council, Commission, and EP – accountable for policy failures. If the EU were a system with a genuine electoral contest to determine the make-up of government and the direction of policy, these critics continue, then the outcome of European elections would have a direct effect on what European leaders do, forcing them to assume responsibility for the results of the policies they initiate. This is of course a very big 'if'. The problem is that such an EU would be radically different from the present one, and those who propose true European elections do not tell us how such elections would fit with the approach to European integration followed for the past half a century. For instance, how could an electoral process capable of influencing the direction of EU policy be made compatible with the Community Method's top-down approach, or with the Monnet method of integration by stealth? In fact, carried to its ultimate logical consequences, the argument suggests that the EU's democratic deficit can be solved by nothing less than transforming the present Union into something very similar to a fully fledged federal state. Unfortunately, a European super-state is precisely what neither the national governments, nor the people they represent, seem to want (see chapter 1). Hence the paradox that to make the EU democratic by a radical reform of the electoral process along the lines suggested by these critics would require going against the preferences of the vast majority of Europeans, and at the same time discarding the integration methods followed so far – methods which, for all their limitations, have delivered some important results. In other words, lacking sufficient popular support for a federal solution, we are faced with the trade-off between democracy and integration mentioned in chapter 1. Before exploring this key point more closely, let us briefly examine the last group of arguments about the democratic deficit and its possible remedy.

Politicians and scholars in this group face a different, but equally severe, trade-off: not so much between integration and democracy, as between integration and social justice – however defined. By and large, these are the same critics whose views were analysed in chapter 5. Rather than applying traditional normative standards, they invoke social standards of legitimacy; the EU's democratic deficit, they claim, is caused less by the absence or insufficient development of the institutions and practices of parliamentary democracy, than by the failure of the Union to ensure sufficient equality and social justice. In other words, the culprit is the failure of the political leaders to develop a European welfare state, or at least to give the Union a greater role in the transnational redistribution of income. By the social standards prevailing in the member states, they point out, the EU is a 'welfare laggard' and on this count cannot win the social acceptance and democratic legitimacy enjoyed by national welfare states. They fear, furthermore, that competition between the different national welfare regimes could lead to regime-shopping, social dumping, and far-reaching deregulation of labour markets. A fully fledged social policy at European level would not only prevent such negative developments; it would also enhance the legitimacy of the EU just as, in the past, social policies proved to be an essential source of democratic legitimacy for the nation state. Unfortunately, it is more likely that the result would be exactly the opposite of what the advocates of 'Social Europe' hope to achieve (see chapter 5).

In sum, normative arguments using standards derived from national models of parliamentary democracy are exposed to the analogical fallacy, as are arguments advocating standards of social legitimacy derived from the experience of the national welfare states. The proponents of social standards of legitimacy also fail to show how such standards could be implemented without a radical recasting of the present EU, along lines the majority of European voters seem to reject. These objections are considered in somewhat greater detail in the two following sections.

The Analogical Fallacy

No more serious pitfall threatens the student of the European Union than the idea of assessing its institutions and decision processes using the same criteria that apply to the national level. Some examples of misleading analogies were given in the preceding pages, and in the previous chapter, in connection with the model of Social Europe, but the analogical fallacy is quite widespread. Thus, in spite of some undeniable structural analogies, one cannot understand the real nature of the European Parliament using the same conceptual categories which have proved useful in analysing national parliaments. The EP does not differ from the legislatures of parliamentary democracies only because it lacks their power to tax and spend, to initiate legislation, and to validate a government's actions. Another fundamental difference is the absence of the traditional government–opposition dialectic. The consequences of this absence are quite significant: being denied an appropriate political arena in which to hold European governance accountable, voters are almost pushed into organizing opposition to Europe (Mair 2007). Hence the transformation of popular referendums on new treaties into contests for or against the EU. The *sui generis* nature of the EP is also revealed by the attitude of its members: many MEPs see themselves as policy specialists rather than as partisan politicians, and insist that the Commission should be a neutral institution, and that individual commissioners should forget their party affiliation, if any (Magnette 2001). This attitude may also account, at least in part, for the fact that the EP has never seriously contested the Commission's monopoly of legislative initiative.

In sum, the EP cannot represent a (non-existent) European people in the same sense in which a national parliament represents a historically defined demos, and thus cannot represent, even in theory, a common interest which is more than the sum of the various national interests. Individual interests, on the other hand, are still largely rooted at the national level, and hence find their natural expression in national parliaments and political parties. In fact, when important national interests are at stake, the EP tends to vote along national, rather than party, lines. One example among the many that could be cited is July 2001, when the EP turned down a Commission proposal for a Takeover Directive; the MEPs voted overwhelmingly to protect national economic interests, rather than the 'common interest' in the integration of Europe's capital markets, or even according to party-political (left–right) positions (Knudsen 2005). Given that in the enlarged EU structural differences among the national economies have increased significantly, one may expect that this process of 're-nationalization' of the European Parliament will acquire momentum in the future.

All this explains why the real arena of democratic politics continues to be the nation state, and why European elections are 'second-order elections' – useful perhaps to gauge the popularity of the incumbent *national* government, but meaningless as an arena where European issues would be debated and settled. It also explains why voter participation in European elections has been constantly decreasing, and why the EP does not enjoy sufficient democratic legitimacy to be able, in turn, to legitimate European policies, or other European institutions like the Commission. The key point that must be understood is that the institutional architecture of the EC/EU is based on the representation of *corporate* (national and supranational), not individual, interests – as in the old, pre-democratic model of governance known as 'mixed government' (Majone 2005: 46–51). It is therefore not surprising that the application of modern notions of representative government to the European institutions, and to the EP in particular, is more misleading than heuristically helpful. The limitations of the EP as an institution of general representation of a non-existent European people were implicitly acknowledged by the now defunct Constitutional Treaty and by the Lisbon Treaty, with their proposals to assign a larger role to the national parliaments in the process of European integration. We may conclude that, whatever useful role the EP may play in the institutional architecture of the EU, it cannot be evaluated by the same standards we apply to national legislatures.

Similarly, the European Commission is often referred to as 'the European executive', but the label is, again, more misleading than useful. As already mentioned, the constitutional model of the EC/EU is not based on the principle of separation of powers, hence it is impossible to map functions onto specific institutions. In particular, there is no neatly identifiable European executive, since executive powers are exercised for some purposes by the Council acting on a Commission proposal, for other purposes by the Commission under delegation from the Council, and overwhelmingly by the member states in implementing European policies on the ground. The most striking violation of separation-of-powers is of course the monopoly of legislative initiative the Commission enjoys under the classic Community Method. Because of this monopoly, the Commission plays a role in the legislative process at least as important as its executive role, when it implements the rules the Council lays down. No comparable institution exists at national level, so that evaluative norms derived from the experience of modern constitutional democracies are again wholly inapplicable.

Since the establishment of EMU, worries have also been expressed about the democratic deficit of the European Central Bank. It is perhaps less widely appreciated that what has just been said about the impossibility of applying standards distilled from national practices to *sui generis* institutions like the EP and the Commission applies to the ECB as well. Specifically, there seems to be no historical precedent of an independent central bank operating without the political counterweight provided by a fully fledged government. Attention has already been called to the fact that the ECB's extremely high level of independence was meant to compensate for the serious shortcomings of macroeconomic governance at European level. But precisely because of those shortcomings, formal and informal mechanisms used to temper the independence of a national central bank are not available to EU policy-makers. In any case, the normative concerns raised by this abnormal situation should be addressed to the European leaders who designed the institutional framework of EMU, rather than to the Bank itself (see the following section).

In sum, the Commission, the European Parliament, the ECB, and also the Council of Ministers are so different from superficially analogous national institutions that to apply to them normative standards derived from the democratic practice of the member states is to commit a 'category mistake'. A category mistake, according to Gilbert Ryle (1949), consists in discussing certain facts as if they belonged to one logical type or category, when they actually belong to another. Thus it is a category mistake to talk about a university in the same terms in which one talks of its departments, professional schools, or administrative offices: the university is not identical with any one of these units; rather, it is the way the units are organized. The pitfall lies in thinking of the university as if it stood for an extra member of the class of which departments, schools, and offices are members. A similar category mistake consists in assessing the EU and its institutions by means of the same criteria we adopt at the national level – as if the Union were a state and not an organization or association of corporate bodies: the member states and the European institutions (Majone 2005: 24–5).

The Big Trade-Off: Democracy and Integration

The nature of the European polity as a system based on the representation of corporate, rather than individual, interests ('mixed government') appears most clearly in the Community Method. The institutional and normative significance of this method has been emphasized in several of the preceding chapters. In chapter 1 it has been linked to the difficult decision of the founding fathers of the EEC to sacrifice democracy on the altar of European integration. Today Euro-leaders are still divided on the merits of the method, and especially over whether or not it should be generalized, i.e. extended to all areas of activity of the EU, including foreign policy and defence. Also, the popular view of the EU as a polity run by unaccountable bureaucrats rests, in the final analysis, on a simplistic, though not wholly mistaken, understanding of the ways the method operates in practice.

Some authors have proposed to distinguish between a 'classic' Community Method, derived from the treaties, as interpreted by the ECJ, and some updated version of it, which would include such recent reforms as the non-binding Open Method of Coordination (OMC), and more efficient decision-making rules in the Council – primarily the replacement of unanimity by qualified majority even in areas close to the core of national sovereignty. The validity and/or usefulness of such innovations have been questioned by a number of analysts, however. There seems to be a growing consensus in the literature that OMC has fallen far short of expectations. It has also been argued that OMC and other informal and non-binding new modes of governance, far from enhancing the legitimacy of EU policy-making, threaten to do precisely the opposite. This is because they lack the certainty, transparency, and legal protection that are provided by the classic Community Method (see Idema and Kelemen 2006 for a good survey of the relevant literature).

Proposals to make the Community Method more efficient by generalizing qualified majority voting raise yet more serious normative problems. The reformers point out that in an EU with twenty-seven members, governance will be practically impossible without extending Qualified Majority Voting (QMV) to all areas of EU policy-making. The rule of unanimity, they say, is both inefficient and unjust since it gives the possibility to any country, even a very small one, of imposing the status quo on the other members of the Union. As I have shown elsewhere, such proposals, if implemented, would actually undermine the very approach they are supposed to improve (Majone 2005: 53–9). An essential feature of the Community mode of governance is that the nature of the prevailing interests determines the method of decision-making. This means that each subject matter has its own decision-making procedure according to the nature of the interest receiving special protection under the treaties: a unanimous vote in the Council in policy areas of particular relevance to national sovereignty; QMV in matters where national interests have to be reconciled with the common interest; autonomous powers of decision to the Commission where supranational interests should prevail. This being the case, the proposal to extend QMV to all areas of EU policy-making, far from strengthening the traditional method, would actually subvert it. The principle that decision rules should be tailored to the nature of the various interests deserving protection is one of the main results of the modern theory of collective choice as developed by James Buchanan and Gordon Tullock (1962). The reason why collective activities should *not* be organized through the operation of the same decision rule for all subject matters is that the costs of collective decision-making to the individual members of the group vary considerably from issue to issue. In general, the more important the issue, the greater the majority required for a collective decision. When basic interests of individual members of the group have to be protected against the potentially negative consequences of a decision, unanimity – or something close to it – is the optimal decision rule.

In the EU context, two more observations are relevant. First, if efficiency in decision-making were the only relevant criterion, then it would be necessary to get rid of the co-decision procedure as well, under which the EP enjoys the same status as the Council in the law-making process. In fact, it has been demonstrated that in areas where the QMV rule applies, decision-making speed did not accelerate, but actually deteriorated, largely because of the delays stemming from the complex procedures required by co-decision. Second, it is ironic that the Commission, which is among the strongest advocates of generalized QMV, should oppose the veto power that the unanimity rule, where it applies, gives to each member state: with its monopoly of legislative initiative, the Commission also enjoys a power of veto (or at least 'pre-veto') over legislative ideas it dislikes. In sum, recent proposals to extend the Community Method in various directions are hardly convincing, either empirically, theoretically, or normatively. In the following analysis, which is concerned with this method as one of the roots of the EU's democratic deficit, it appears therefore preferable to stick to the traditional view, as it is stated, for instance, in the Commission's White Paper on *European Governance* (Commission 2001a: 12).

According to this document, the Community Method rests on three principles:

1. The Commission is independent of the other European institutions; it alone makes legislative and policy proposals. Its independence is meant to strengthen the ability to execute policy, act as guardian of the treaties, and represent the Community in international negotiations.
2. Legislative and budgetary acts are adopted by the Council of Ministers and the European Parliament, always on a proposal made by the Commission.
3. The European Court of Justice guarantees the maintenance of the balance among European institutions, and respect for the rule of law.

It is especially important to understand what is implied by the Commission's monopoly of agenda-setting. First, other European institutions cannot legislate in the absence of a prior proposal from the Commission. It is up to the latter to decide whether the Community should act and, if so, in what legal form, what should the content be, and which implementing procedures should be followed. Second, the Commission can amend its proposal at any time while it is under discussion, but the Council can amend the proposal only by unanimity. On the other hand, if the Council unanimously wishes to adopt a measure that differs from the Commission's proposal, the latter can deprive the main Community legislator of its power of decision by withdrawing its own proposal. As was argued in chapter 2, such a sweeping delegation of legislative powers to a non-elected body was a response to the crisis of the mid-1950s. After the collapse of the plans for a democratic, pre-federal European Political Community, the architects of the EEC faced a situation never contemplated by the federalists of the first post-war decade: the existence of a trade-off between democracy and integration – which the fathers of communitarian Europe consistently resolved in favour of integration. The implications of this choice did not appear as serious to them as they appear to us today because it was expected that the competence of the EEC would remain so narrow that the indirect legitimacy provided by the democratic character of the member states would suffice. Recall that even Robert Schuman (see chapter 2), father of the ECSC and 'European saint', thought that the competence of the supranational institutions should be limited to technical problems, and should not extend to functions involving the sovereignty of the member states. Likewise at the national level, after all, certain technical tasks are delegated to non-majoritarian institutions (see the following section). The relatively limited scope of the original plans explains why the debate about the democratic deficit started only after the SEA expanded significantly both Community competences and the domain of application of majority voting. What was originally a marginal trade-off – a small sacrifice of democracy for the sake of greater efficiency in limited areas of economic integration – became a surrender of basic principles of representative democracy as the competences of the EU kept growing.

Despite the widening gap between supranational powers and democratic legitimacy, most critics of the democratic deficit are reluctant to admit that the root cause of the phenomenon they deplore lies in the priority given to the promotion of integration. Less realistic than the founders, they would like to have both – more integration *and* more democracy – and grope for ways of resolving the basic dilemma without either questioning the logic of the method pursued so far, or admitting the lack of popular support for a fully fledged European government. However, all attempts to increase the legitimacy of the EU by such devices as the direct election of the EP and the steady expansion of its powers, the symbolism of EU citizenship, and the launch of various

'social' programmes – from the agricultural, regional, and cohesion policies to pro-labour regulations – have failed, for the simple reason that they
do not tackle the underlying problem.

The sacrifice of democracy in favour of European integration was of
course acceptable to Jean Monnet – no great admirer of majoritarian
politics – and to his cryptofederalist followers, determined to expand
supranational competences by all possible means. The willingness of integrationist leaders to sacrifice democracy for the sake of deeper integration
was again revealed at the time of the Maastricht Treaty, when it was decided
to give quasi-constitutional status (i.e. a treaty basis) to the independence of
the ECB. Before monetary union, the independence of national central
banks had only a statutory basis. This meant that in principle national
parliaments could always change the rules if they thought the central bank
was using its independence in a manner of which they did not approve. This
was true of the German Bundesbank and is still true of the Bank of England
or of the US Federal Reserve. Instead, to change the rules under which the
ECB and its national counterparts, as members of the European System of
Central Banks (ESCB), operate requires a treaty revision acceptable to all
the member states – a complex and politically hazardous procedure. The
net result is that the national parliaments of the members of the euro-zone
have lost any control over monetary policy, while the EP has no authority
in this area. The ECB is free to operate in a political vacuum since there is
no true European government to balance its powers, and even the institutions of economic governance are still poorly defined. In contrast, an
independent central bank like the Federal Reserve is placed within a
political structure where Congress, the president, and the Treasury supply
all the necessary political counterweights.

It should be noted that, unlike its American counterpart or the Bank of
England, the ECB enjoys both *instrument* independence and *goal* independence. When a central bank enjoys only instrument independence, it
is up to the government to fix the target – say, the politically acceptable
level of inflation – leaving the central bank then free to decide how best to
achieve the target. Because of the grant of both instrument and goal
independence to the ECB, some scholars complain about the democratic
deficit of the European Central Bank, asserting that in order to reduce
this deficit the ECB should evolve towards a governance model excluding
goal independence (Gormley and de Haan 1996). Unfortunately, these
analyses and the proposed solutions once again evade the deeper issue.
As noted in the preceding section, the ECB's exceptionally high level
of independence was meant to compensate for the shortcomings of

macroeconomic governance at European level. Because of the decision to pursue monetary integration in the absence of political agreement on crucial institutional and policy questions, the formal and informal mechanisms to temper the independence of national central banks are not available at EU level. For example, some economists have concluded that the socially optimal delegation of monetary policy is not to a completely independent central bank; in order to maximize social welfare, governments should have the option of overriding the central bank's decisions under some circumstances. Thus, the 'optimal' central bank should follow a non-linear decision rule: in case of small output shocks it determines the acceptable inflation level independently, while in the case of large disturbances it follows the government's preferences. But since at European level there is no secretary of the treasury or finance minister, hence no generally accepted political counterweight to the central bank, it is not obvious how appropriate procedures for overriding ECB decisions could be designed and enforced.

Some EU leaders, such as French president Sarkozy, think that the governments of the members of the euro-zone should have a greater say in the making of European monetary policy, especially in decisions concerning exchange rates: an excessive appreciation of the euro, they protest, is damaging the national economies. In March 2008, while the euro was reaching new record levels against the dollar, the Director General of the International Monetary Fund, Dominique Strauss-Kahn, joined the debate attributing the overvaluation of the European currency to the excessive power of the ECB. According to Strauss-Kahn, the ECB fulfils its statutory duty of containing inflation, but the absence of a treasury minister of the EU means that at European level concerns about inflation de facto prevail over concerns about growth: the ECB is overpowering precisely because it has no political counterweight (cited in Agence France-Presse 2008). However, it is known that Germany, supported by other members of the former D-mark bloc, is resolutely opposed to any significant change in the present framework of economic governance. The ECB itself strongly resists any external interference over its own decisions. Precisely for this reason it does not wish to be considered a 'European institution', as had been suggested during the drafting of the Constitutional Treaty. The fear is that having the same legal status as the Council, the EP, the Commission, and the Court of Justice could entail some commitments – e.g. expectations of institutional cooperation and of consultations before taking certain decisions – which could threaten the ECB's total independence. Under the EC Treaty, the ECB is simply a 'body', hence it is free of the 'constitutional glue' that is supposed to hold together the European 'institutions' – those listed as such in the treaty.

Again, it has been stressed that because of the absence of an effective system of economic governance at European level, complete political insulation of the ECB is necessary to the credibility of the new common currency. Now, this insulation was imposed by Germany on the other member states as a non-negotiable condition for giving up the Deutschmark in favour of the euro. This being the situation, it is pointless to lament the 'democratic deficit' of the ECB without first questioning the wisdom of a monetary union introduced not for sound economic reasons, but in order to advance the integration process, and to favour particular national interests. Those critics who look to the Federal Reserve as the better model – being as it is politically more accountable, and not exclusively concerned with price stability – forget that the American central bank operates within the framework of a system of government capable of providing all the necessary checks and balances. Early in 1951, for example, there arose a serious conflict between the Treasury and the Fed about the appropriate level of interest rates. With the help of the US president, the conflict was eventually settled by means of the 1951 Treasury–Federal Reserve Accord – a delicate compromise in which the Treasury accepted slightly higher rates and granted some flexibility to the Fed (Greider 1987: 327–8). In the interpretation of one scholar, the Accord 'defined quite clearly that the Fed was a political agency whose power depended on the balance of political support it could attract from its key constituencies: the President, the Treasury, interest groups like bankers, and Congress' (Kettle 1986: 80).

To recapitulate, scholars who lament the EU's 'democratic deficit' in its different facets, and suggest possible solutions, tend to focus on epiphenomena, when they should go back to first principles in order to identify underlying causes and possible remedies. Without going back to first principles there is no hope of understanding, let alone resolving, the legitimacy problems of the EU. In the case of the ECB, going back to first principles means recognizing that crucially important mechanisms of economic governance should have been agreed upon long before the introduction of the common currency. Until these holes in the policy-making machinery are filled, authority over the entire domain of monetary policy will continue to flow, by default, to the ECB, but responsibility for the deficit of political accountability should be attributed less to the central bank than to those who hoped to make monetary union the capstone of a

European federal structure – a classic example of the cryptofederalist strategy of fait accompli (see chapter 3). In the case of the Community Method, a reassessment of the situation should begin by asking whether the normative costs entailed by the Commission's monopoly of legislative and policy initiative are still acceptable in terms of actual results. Recent events like the string of negative referendums, and growing disenchantment with European integration justify doubts on this score. At the same time, Commission executives, well aware of the strategic importance of agenda control, look for every possible occasion to expand its scope. This can only aggravate the democratic deficit, and even in efficiency terms one can doubt the wisdom of extending the Commission's control of the policy agenda to areas such as Justice and Home Affairs, where the national governments enjoy a clear advantage of expertise and material resources. During a five-year transitional period, 1999 through 2004, both the national governments and the Commission were entitled to advance policy proposals for the 'communitarized' parts of JHA. Given the Commission's limited experience in this area, and the political salience of the issues arising in JHA, the decision to allow a competition of policy ideas, from both national and supranational sources, was wise. The traditional Commission monopoly was reintroduced at the end of the transitional period, but this writer is not aware that any of the scholars who worry about the EU's democratic deficit criticized the exclusion of the democratically legitimated national governments from policy initiation in such a politically sensitive area.

Legitimation through Distinctive Institutional Competence

The most striking aspect of the academic debate on the democratic deficit is the neglect of the continuous expansion of Union powers as a possible cause of the legitimacy problem. In the vast literature on the subject it is hard to detect any awareness that one of the roots of the problem may be the bulimia of the European institutions. On the contrary, the proposed solutions that have received most attention in academic and political discourse, such as extending the powers of the EP, expanding the use of QMV, or recasting the EU along the lines of 'Social Europe', presuppose, and thus implicitly justify, a further expansion of Community competences. The possibility of reducing the democratic deficit by drawing more precise limits on the powers exercised by the supranational institutions is seldom, if ever, mentioned – though this was the basic reason for inserting in the Maastricht Treaty Article 3b (now Article 5 EC) on the principle of subsidiarity. The explication of the principle in terms of comparative efficiency ('the Community shall take action ... only if and in so far as the objectives of the proposed action cannot be sufficiently achieved by the Member States and can therefore ... be better achieved by the Community') obscures the normative intent of the drafters of the article. The normative bite of Article 3b is in its first sentence – 'The Community shall act within the limits of the powers conferred upon it by the Treaty' – suggesting that in the past the supranational institutions repeatedly made use of their delegated powers in ways not approved of by at least some of their political principals. This sentence enunciates the principle of attributed (or limited) powers, and Professor Dashwood was referring to it when he wrote that after Maastricht 'The notion of a Community continuously moving the boundary posts of its own competence is ruled out of court' (Dashwood 1996: 115).

European institutions have no inherent powers – they possess only those conferred on them by the member states in the treaties. The question, therefore, is how far the powers so conferred may be expanded by indirect means, such as judicial interpretation or the creation of subsidiary powers under Article 235 of the Rome Treaty (now Article 308 EC). In the euphoria created by the Single European Act and the highly successful marketing of the 'Europe '92' campaign, it became tempting to imagine that there was no effective barrier to the continuous, if incremental, expansion of Community competences. European lawyers could refer to the broad interpretation given by the European Court to Article 235, which enables the Council to take appropriate measures in cases where, 'in the course of the operation of the common market', action by the Community is found to be necessary to attain one of its objectives, and there is no specific treaty-based power available for that purpose. Reviewing the effect of Article 235 as a whole, before the Maastricht Treaty, Hartley (1991: 108) wrote that 'it confers what can only be termed a general legislative power. For this reason, the theory of limited powers does not seem to be part of Community law, except to the extent that the Community may legislate only within the general area covered by the Treaties'. Indeed, since the early 1970s the Council and the Commission had made liberal use of this article to expand Community competences or to broaden the reach of Community legislation in many policy areas, e.g. social and regional policy, energy and environment, scientific and technological research and development, and cooperation agreements with third countries. Article 235 was used to accomplish 'the trick of self-levitation through pulling on its own boot straps' (Dashwood 1996: 123): in other words, to amend the treaty without following the normal democratic procedures of ratification and approval by national parliaments or popular referendums. The question whether Community action was actually necessary was considered by the European institutions as a matter within their complete discretion.

Interestingly enough, the European Convention responsible for drafting the Constitutional Treaty considered the possibility of scrapping Article 308 of the EC Treaty (former Article 235), but had to retreat in the face of determined opposition by the Commission and by integrationist groups – which, Peter Norman (2003) informs us, were overrepresented among the *conventionnels*. It has been argued that the article has rarely been used in recent years, hence not much would have been lost in discarding it, while the message would have reassured all those who fear that the creeping expansion of Union powers will not abate (Micossi and Gros 2006). This reluctance to consider the possibility of reducing the democratic deficit by a more precise delimitation of powers is rather surprising, since an analogous problem is well known at the national level. The delegation of powers to institutions that are not accountable to the voters or to their elected representatives, such as independent central banks and regulatory authorities, is a significant feature of the governance structure of all contemporary democracies. As discussed in the next chapter, a strong rationale for delegating powers to institutions independent of the electoral cycle is to increase the credibility of long-term policy commitments. The delegation of powers to 'non-majoritarian' institutions is meant to restrain the temptation of democratic politicians to assign greater weight to short-term considerations and to default on long-term commitments. At the same time, in a democracy, important policy choices are supposed to be taken by politically accountable leaders, so that democratic-deficit problems can, and do, arise also at the national level. How are such problems resolved there? Historically, courts of law are the first, and still the most important example of non-majoritarian institutions. The problem of the democratic legitimacy of judicial decisions has been especially felt in the United States, where federal courts may strike down a law enacted by Congress, and as such presumably expressing the preferences of the majority of American voters.

The legitimacy problem is particularly acute when the US Supreme Court engages in 'non-interpretive' review, i.e. when it makes the determination of constitutionality of a given policy by reference to a value judgement other than one embodied, even if only implicitly, either in some specific provision of the Constitution or in the overall structure of government as set up by the Constitution. A rich body of literature deals with the issue of judge-made constitutional law, and with the role and justification of the Supreme Court as a non-majoritarian, or even anti-majoritarian, institution (for a useful survey see Wolfe 1986). Of immediate relevance to our topic is Jesse Choper's 'functional' analysis of the role of the Supreme Court (Choper 1983). The thesis of this distinguished constitutional lawyer is that, despite the anti-majoritarian character of judicial review, the Court must exercise this power in order to protect individual rights which are not adequately represented in the political process. At the same time, however, the Court should decline to exercise judicial review in other areas in order to minimize the tension between this formal power and democratic dialectic, and to economize on its own legitimacy resources. What Choper proposes is a plan to use these scarce resources only where strictly necessary. The functional justification of judicial review in the area of individual rights is that the judiciary has an essential ingredient for this task, which is lacking in the political branches of government: it is 'insulated from political responsibility and unbeholden to self-absorbed and excited majoritarianism' (Choper 1983: 68). In areas like relations between the states and the federal government, and in questions having to do with separation-of-powers, on the other hand, the Court's involvement should be drastically restricted. The resolution of such issues should be left to the political process, where the states, Congress, and the presidency are all adequately represented, and can thus defend their interests there. In sum, the Supreme Court should be active only in areas where it enjoys, in Choper's phrase, a *distinctive institutional competence* – where it has a clear comparative advantage with respect to all other institutions.

With reference to the preceding discussion, Choper's criterion could be labelled 'horizontal subsidiarity'. Applying the criterion to the EU context, it may be argued that the role of the Court of Justice could not be played as effectively by any other European institution. Also the EP enjoys a distinctive institutional competence as the only supranational body consisting 'of representatives of the peoples of the States brought together in the Community' (Article 189 EC); and this despite the fact that it is quite unlikely that the EP will ever reproduce the national model. The ECB, too, can reasonably claim to enjoy a distinctive institutional competence to manage the common currency. It has already been noted that the Bank's exceptional degree of political independence was meant to compensate for the serious weakness of macroeconomic governance at European level. Whatever the doubts about the macro-economic wisdom of the Bank's well-nigh exclusive commitment to price stability, from the point of view of accountability this explicit, treaty-based commitment has the advantage that the performance of the ECB can be gauged against the rod of the regular statistics of inflation in the euro-zone. In this sense, at least, the ECB is an accountable, thus to some extent legitimated, non-majoritarian institution; its task is precisely, some would say too precisely, delimited.

The same cannot be said about the Commission, hence it is much more difficult to identify its distinctive institutional competence. Most EU policies are regulatory in nature, and in this respect the Commission may be considered a sort of super-agency. Still, it has been assigned a variety of other functions – executive, legislative, and quasi-judicial. This multiplicity of functions expands the scope of the Commission's discretionary choices, greatly complicating the task of evaluating the overall quality of the institution's performance. And because of the multiplicity of distinct tasks assigned to this body, it is extremely costly to dismiss it even when there is intense dissatisfaction with how it carries out one particular task. The collegial nature of the Commission further complicates matters, since the EP has been understandably reluctant to dismiss the entire college in order to sanction a single commissioner. Moreover, the Commission's control of the legislative and policy agenda allows it to pursue objectives of political integration and self-aggrandizement while claiming to solve specific policy problems. As a result, both political accountability and accountability by results are reduced to vanishing point.

In conclusion, non-majoritarian institutions – whether they operate at national or supranational level – have a limited moral capital from which they can draw. Therefore they should carefully husband their scarce normative resources, limiting their interventions to problems no other institution in the system can resolve as effectively. It is precisely this form of self-discipline which the principle of subsidiarity was meant to impose, but which the European institutions have been reluctant to exercise, and students of European integration unwilling to consider as a possible solution to the democratic-deficit problem. In fact, public opinion seems to be more concerned than academia about the continuous expansion of supranational powers in the absence of any clearly envisaged end-state. The difference between the indefiniteness of the European integration process and the tangible goals of the nineteenth-century national unification movements, say in Germany and Italy, is indeed striking.

Europa: Geht's nicht eine Nummer kleiner?

'Europe: couldn't we have it one size smaller?' The title of an article that appeared in the German weekly *Die Zeit* a few years ago expresses well the feelings of many Europeans about the apparently unstoppable growth of EU competences, and the steady expansion of its borders. While elite opinion prefers to ignore the accretion of supranational powers as a cause of the democratic deficit, public opinion tends, if anything, to exaggerate the extent of the phenomenon. For instance, the survey conducted by the German TV channel, ZDF, on the occasion of the fiftieth anniversary of the Rome Treaty (see chapter 1), disclosed that 41 per cent of respondents thought the EU has an excessive influence on decisions taken in Germany, while 46 per cent thought the European integration process is moving ahead too fast. Large-scale eastern enlargement, on the other hand, is viewed by many people in Western Europe as a reproduction of globalization within the boundaries of the EU, and the vehement popular opposition to the Bolkestein General Services Directive was a clear demonstration of widespread *Angst* (see chapter 4). Just as people no longer see any natural limits to the extension of the Union's borders, regardless of socioeconomic problems and geopolitical risks, so they begin to realize that the open-ended commitment to 'ever closer union of the peoples of Europe' may be used to justify the steady growth of European competences. Perhaps more than anything else, it is this idea of integration as an infinite process, with no definite goal in view, that worries people. Hence the impression that there is no effective barrier to the continuous, if incremental, expansion of supranational powers. In 1990 a prominent legal scholar, and member of the European Court of First Instance, could write that 'there is no nucleus of sovereignty that the Member States can invoke, as such, against the Community' (Lenaerts 1990: 220). When these words were written, few people appeared to object to them, or even to take notice. The rejection of the draft Constitutional Treaty and the serious concerns of EU leaders about final ratification of the new Lisbon Treaty after the Irish No, show how much the public mood has changed since 1990.

According to some scholars, worries about 'creeping competences' are unjustified because the powers of the EU compared with those of the national governments remain quite restricted. This is a misleading argument. The appropriate standard to assess the extent of Union powers is not the omnicompetent, though democratically legitimated, national welfare state, but rather the modest level of material and normative resources available to European policy-makers. In the language of Walter Lippmann (1943), a policy is solvent only when commitments and available resources have been brought into balance. EMU is a good example of a European policy whose commitments and resources – political, institutional, and normative – have not been brought into balance, with the consequences discussed above and in earlier chapters. In view of the growing doubts about the wisdom of forcing monetary union before reaching any agreement on political union, and of the failure of EMU to produce the promised results – in terms of price stability, employment, productivity and, not least, international status – it is not surprising that the euro was cited by one-third of Dutch voters as one significant reason for their rejection of the Constitutional Treaty (Frankenberger 2005). Already, in June 2000, a Danish referendum had rejected the Maastricht Treaty and, in particular, the third and final stage of EMU, causing European commissioner Guenther Verheugen to admit that the decision to proceed with monetary union had been taken 'behind the backs of the population'.

Large-scale enlargement is another example of an EU policy exhibiting a serious mismatch between commitments and available resources. As we know, socioeconomic conditions in the EU-27 are so heterogeneous that income inequality is today greater in the EU than in the United States. One important consequence of heterogeneity has been noted in the preceding chapter: the model of a Social Europe strongly committed to furthering socioeconomic equality, or at least greater interstate cohesion through income transfers, is no longer credible. The financial resources of the Union are simply inadequate to the task on the scale the new situation would require, while the wealthier member states refuse to increase the EU budget. Ever optimistic, Euro-leaders count on a quick convergence of the new member states towards the average level of affluence of the older members, but it has already been pointed out that the experts do not share this convenient belief. Even if the optimists were right, the underlying problem would not be resolved for the simple reason that the enlargement process is far from being concluded. All the Balkan countries, as well as Turkey, the Ukraine, and Georgia are actual or potential candidates for EU membership.

Commitments and resources are likely also to be mismatched in the case of recent attempts to promote economic growth and political stability in countries bordering the EU, such as the 'European Neighbourhood Policy' proposed by the Commission in 2004. This policy aimed to include, in addition to the twelve partners of the Euro-Mediterranean

Partnership (the 'Barcelona Process'), the western Balkans, Russia, Ukraine, Belarus, Moldova, Georgia, Armenia, and Azerbaijan. The main components of this ambitious regional commitment were not only the familiar ones of trade liberalization and regulatory alignment, but also cooperation on justice and home affairs, and foreign policy. This particular proposal has been overshadowed by French president Sarkozy's dramatic announcement, in July 2008, of a 'Union for the Mediterranean' open to all the twenth-seven present members of the EU, the twelve members of the Barcelona Process – from Morocco and Algeria, to Israel, Lebanon, Syria, and Turkey – and to all remaining Mediterranean countries: Croatia, Bosnia, Montenegro, and Monaco. It should be noted that the Barcelona Process, of which Sarkozy's project is supposed to be an updated and more pragmatic extension, produced very few concrete results, despite the fact that since 1995 the EU has invested €9 billion in it. The Barcelona Declaration of 28 November 1995 – the centrepiece of the Euro-Mediterranean Partnership – had pledged the EU and the neighbouring Mediterranean states to establish a Mediterranean Free Trade Area by 2010, but this goal has not yet been achieved: only Tunisia agreed, in 2008, to a free-trade arrangement with the EU, limited to industrial products. Negotiations concerning agriculture, fisheries, and the liberalization of services started in 2008, and only between the EU and Egypt, Morocco, Tunisia, and Israel. The prospects of peace in the Middle East are as uncertain now as in 1995; the wealth gap between North and South has actually widened; while the cultural and social partnership has suffered from the growing obstacles to the circulation of people. These failures have convinced the French president to restrict the goals of his Union for the Mediterranean to a limited number of projects in the areas of environment, transportation, solar energy, and education. Even so, many governments of the region continue to doubt its usefulness.

Not surprisingly, EU leaders are beginning to worry about the 'absorption capacity' of the Union, not only in terms of membership, but also of foreign commitments. Indeed, during the period 2000–2004 when Pascal Lamy was Trade Commissioner, the Commission, in a rare display of self-restraint, resisted new regional or bilateral initiatives. This is also the position of the critics of 'European Bonapartism' (see chapter 2), who call attention to the many internal and external conflicts in the EU's 'near abroad' – not only the unresolved Arab–Israeli conflict, but also Islamic terrorism in Algeria, the Kurdish problem in Turkey, and rising tensions between Russia and former members of the Soviet Union like Georgia and Ukraine. Experience has shown that 'soft power' is hardly sufficient to resolve such conflicts (see chapter 7), but the EU does not have stronger means to credibly promote stability in some of the most explosive regions in the world. While third countries continue to remain sceptical about the role the EU can play in the new world order, Europeans are becoming more insistent in their demand for greater policy effectiveness.

Democracy in the EU: A Merit Good?

From the volume of academic writings on the democratic deficit and the frequent expressions of concern by Euro-leaders, one could infer that the stunted development of democracy at European level is a burning issue for many, if not most, EU citizens. As noted above, this is not really the case. After both the French and Dutch referendums, only tiny percentages of interviewed voters gave 'not democratic enough' as one of the motivations for their rejection of the Constitutional Treaty. In addition, the Irish NO to the Lisbon Treaty did not seem to be significantly influenced by concerns about the democratic deficit. Eurobarometer data convey the same general impression of a non-issue, as far as the citizens at large are concerned, but the best evidence is provided by the electoral statistics, which show the lack of popular interest in taking advantage of the democratic opportunities offered to EU voters. As we know, turnout in EP elections has constantly declined since 1979, and an even lower turnout than the 45.7 per cent of 2004 is feared at the 2009 elections. Moreover, the aggregate data conceal a great variability of turnout rates across member states and elections. For instance, at the 1999 elections, when the overall rate was 49.4 per cent, less than 30 per cent of the eligible voters in the Netherlands – one of the six founding members of the EEC – bothered to vote for the EP. In the same year, the Finnish turnout was less than half the previous Finnish turnout at the previous European elections. In 2004 the disappointing overall turnout of 45.7 per cent would have been even lower, except for the fact that in Italy the European elections had been combined with regional and local elections. This variability of participation rates is largely due to the fact that European elections, as we know, are not about European issues, but about national issues, national political parties, and national governments in office. After half a century of elite-driven integration, people continue to consider the nation state the natural (and proper) arena of democratic politics.

Thus it would appear that the democratic deficit of the Union, however defined and whatever its underlying causes, concerns some political leaders and a number of academics more than the mass of European voters. Rather than a popular sentiment – like that voiced by the Chartist and other movements for democratic reform in nineteenth-century Europe – the quest for more democracy at European level seems to be largely an expression of elite preferences, something similar to the demand for stricter environmental standards. One frequent justification for EU environmental policy appeals to the idea that environmental quality is a 'merit good' which should be made available to all the citizens of the Union. Merit goods are defined as goods or services, e.g. primary education or seat belts in cars, which the government compels individuals to consume. The rationale usually offered for this form of paternalism is that the government is entitled to act because it knows what is in the best interest of the citizens better than they themselves do (Stiglitz 1988). In the case of EU environmental programmes, supranational paternalism also implies that some member states might undervalue the benefits of environmental protection or overestimate the corresponding costs, so that the calculus of benefits and costs would be done more accurately at European level. Both implications are extremely doubtful (Majone 2005: 120–22). It is simply arrogant to suggest that the voters in some member states lack the means to make their preferences about environmental quality known to their elected representatives, or to punish them if national policies do not adequately reflect majority preferences. This point deserves to be emphasized because a major success of EU environmental policy, according to some commentators, consists precisely in having forced some member states to 'ratchet up' their environmental standards. Such arguments overlook a general principle repeatedly stressed in previous chapters: if national preferences for environmental quality, or for other public goods, vary significantly across countries, for example because of different levels of socioeconomic development, then uniform European standards, even minimum ones, will reduce aggregate welfare. Anyway, it is highly improbable that European institutions can make a more accurate assessment of the costs and benefits of environmental protection than the national authorities.

If the suggested justifications of EU-level paternalism are dubious, the underlying reason for viewing democracy as a merit good – something that people should have, whether or not they have a demand for it – is clear, and perfectly consistent with the general philosophy of crypto-federalism. The notion of merit good has always provided an important rationale for government intervention and policy centralization. In the United States, for example, the doctrine developed in the 1960s and

1970s, according to which environmental quality is a merit good and as such should be available to all Americans qua Americans, justified a formidable shift of competences for environmental policy-making from the states to the federal government. In the EC, some 150 separate pieces of environmental legislation were adopted before it was decided that 'environmental protection requirements shall be a component of the Community's other policies' (Article 132(2) of the Single European Act). Those writers who define the democratic deficit as 'the gap between the powers transferred to the Community and the efficacy of European Parliamentary oversight and control' (Williams 1991: 155) find the view of democracy as a merit good especially attractive. To them, any increase in the power and influence of the EP provides sufficient justification for a corresponding transfer of powers to the European level.

The Accountability Deficit

In the EU the real problem – in the sense of a condition about which something could be done without a root-and-branch reform of the current approach to European integration – is not the democratic deficit, but the accountability deficit: a good accountability framework, rather than imperfect imitations of national parliamentary institutions, should be the goal of those who wish to enhance the legitimacy of the Union. I have explained at some length why democracy, as we know it at the national level, cannot be replicated at European level – unless and until a majority of EU citizens are persuaded to support a federal super-state. At present, the democratic deficit could be reduced – e.g. by setting more precise limits to the powers of the European institutions; by giving a greater say to national parliaments on matters related to the vertical division of competences; and by making it easier for the European Parliament to censure the Commission on questions of policy – but could not be eliminated. On the other hand, the problem of establishing an effective system of accountability, while less daunting than the elim-ination of the deficit, has become more urgent since the launch of EMU and the start of an indefinite enlargement process. Now, for the first time, the practical impact of European policies – whether on interest rates, on labour markets, or on immigration – is felt by the average EU citizen, not just by elites and special-interest groups. This is why an effective system of accountability has become so important, even as we realize the diffi-culty of resolving the more fundamental problem.

In this respect, the EU represents an important special case of the general issue analysed by Ruth Grant and Robert Keohane in an important recent paper on 'Accountability and Abuses of Power in World Politics' (2005). The problem discussed by these scholars is how to secure accountability in situations where the traditional standards of democratic accountability are either inapplicable or unenforceable. The first step towards understanding the general issue is to recognize that accountability to the voters, or to their elected representatives, is only one dimension of accountability – important, but not always the most relevant one. In the context of democratic polities, accountability to one's peers, to expert opinion, to stakeholders, or to particular segments of public opinion, may be the most appropriate way of explaining the reasons for one's decision, and of activating other accountability mechanisms. At international (or supranational) level, on the other hand, the very meaning of democracy, hence of democratic accountability, is contested. Hence, the definition given by Grant and Keohane is necessarily general: '*Accountability* ... implies that some actors have the right to hold other actors to a set of standards, to judge whether they have fulfilled their responsibilities in light of these standards, and to impose sanctions if they determine that these responsibilities have not been met' (Grant and Keohane 2005: 29). Whatever the political and institutional context, then, accountability involves two judgements: evaluating the outcome of a decision, and/or the quality of the decision-making process, in terms of a given set of standards; and imposing appropriate sanctions if decision-makers did not fulfil their responsibilities under those standards. Using these two parameters, it is not difficult to see why the EU suffers from a serious accountability deficit.

To begin with, we know that European policies are often initiated less to solve concrete problems than to drive forward the integration process, or to facilitate political deals between member states. It follows that there are few incentives to seriously evaluate actual policy outcomes, unless the budgetary costs of the policy become intolerable. This explains why ineffective policies – such as the conservation part of the Common Fisheries Policy mentioned in chapter 1 – can survive, unexamined and unchallenged, sometimes for decades. In this, as in many other cases, actual policy outcomes play a subordinate role at best, while the politically relevant objectives are never spelt out: tacit knowledge replaces public discussion. Policy evaluation is further complicated by the habit of pursuing several objectives with the same policy instrument. We know that this characteristic feature of the Monnet method of integration by stealth tends to produce suboptimal results; but it also complicates the evaluation process by allowing the policy-makers to reorder policy priorities as they see fit, or to make the means a goal, and the goal a means (see chapter 3).

Moreover, the treaty-based independence of the European institutions implies *inter alia* that many of the traditional modes of sanctioning are absent. In particular, all European treaties emphasize the apolitical character of the Commission, insisting on its complete independence 'from any government or from any other body'. Up to a point, insulation from the political process makes sense if we think of the Commission as the guardian of the treaties or as an independent regulatory authority. That was indeed what the institution was intended to be originally. In time, this independent institution has become a highly politicized body that takes decisions involving political judgement and a high degree of discretion. In spite of these developments, the framework of political accountability has remained quite weak. As we saw in previous sections of the present chapter, for example, it is quite difficult for the EP to censure the Commission on a question of policy. The conclusion is that the accountability deficit, like the democratic deficit, is built into the institutional architecture of the EU. Still, greater concentration on the Commission's core competences, and a more precise definition of tasks would help reduce the strains on the narrow legitimacy basis of this unelected body, and at the same time facilitate evaluation. As long as integrationist leaders in Brussels and in some of the national capitals keep thinking of the Commission as the kernel of the future government of Europe, rather than as a specialized institution with a well-defined mandate, it will be difficult to design robust accountability mechanisms.

The recent proliferation of semi-independent European regulatory agencies has become another significant cause of the accountability deficit. The main problem, it should be noted, is not the excessive discretion of the agencies; on the contrary, the problem is that agency heads are not allowed to take final decisions, and therefore cannot be held responsible for the outcomes of the regulatory process. EU agencies do not have the powers usually granted to national regulatory authorities: even the European Medicines Agency (EMEA), which comes closest to being a fully fledged regulatory body, does not take decisions concerning the safety and efficacy of new medical drugs, but must submit its opinions concerning the approval of such products to the European Commission, which then decides. Similarly, the European Food Safety Authority (EFSA) is only allowed to assess risk, not to manage it. Only the Commission can make final determinations concerning the safety of our food.

As long as agencies like EMEA and EFSA have no authority to take final and binding actions, but must share responsibility with the Commission and a variety of committees of national experts, accountability is reduced to vanishing point. But regulatory failures like the BSE ('mad cow' disease) disaster are always possible, and in such cases citizens want to know who to blame. This legitimate demand cannot be satisfied under the present institutional arrangements. In the case of the Food Safety Authority, for example, the tension between the desire to improve the scientific credibility of Community regulations after the BSE disaster, and the refusal to delegate regulatory powers to the agency has been temporarily resolved by the doubtful expedient of an institutional separation of risk assessment – the task assigned to the Authority – and risk management, which remains the responsibility of the Commission. Such institutional separation has been tried before, in the United States and elsewhere, usually with disappointing results. The separation of risk assessment and risk management is problematic because while the two functions are conceptually distinct – one dealing with scientific issues, the other with economic, legal, and political issues – they are closely intertwined in practice. The setting of regulatory priorities, for instance, entails economic, political, and scientific judgements that cannot be easily separated. But if risk assessment and risk management are not separable in practice, then it follows that both efficiency and accountability are best served when the head of an expert agency, rather than a collegial body of political executives and bureaucratic generalists like the Commission, is personally responsible for the outcomes of the regulatory process (Majone 2005: 96–9).

The conclusion is that a less rigid interpretation of the Commission's rights and privileges under the treaties would help reduce the accountability deficit, just as a less rigid enforcement of the Commission's monopoly of policy initiation would contribute to a reduction of the democratic deficit (see above). The difficulty of fitting European regulatory agencies into a scheme of governance devised half a century ago is an illustration of the general phenomenon discussed in the following chapter: the growing obsolescence of the traditional integration methods.

7

The Obsolescence of the Traditional
Integration Methods

Delegation of Powers

Informed observers like the American international lawyer D. E. Rosenthal, whose critical comments on the political powers of the non-elected Commission were quoted in chapter 1, find the extensive delegation of powers to supranational institutions one of the most striking features of the constitutional architecture of the EC/EU. The member states of the EU, Miles Kahler writes, 'have delegated more important and extensive functions to European institutions than has been the case with the members of other international or regional institutions. The Commission, for example, surpasses even the strong secretariat of an international organization' (Kahler 1995: 85). Indeed, the Commission's monopoly of agenda-setting – arguably the key provision of the classic Community Method – is unique. Such broad delegation of powers presupposes a fiduciary relationship between the principals, the member states, and their agents, the European institutions. Hence the progressive restriction of the scope of delegation should be an indication of growing mistrust between national principals and supranational agents. This is actually the case, but before reviewing the evidence a few general comments on the logic of delegation might be helpful. For a more detailed discussion of this topic the interested reader is referred to a previous work (Majone 2005: 64–82).

  Why do political principals choose to delegate some of their powers to agents rather than exercise those powers themselves? A number of reasons have been debated in the literature, ranging from delivering private benefits to favoured constituencies to avoiding making unpopular choices. However, the most significant reasons for delegating powers – and the ones to be considered here – are two: first, to reduce decision-making costs, for instance by taking advantage of executive-branch expertise; and, second, to enhance the credibility of long-term policy commitments. The main difference between these two modes of delegation may be stated as follows. In the former case – the *agency mode*, where the main purpose of delegation is the reduction of decision-making costs – the key problem facing the political principals is bureaucratic drift, i.e. the ability of the agent to enact outcomes differing from the policies preferred by those who originally delegated powers. Since controls are never perfect, there will always be a discrepancy between the policy enacted and what is implemented, and this partial non-compliance is the source of *agency costs*. The situation is quite different when credibility is the main reason for delegating powers. An agent who simply carries out the principal's directives cannot enhance the latter's credibility, so the second mode of delegation – the *fiduciary mode* – implies that the delegate should be independent, although the degree of independence will vary with the nature of the task and the seriousness of the credibility problem. This means that the best strategy for the credibility of a long-term policy commitment is often to choose a delegate whose policy preferences differ from the preferences of the delegating principal(s).

The failure to distinguish between the agency and the fiduciary modes of delegation has led to the overlooking or misinterpretation of important aspects of EU governance. For instance, the standard principal–agent model has been applied with some success to the analysis of the so-called comitology system – the cumbersome system of committees of national administrators and experts who are supposed to oversee the exercise of the Commission's implementing powers. However, agency theory offers no useful insights into the rationale for the treaty-based independence of the same institution in the performance of its fiduciary duties. From the perspective of agency theory, the independence of the Commission would be a failure of the control mechanisms established by the member states (see, e.g., Pollack 1997), but this view ignores the fact that this independence is in fact prescribed and guaranteed by the founding treaties.

Furthermore, the notions of efficiency that apply to these two modes of delegation are different. Since the main purpose of delegation in the agency mode is to reduce decision-making costs, an efficient mechanism of delegation is one which minimizes agency costs, ex ante through a careful selection of the agents, and ex post by means of strict procedural and substantive controls. In the case of fiduciary delegation, the proper concept of efficiency refers to the minimization of *political transaction costs* related to the problem of achieving credible commitments. The time limit inherent in the requirement of elections at regular intervals implies that the policies of the current majority can be subverted by a new majority with different, and perhaps opposite, interests. Because political property rights, in the sense of authority to make public policy, are ill-defined, it is difficult for democratic policy-makers to credibly commit themselves to long-term policy goals. Lack of an appropriate 'technology of commitment' is a political transaction cost – the cost of using the democratic voting mechanism – just as Ronald Coase's (economic) transaction cost is 'a cost of using the price mechanism' (Coase 1988: 38). Much of transaction-costs economics is preoccupied with the efficiency of institutional responses to such market failures as imperfect competition, insufficient provision of public goods, or negative externalities. Similarly, (political) *transaction-costs efficiency* (Breton 1996: 20) is basically preoccupied with various possible failures of political markets – failure of mechanisms like voting, logrolling, party competition, or policy commitments – and with the efficiency of institutional responses to such failures: legislative committees, seniority, reputation, or fiduciary delegation.

Time-inconsistency – the tendency of democratic policy-makers to compromise long-term goals for the sake of short-term electoral benefits – is an important example of political-market failure: governments are worse off because of their inability to credibly commit themselves to the optimal long-run policy. This is precisely the problem addressed by the fiduciary delegation of powers to the European Commission. By their ratification of the treaties the member states have indicated their commitment to the process of European integration. However, the national representatives in the Council of Ministers, usually elected politicians, could be inclined to renege, de facto, on this commitment for short-run political advantages. Thus, they might introduce measures whose practical effect would be to set back the clock of integration. The Commission's monopoly of legislative and policy initiative is best understood as an attempt to solve this time-inconsistency problem. Whether the delegation of agenda-setting powers to an independent supranational institution is still a transaction-cost-efficient response to the commitment problem is a question we shall examine in the section on 'The Community Method' below. The remainder of the present section is devoted to a discussion of the crisis of fiduciary delegation first revealed by the Maastricht Treaty.

Speaking of delegation of powers to the European institutions, one has to keep in mind that the latter have no inherent powers – they possess exclusively those powers conferred on them by the member states in the treaties. As was seen in the preceding chapter, the European institutions have made liberal use of Article 235 of the Rome Treaty to expand Community powers or to broaden the reach of Community legislation in a number of policy areas. But as Alan Dashwood (1996) pointed out, after the Maastricht Treaty Article 235 makes sense only if the reference to the attainment of a Community objective 'in the course of the operation of the common market' is taken seriously. That means that subsidiary powers may be created under this article in direct connection with the policies lying at the core of the Community, but not for other programmes, no matter how worthy their objectives – an opinion now shared by the ECJ, as we shall see. The principle according to which the Union enjoys merely those powers *explicitly* conferred on it by the treaties is stated even more forcefully by Articles 4 and 5 of the new Treaty of Lisbon. This insistence on the narrow scope of implied powers is one symptom of the crisis in the fiduciary relations between member states and European institutions.

The frequency of treaty amendments since the late 1980s is another, even clearer, indication of the severity of this crisis. For about thirty years the powers of the Community and the reach of European law were expanded, sometimes dramatically, without any formal treaty amendment. Starting with the Maastricht Treaty, the national governments have taken the initiative in the amendment process, and have used this process to define new competences in a way effectively restricting the exercise of Community powers (see the next section). As long as the scope of European law was limited, and trust in the self-restraint of the supranational institutions was maintained, the simplified procedure for adapting the original agreement by means of Article 235 had an obvious appeal. Since the SEA significantly expanded Community powers, however, the member states have been willing to pursue the more complex procedure of formal treaty amendment, rather than delegate to the Commission and the Court of Justice the task of deciding whether Community action in a given area is needed, and which form it should take. After the SEA, intergovernmental conferences for the purpose of treaty revision have taken place every few years. Treaty amendment has become almost a routine procedure, initiated as soon as a new treaty is accepted by all the member states.

To appreciate the implications of this development, it may be helpful to think of European treaties as *incomplete contracts*. In the terminology of the law-and-economics literature, an incomplete contract is an agreement that does not fully and unambiguously describe all relevant contingencies, for the simple reason that not all possible contingencies could even be imagined at the time of negotiation. Now, incomplete contracting leads to problems of imperfect commitment. There is a strong temptation to renege on the original terms of the contract because what should be done in case of an unforeseen contingency was left unstated, or open to interpretation. One possible remedy to contractual incompleteness is an arrangement known as *relational contracting*, whereby the parties agree on general principles rather than detailed plans of action. A relational contract settles for a general agreement framing the entire relationship, recognizing that it is impossible to concentrate all bargaining at the ex ante contracting stage. In relational contracting the task of interpreting the original agreement in light of unforeseen circumstances may be delegated to one of the parties, or else to a third party. A relevant consideration is that the delegate should have much to lose from a damaged reputation. It follows that the delegate is likely to be a person (or an institution) with a longer time horizon, more visibility, and greater frequency of transactions than the other contractual partners (Milgrom and Roberts 1992: 130–41).

The Treaty of Rome is a good illustration of a relational contract. With a few exceptions, the treaty only provides general principles and policy guidelines, and delegates to the European institutions the tasks of specifying the concrete measures to be taken in order to achieve the broad treaty objectives in a constantly evolving situation. In this perspective, Article 235 is part of the general response of the member states to the contractual incompleteness typical of all treaties and constitutional documents; no such provision would have been necessary if the treaty framers had been infinitely wise and prescient. The fact that since the SEA the national governments, unwilling to rely on the supranational institutions to determine the limits of implied powers, have taken the initiative in treaty amendment – in spite of the political risks involved in the subsequent ratification process – shows how serious the loss of confidence in the self-restraint of the supranational institutions has become. The reputation of these institutions is no longer good enough to convince the member states to keep delegating to them the crucial task of adapting the collective agreement to new contingencies.

The Rise and Decline of Harmonization

Harmonization of national laws and regulations is one of the three legal techniques the Rome Treaty made available to the Commission for establishing and maintaining a common European market – the other two techniques being liberalization and the control of anti-competitive behaviour. Limitations imposed on the use of the harmonization technique by the more recent treaties are another indication of a progressive loss of trust in the supranational institutions. The Treaty of Maastricht defined for the first time new European competences in a way that actually limits the exercise of Community powers. For example, Article 126 (now Article 149 EC) adds a new legal basis for action in the field of education, but policy instruments are restricted to 'incentive measures' and to recommendations: harmonization of national laws is explicitly ruled out. Likewise, Article 129 (Article 152 EC) creates specific powers for the Community in the field of public health protection, but this competence is highly circumscribed as subsidiary to that of the member states. Harmonization is again ruled out, though the article states that health-protection requirements shall form a constituent part of the other Community policies. The other provisions of the treaty – defining new competences in areas such as culture, consumer protection, and industrial policy – are similarly drafted. Unwilling to continue to rely on implicit powers, which seemed out of control, the framers of the TEU opted for an explicit grant that delimits the mode and the reach of action (Weiler 1999). Such has been the approach followed thereafter by the Amsterdam and Nice treaties, and by the Lisbon Treaty.

In its Tobacco Advertising judgment of October 2000 – annulling for the first time a measure adopted under the co-decision procedure – the ECJ showed how seriously the limits of the Community's powers are taken today. Germany, which had been outvoted in the Council, protested that Directive 98/34 prohibiting all forms of tobacco advertising was a disguised public-health measure, while the EP and Council contended that the treaty allowed the Community to adopt any measure to regulate the internal market, and not just those to liberalize trade. The Court held that the European legislator could not rely on other articles to circumvent the explicit prohibition in Article 152 EC of harmonization of health measures. It argued that recourse to Article 95 EC (on the harmonization of national laws and regulations) must be aimed at improving the conditions of the internal market, not at market regulation in general. As the requirements for resorting to Article 95 had not been fulfilled – the prohibition neither facilitated trade nor contributed to eliminating distortions of competition – the directive was annulled. Such care in spelling out the limits of the conferred powers has been viewed by several legal scholars as reflecting a lack of confidence in the capacity for self-restraint of the supranational institutions. Professor Dashwood, whose opinion anticipating the philosophy of Tobacco Advertising has been reported in the preceding section, has pointed out that in the 1960s

> harmonization tended to be pursued not so much to resolve concrete problems encountered in the course of constructing the common market as to drive forward the general process of integration. This ... was bound to affect the judgment of the Commission, inclining it towards maximum exercise of the powers available under Article 100 and towards solutions involving a high degree of uniformity between national laws.
>
> (Dashwood 1983: 194)

As a matter of fact, from the early 1960s to about 1973 – the date of the first enlargement of the Community – the Commission's approach to harmonization was characterized by a distinct preference for detailed measures designed to regulate exhaustively the problems under consideration, to the exclusion of previously existing national laws and regulations – the approach known as 'total harmonization'. Under total harmonization, once European rules have been put in place, a member state's capacity to apply stricter rules by appealing to the values mentioned in Article 36 of the Treaty of Rome – such as the protection of the health and life of humans, animals, and plants – is out of the question. Total harmonization corresponds to what, in the language of American public law, is called 'federal preemption', and does indeed reflect early federalist aspirations. For a long time the ECJ supported total harmonization as a foundation stone in the building of the common market (Weatherill 1995). By the mid-1970s, however, the limitations of the approach had become clear, while mounting opposition to what many member states considered excessive centralization convinced the Commission that this instrument had to be used so as not to interfere too much with the regulatory autonomy of the national governments. The emphasis shifted from total to optional and minimum harmonization – and to mutual recognition.

The idea that economic integration demands extensive harmonization of national laws and regulations has been criticized by a number of distinguished economists since the early years of the European Community. According to Harry Johnson, for instance, 'The need for harmonization additional to what is already required of countries extensively engaged in world trade is relatively slight ... The problems of harmonization are such as can be handled by negotiation and consultation according to well-established procedures among the governments concerned, rather than such as to require elaborate international agreements' (Johnson 1972, cited in Kahler 1995: 12). Against the harmonization bias of the literature on economic integration of the post-war years, Johnson argued that the gains from harmonization should be weighed against the welfare losses caused by harmonized rules not tailored to national preferences except in a rough, average sense. The welfare loss entailed by centralized harmonization has become a major theme in the more recent literature on free trade and harmonization (Bhagwati and Hudec 1996); it is certainly an issue that has been ignored for too long in the EU.

Arguments presented in previous chapters suggest that growing heterogeneity in the enlarged Union will contribute to the obsolescence of harmonization even more than will the member states' distrust of the supranational institutions. Significant inter-country differences in socio-economic conditions are necessarily mirrored in a diversity of national priorities and policy preferences, and this implies that welfare-enhancing regulations have to be different rather than harmonized. When socio-economic conditions vary significantly mutual recognition also meets intense political resistance – as shown by the fate of the Bolkestein draft of the Services Directive (see chapter 4). In short, every new enlargement is likely to change the calculus of the benefits and costs of harmonization, hence to make the achievement of a single European market more problematic – an important point to which I return in the next chapter. For the time being it is enough to recall that the version of the Services Directive that was finally approved triggered a backlash from East European countries, which as low-cost countries would stand to benefit most from price competition among services providers.

Institutional Balance

The principle of institutional balance, another key element of the classic Community Method, was first stated by the European Court of Justice in the case *Meroni* v. *High Authority* (case 9/56[1957–8] ECR 133). This case relates specifically to the ECSC Treaty, but the Meroni doctrine continues to be considered 'good law', and to act as a rigid barrier to the delegation of regulatory responsibilities to institutions or bodies not explicitly named by the treaties. To appreciate the meaning of this principle in the political culture, as well as in the law and policy of the EU, we must keep in mind that each European institution is the bearer of a particular interest which it strives to protect and promote. Institutional balance does not imply an equal allocation of power among the European institutions, but only that the relative position of each institution, as defined by the treaties in each policy domain, should be preserved. Because what counts is relative, rather than absolute, position (as in realist theories of international relations, see, for example, Kennedy 1987), the implications of the principle of institutional balance are more far-reaching than may appear at first sight. They explain, *inter alia*, such features of the Community system as the reluctance of the European Parliament to challenge the monopoly of legislative initiative granted to the unelected Commission; the Commission's refusal to delegate rule-making powers to European agencies; and, not least, the striking difference between EU politics and democratic politics. These and other implications may be better understood if we view the Community system in historical perspective. While this system is unique among contemporary polities, in important respects it is quite similar to the 'mixed government' of *ancien-regime* Europe – 'mixed' in the sense that different corporate interests were involved in the law-making process. Since I have discussed this structural similarity at some length in a previous publication (Majone 2005: 46–51), a brief summary will suffice here. According to the philosophy of mixed government, the polity is composed not of individuals, but of corporate bodies (such as Monarchy, Lords, and Commons in eighteenth-century England) balanced against each other and governed by mutual agreement rather than by a political sovereign – in England sovereignty pertained not to the monarch, but to 'the king in Parliament'. In practice, the corporate members constituting the mixed polity were interested less in policy-making per se than in preserving the balance of 'privileges' and rights: rights of the territorial rulers as against the estates, and vice versa, or the respective rights of each estate vis-à-vis the others. Hence, the prime theme of the internal political process was the tug-of-war among autonomous power centres over the extent and security of their respective jurisdictional prerogatives and immunities; in other words, the maintenance of the relative position of each corporate member of the polity.

Such a political process is of course very different from the politics of modern democracies, where the main aims of the electoral contest are the control of political power and the formulation and implementation of public policy. Unlike in modern democracies, in the EC/EU there is no central power to conquer in a competition among political parties, while policies are not made by a majority government, but are the (often epiphenomenal) result of bargaining among the three law-making bodies – Council, Commission, and EP, each representing different interests. Not surprisingly, the language of majoritarian politics – government and opposition, party competition, left and right – has very limited currency in this context. As in the old mixed government, the prime theme of the internal political process is the contest among autonomous institutions over the extent and security of their respective competences. This explains why in many votes the EP does not divide along party lines, presenting instead a united front against the other institutions – sometimes against the Commission, more often against the Council. The logic of mixed government also explains why institutional balance is considered so important. The rule that 'each institution shall act within the limits of the powers conferred upon it by this Treaty' (Art. 4(1) of the Rome Treaty, now Art. 7(1) EC), when read in the light of the principle of institutional balance, means that each institution: (1) has the necessary independence in exercising its powers; (2) must respect the powers of the other institutions; and (3) may not unconditionally assign its powers to other institutions or bodies. Hence the refusal to delegate rule-making powers to independent European agencies, regardless of the advantages such delegation would have in terms of policy effectiveness and public accountability.

The refusal to adopt the independent-agency model, a model whose advantages are today generally acknowledged, is a striking demonstration of the difficulty of modernizing the traditional methods of governance. The design of the Community system as a latter-day version of mixed government, with representation of interests and institutional balance as its organizing principle, is one of the roots of the difficulty of reforming an outdated institutional architecture. As J. P. Jacqué has argued, under the Community Method it is impossible for European institutions to achieve more than incremental adjustments: 'For a significant evolution to take place it would be necessary for an institution to forgo exercising its prerogatives to align its position on that of another institution. This is hardly conceivable since each institution is the representative of interests which it is its duty to protect' (Jacqué 1991: 252, my translation). This resistance to institutional innovations is one of the reasons why the Community Method, for several decades the engine of the integration process, is increasingly perceived as being too rigid to accommodate the needs of an ever more complex and diverse polity.

The Community Method: Still Viable?

Somewhat belatedly, EU leaders have acknowledged that 'the pace of enlargement must take the Union's absorption capacity into account', and have started to worry about 'the perception of enlargement by citizens ... and the need to explain the enlargement process to the public', (see chapter 4 and European Council 2005). It is, however, difficult to see how, having already admitted ten countries from Central and Eastern Europe, the Union could refuse to admit, sooner or later, Croatia, Montenegro, Bosnia-Herzegovina, Serbia, Kosovo, Macedonia, and Albania, as well as Moldova, Ukraine, and, possibly, Turkey and Georgia. It looks improbable that there will be another big bang enlargement as in 2004, but before too long the EU will comprise more than thirty countries at vastly different levels of development, and with correspondingly different policy preferences and national priorities. What has been said about the growing reluctance of the member states to delegate powers to the supranational institutions, the difficulty of harmonizing national laws and regulations, and about the rigidity of the present institutional framework – not to mention the difficulty of crafting common positions on foreign policy and security issues – will be *a fortiori* true in the future Union.

It is indeed hard to imagine how the Community Method – designed for a small group of fairly homogeneous West European countries, mostly averse to nationalism and willing to sacrifice important elements of national sovereignty for the sake of closer integration – could survive more or less intact in a completely different environment. It seems much more likely that the EU of the future will be characterized by flexible institutional arrangements like those variously described in the literature as 'variable geometry', 'Europe à la carte', 'multi-speed Europe' (these and related terms are defined by H. Wallace 1998), or by even more radical institutional designs (see the next chapter). In this scenario, the scope of the Community Method would have to be restricted – rather than extended or even generalized, as optimists in Brussels were still advocating in 2002 at the time of the Convention on the Future of Europe – and some of its key principles either abandoned or extensively reformed. Only those who continue to believe that the integration process can move in just one direction can imagine that a radical reform of the Community Method must spell the end of the idea of European unity. Even a convinced federalist like Joschka Fischer was prepared to give up the received integration methods in favour of a different, more democratic, approach to political integration (2000). It will be recalled that the project presented by the former German foreign minister in his Berlin speech of May 2000 assumed that the irrevocable commitment to a fully fledged federal union would be preceded by a period of intense *intergovernmental* cooperation, during which supranational institutions would no longer play a significant role. More logically consistent, or perhaps more intellectually honest, than other federalists, Fischer openly expressed his doubts that a democratic federation of democratic states could be established by means of democratically unaccountable institutions (see chapter 2).

On the other hand, those who think that the federalist project is unfeasible, or perhaps undesirable, but do not reject the idea of European solidarity, must see that institutions like the Commission and the Court of Justice are needed in order to make sure that the common rules, freely accepted by all the members of the Union, are enforced in good faith. For this purpose the Commission's loss of power in some domains might have to be compensated for by strengthening its power to veto national decisions contrary to the common rules. In practice, such a development would represent a return to the primacy of negative integration, in the original spirit of the Treaty of Rome. The proliferation of Community programmes of doubtful effectiveness has been abetted by the mistaken idea of the superiority of 'positive' over 'negative' integration. As mentioned in chapter 5, the distinction between these two approaches goes back to the earliest studies of regional economic integration but the Treaty of Rome itself did not attach any normative connotation to it. More recently, positive integration has often been identified with positive values like deeper integration and social cohesion, while negative integration has been associated with deregulation, an alleged neo-liberal ideology, and the prevalence of narrow economic interests. The champions of positive integration tend to forget that the progressive merging of heavily regulated national markets would have been impossible without negative integration, as explained in chapter 3. In this sense, treaty-based rules of negative integration, such as the competition rules, are *constitutive* rather than merely contingent, like most measures of positive integration.

In comparing the two modes of integration, another factor, as we have seen, must be taken into account. While the actual outcomes of positive integration are uncertain, in part because of their dependence on implementation by national bureaucracies with their different methods and uneven levels of efficiency, the results of negative integration are clear-cut, and generally implemented, albeit reluctantly, by the affected member states. The strength of negative integration was again revealed by the ECJ's decision of October 2007 against a German law protecting Volkswagen from hostile takeovers – an impressive demonstration of the power of negative integration, and a significant legal victory for the Commission, which, in an effort to get rid of the law, had taken the German government to court in October 2004. This victory followed the Microsoft decision to surrender in its nine-year battle with the Commission over its dominance of the software market. Microsoft agreed to apply the decision globally, thus acknowledging that the Commission's reach as a competition regulator extends beyond Europe. Comparing these victories with the failure, or limited success, of so many measures of positive integration (see, for example, Majone 2005: 111–38) we can see that negative integration still works – at least in a number of important cases.

Under a negative-integration regime, most regulatory responsibilities would be left with the people who are most directly affected by a given problem, and who have to bear the cost of regulation. The tasks of the European institutions would primarily consist in monitoring the behaviour of national regulators, to make sure that they do not abuse their autonomy for protectionist purposes, or to violate rights guaranteed by European law. Where the functional requirements of the common market, or of international trade, call for some type of ex ante harmonization, this can be achieved by a variety of methods: information exchange, greater reliance on international standards, or self-regulation. Centralized, top-down harmonization would become an option of last resort, while under the old Community Method too many harmonization claims were driven by a political agenda rather than by genuine concerns about the integrity of the Single Market.

On the occasion of the celebrations for the fiftieth anniversary of the Rome Treaty, some official speakers attributed the accomplishments of half a century of integration to the invention by the founding fathers of an original institutional setting, having in the Community Method its most significant expression. As argued in previous chapters, however, the continuous expansion of the scope of the method is also one of the main causes of the EU's democratic deficit. In choosing a high level of institutionalization as their approach to integration, the founding fathers overlooked the fact that 'It is not institutions that create a sense of belonging, but a sense of belonging which makes institutional constraints acceptable' (Guéhenno 1993: 79). Acceptance of institutional constraints is particularly problematic when the effectiveness of the institutions begins to be questioned, or is at any rate less obvious than official claims pretend. The causal role of the Community Method should be most visible in the area of economic integration, and yet according to most economists and economic historians, the contribution of the institutional setting invented by the founders to the growth of Europe during the three 'glorious decades' 1945–75 has been limited (see chapter 1, and *passim*). After the early phase of rapid catch up with the United States, development stagnated and even regressed, so that the desire to improve poor economic performance has guided EU policy over the last thirty years. In spite of ambitious projects such as EMU and the Single Market, the Community Method has thus proved unable to reverse, and even to stop, the steady deterioration of the relative position of the EU as a whole with respect to its major international competitors.

Moreover, if it is true that the Community Method puts the European Commission 'at the heart of the Union' as some authors have asserted, then it follows that the political weakness of this institution since the end of the Delors era could not but reduce the effectiveness of the method. Centrally positioned in the institutional architecture of the EC/EU, the Commission has been able to play a number of roles not explicitly envisaged by the treaties. For instance, it has often been a broker and mediator of interests at several points of the policy process; in particular, in Council of Ministers meetings, which it attends at all levels – working parties, permanent representatives, and ministers – as a non-voting but nonetheless traditionally influential participant. Closely related to, and partly overlapping with, its role as 'honest broker', the Commission has been a facilitator of EU decision-making by presenting itself as the body best able to provide the necessary information.

But even aside from the Commission's present political weakness and the growing distrust of the member states, its role as honest broker, mediator, and facilitator was bound to decrease in time, the reason being that the significance of such functions is inversely related to the level of available information. In an information-poor environment productive interchange is made possible by the presence of persons or institutions in a position to know the resources, constraints, and preferences of the potential transactors. In an information-rich environment, on the other hand, transactions can be carried out directly by the interested parties. This is the gist of the arc-of-information hypothesis advanced by Miles Kahler in an important study of international institutions and economic integration (Kahler 1995). According to this hypothesis, when information about national preferences is scarce and expensive, a substantial degree of information-gathering is required before strong, centralized institutions can emerge; when information is plentiful and cheap, decentralization is likely to be more efficient in transaction-costs terms. In other words: 'when levels of information are very low, formal and centralized institutions cannot be constructed; when they are high, such institutions are unnecessary' (Keohane 1995: 142). With specific reference to the EU, Kahler conjectured that 'Europe's highly centralized institutions may seem less necessary as economic integration and political understanding produce an increasingly information-rich environment' (Kahler 1995: 123). He cited mutual recognition and the debate on the principle of subsidiarity since the Maastricht Treaty as evidence supporting his hypothesis of growing decentralization. True, neither subsidiarity nor mutual recognition have proved sufficiently robust in practice to directly affect the institutional evolution of the EU, but, as will be discussed in chapter 8, the prediction of eventual institutional decentralization is likely to prove correct – although not exactly for the reasons mentioned by the American scholar.

Intergovernmentalism

In the literature on European integration, policy cooperation based mainly on interactions between the relevant national policy-makers, with relatively little involvement by the EU institutions, is known as 'intergovernmentalism'. This label does not really capture the nature of the cooperation taking place outside the Community Method in such areas as foreign and security policy or monetary policy. Helen Wallace has rightly pointed out that intergovernmentalism resonates too much of cooperation between governments in international organizations whose role is limited to providing secretariat services and a forum for debate. She suggests a different label, 'intensive transgovernmentalism', to connote those situations in which the member states have been prepared to commit themselves to rather extensive engagements and discipline, but have judged the Community Method to be inappropriate or unacceptable. The main institutional characteristics of this mode of policy-making are: the active involvement of the European Council in setting the overall direction of policy; the predominance of the Council of Ministers in consolidating cooperation; the limited or marginal role of the Commission, and the virtual exclusion of the EP and ECJ from the policy process; the involvement of a distinct circle of national policy-makers, e.g. central bankers or foreign ministers; the opaqueness of the process to national parliaments and citizens; and the ability on occasion to deliver substantive joint policy (H. Wallace 2005: 87–8).

The Common Foreign and Security Policy (CFSP) and EMU are the prime examples of transgovernmentalism. All measures the Union adopts under the CFSP originate with the European Council and the Council of Foreign Ministers. The former body defines the principles and general guidelines and decides on 'common strategies'; the latter adopts 'common positions' and 'joint actions' – operational decisions with financial implications. Before the Treaty of Amsterdam the member states had an exclusive right of agenda-setting in CFSP, whereas they now share this right with the Commission. The Commission is 'fully associated' with the work carried out in this policy area, though the fact that its right of initiative is not exclusive implies that it does not here enjoy the other prerogatives coming with that right. Thus, while under the Community Method the Commission can generally amend or withdraw its proposal at any time before the Council has taken a decision, outside the sphere of the Community Method decisions to be taken in the Council are not affected by amendment or withdrawal of a proposal. What is even more significant, the creation by the Amsterdam Treaty of the High Representative for the CFSP – with the task of contributing to the formulation, preparation, and implementation of the policy decisions – further restricts the Commission's power to influence policy developments. To the extent that the Commission does have a role in the CFSP, it is primarily because of its treaty-based powers in the area of external economic relations, including sanctions, and development policies. As for the other European institutions, the Council is entitled to act without seeking the opinion of the EP, and the Court of Justice has no power of judicial review with respect to decisions relating to the CFSP. The Court's jurisdiction is limited to ensuring that no measure taken in this context detracts from the rights and duties imposed by the treaties.

The label 'intergovernmentalism' is even less appropriate in the case of EMU. Under EMU, monetary policy is the sole responsibility of the European Central Bank, which is completely independent from the other European institutions, as well as from the national governments. The Commission has been an intermittent player in the process that led to EMU. It made important contributions, first with Roy Jenkins and then with Jacques Delors, at key points; thereafter it has had little influence on the actual negotiations and little involvement in the implementation of monetary policy (Tsoukalis 2000). The Commission's controversial role in monitoring national governments' respect of the Stability and Growth Pact criteria is discussed below. The CFSP and EMU are similar in that they both operate outside the Community Method, but differ in one important respect: while the CFSP is an example of what may be viewed as a kind of 'self-government' by the EU's member states (Majone 2005), under EMU, responsibility for making monetary policy has been practically surrendered to a supranational fiduciary agent, the ECB.

Like the Community Method, transgovernmentalism has achieved some notable results, but also suffered a number of significant failures, as will be seen in the following section. The key point, however, is that neither method, as presently practised, is adequate to meet the challenges of the future. The introduction of the single currency may be considered one of the achievements of transgovernmentalism – at least in a formal sense. Whatever the substantive merits of the project, it has been largely the work of an exclusive network of central bankers, economic and finance ministers, and monetary experts. Doubts concerning the future of EMU are fed in particular by the prospect that, as the Union becomes more heterogeneous, the costs of a one-size-fits-all monetary policy could increase to the point that some members of the euro area may choose to drop out (see chapter 4). A more clear-cut case of success, in spite of the British and Irish decisions to stay out, is the Schengen Agreement, which has largely achieved its goal of lifting border controls between its signatories, and even expanded its membership beyond the EU, with Iceland, Norway, and Switzerland as associate members.

On the other hand, it is easy to find cases where the member states compromised their collective credibility by committing themselves to overoptimistic goals and failing to bring into balance commitments and available resources. The so-called 'Lisbon Agenda' may become the classic example of intergovernmental hubris. It will be recalled that at the summit held in the Portuguese capital in March 2000, the EU Council announced that by 2010 the Union would become 'the most competitive, knowledge-based economy in the world'. The experts knew from the beginning that the goal was in fact beyond reach, because it would have required, among other things, an impossible productivity growth rate of about 4 per cent per annum. In time EU leaders became convinced that it was wiser to drop the target date of 2010, which they did on the occasion of the 2005 Spring European Council. Surprisingly, the press releases following the spring 2007 meeting of the same body reported that the heads of state and government of all twenty-seven member states 'acknowledged the success of the Lisbon Strategy for Growth and Jobs, reflected in higher growth and falling unemployment figures' (EU 2007). As it turned out, what the Council celebrated so enthusiastically was a cyclical upswing, not structural growth, as was shown by the data released by the European Statistical Office in August 2007: the Union was still dragging behind the US on practically all indicators. More realistically, businesses and economists tend to consider the Lisbon economic reform process comatose, if not quite dead.

The history of the Stability and Growth Pact – a European Council resolution adopted at the Amsterdam summit in October 1997, together with two Council regulations on multilateral surveillance and on implementation of the excessive-deficit procedure – also offers ample evidence in support of the cynical view that a commitment that depends on the good will of the member states and the mutual control of the Council of Ministers is not credible. In May 2002, just two months after agreeing with the other EU leaders in Barcelona to move to budget parity by 2004, French president Chirac decided to cut taxes and increase military expenditures, hoping the inflated deficit would help him secure a favourable majority in the forthcoming national elections. At the same time, the interim finance minister announced that France would not reach a balanced budget by the agreed deadline. In October, after winning the elections, the new French finance minister, Francis Mer, defied his European colleagues with his refusal to start cutting the budget deficit in 2003. At the meeting of the Eurogroup finance ministers in Luxembourg on 7 October 2002, all ministers except the French agreed on a programme for cutting deficits. Three of the four countries with the most serious deficit problem – Portugal, Germany, and Italy – pledged to cut their structural deficits by 0.5 per cent each year, starting in 2003; France insisted that it would not start until 2004, so the deadline for the budget adjustment had to be moved to 2006 – only to be moved again later to a more distant date. Peer pressure was not enough to change Mr Mer's opinion that restoring growth to the French economy (and honouring campaign promises) had priority over honouring France's commitment to fiscal discipline.

Of course, the troubles of the Stability and Growth Pact cannot be blamed on any one country. Portugal was the first member state to break the pact in 2001 with a deficit of 4.1 per cent of GDP; but the situation was especially ironic when Germany declared it would be unable to meet the very rules it had devised in order to restrain other, supposedly less virtuous, members of the euro-zone. The German finance minister, who during the campaign for the federal elections of September 2002 had insisted that the deficit would be at 2.9 per cent of GDP, a few weeks later admitted what many – including people in his own department – knew all along, namely that Berlin would not manage to keep its budget deficit below the 3 per cent limit in 2002. Then on 25 November 2003 a majority of the members of the Council of Economic and Financial Affairs (Ecofin) decided to suspend the procedures for excessive deficit initiated by the Commission against France and Germany. Instead, the Council recommended reductions of the structural deficit of the two countries sufficient to bring the deficit below 3 per cent of GDP by the end of 2005. France and Germany promised to do their best to achieve these goals, but this was a political, not a legally binding, commitment. In January 2004 a badly divided Commission decided to bring the decision of the Council before the European Court of Justice. One consequence of the events of November 2003 was sure: the pact would not be altogether discarded, but it would eventually be reformulated along lines set by the Council rather than by the Commission.

This assessment is not contradicted by the fact that on 13 July 2004 the ECJ overturned the decision of the finance ministers to suspend the sanctions procedure against France and Germany. While the ruling partially vindicated the Commission's challenge before the Court to defend the pact, the Brussels executive lost in the second, and more important, part of its case, where it claimed that Ecofin had a duty to adopt the Commission's recommendations. We may safely conclude that the Stability Pact never worked the way it was intended to (see also chapter 3). The reform of the pact in June 2005 in the end eliminated the elements of automatism in the original agreement and introduced considerable room for intergovernmental margins of manoeuvre. As a result, however, the increased uncertainty surrounding the determination of acceptable intermediate budget balances makes it even more difficult for the Council of Ministers to trigger sanctions against errant member states. This was not the best of arrangements; and the political motivations behind it are revealed by the circumstance that the fiscally virtuous member states defended the original pact, while most of those states exceeding, or at risk of exceeding, the deficit threshold sought reform.

The Limits of 'Soft Power'

Paradoxically, intergovernmentalism, even in the enhanced version of 'intensive transgovernmentalism', has most obviously displayed its limitations in domains, such as foreign and defence policy, where the national governments can operate in almost complete independence from the supranational institutions. One underlying reason why results in these areas are generally disappointing is the systematic violation of the basic prerequisite of a credible foreign policy: the capability to bring commitments and available resources into balance. It may appear useless – perhaps also unfair in view of the inherent difficulty of reaching consensus in the EU – to insist on examples of the mismatch of commitments and resources that are only too well known. The purpose of recalling such examples again is not to disparage current efforts to enhance the international role of Europe, but rather to provide an antidote to the official rhetoric – and to the views of those scholars who attempt to buttress this rhetoric with their celebrations of the EU as 'soft power', or even 'quiet superpower'. The first conceptualizations of the international role of the EC/EU as 'soft', 'normative', 'civilian', or 'civilizing' power go back to the early 1970s. In the view of François Duchêne (1972), for instance, the strength and novelty of Communitarian Europe as an international actor were based on its ability to extend its own method of ensuring stability and security through economic and political, instead of military, means. In this way, Duchêne hoped, Europe would develop into the first example in history of a major actor in the international system becoming, in the period of its decline, not the political satellite of a superpower, but the exemplar of a new stage in political civilization. Later writers expanded Duchêne's argument, claiming that the EU is a novel kind of power in international relations, not only because of its emphasis on non-military instruments of foreign policy but also because of its promotion of multilateral solutions, its encouragement of regional cooperation, and because it assigns primacy to conflict prevention, negotiation, and peacekeeping (Sjursen 2006). Menon *et al.* (2004: 11) go as far as claiming that the EU is 'a pioneer in long term interstate peace building ... [it] is one of the most formidable machines for managing differences peacefully ever invented'.

Unfortunately, praise such as this is seldom corroborated by concrete evidence, and its objectivity is in no way heightened by the fact that it corresponds so closely to the EU's own description of its international role. For some years it looked as if the Barcelona Process could provide the perfect example of the EU as a pioneer in peace-building through its promotion of multilateral solutions and encouragement of regional cooperation. The announced objectives of the project were the establishment of peace and prosperity through political dialogue, economic development, and enhanced cultural cooperation and personal contacts among the citizens of the countries of the Mediterranean region. As we saw in chapter 6, by 2005 the EU had invested €9 billion in the Barcelona Process, but with few concrete results. It seems highly unlikely that the goal of creating a free-trade area of the Mediterranean will be achieved. Negotiations concerning other economic sectors only started in 2008, and only with a few countries in the region. Since the project was launched, moreover, the wealth gap between the northern and southern parts of the Mediterranean has increased, while the prospects for peace in the Middle East are as uncertain as ever.

The academic champions of soft-power Europe accept without reserve the official claim that peace and stability in the old continent are the result of European integration – a claim which has been shown to be largely a myth based on the *post hoc, ergo propter hoc* fallacy (see chapter 3). The truth is that after the disastrous results of two world wars in fifty years, West European states had neither the resources nor the will to again use military means to resolve their conflicts. Many scholars working on EU foreign and security policy are unwilling to admit that during the Cold War the member states of Communitarian Europe were able to devote considerably more resources to welfare than to warfare – and thus could bask in the illusion of inaugurating a new phase in the history of inter-national relations – because their security was guaranteed by NATO and by the US nuclear umbrella (Hyde-Price 2006). The real tests of the EU's capacity to manage differences peacefully came after the implosion of the Soviet Union and the end of bipolarity. The limitations of the soft-power approach were never so clearly revealed as in the 1990s – not in distant theatres of marginal interest, but in the EU's 'near abroad', in the former Yugoslavia.

The inability either to convince the Albanians of Kosovo to postpone a unilateral declaration of independence, or to persuade the Serbian government to accept the inevitability of the Kosovar secession of February 2008 is just the latest in a long series of failures of EU-style diplomacy in the Balkans. Promises of substantial economic aid and of a fast-track procedure for the admission of Serbia to the EU proved insufficient to induce that country's leaders to accept the self-proclaimed independence of a region which they consider the cradle of their nation's identity. Addressing the European Parliament a few days after the uni-lateral declaration of independence, the Serbian foreign minister called the proposal of EU membership in exchange for recognition of the Kosovar secession, 'indecent' and announced that Serbia would recall its ambassadors from all capitals recognizing the independence of the formerly autonomous region. Belgrade probably considered the promise of EU membership not only indecent, but also scarcely credible. Since the admission of Romania and Bulgaria in 2007, many current members of the Union oppose any further expansion of the club, at least in the foreseeable future. Given that acceptance of new members must be decided unanimously, therefore, the promise of a fast-track admission procedure for Serbia could not be taken too seriously.

The failure of EU soft diplomacy was made complete by the inability of the member states to reach a common position on the issue of secession. At the EU summit of December 2007, the rotating president of the European Council, German chancellor Angela Merkel, had said that it was essential to present a united front on Kosovo, while the prime minister of Luxembourg warned his colleagues that this question should not be allowed to become 'a permanent problem' for the EU. Despite the entreaties and the warnings, some members of the Union chose to follow the example of the US and France in recognizing Kosovo's independence immediately, others decided to wait and see how the situation would evolve; while Spain, backed by Romania, categorically refused diplomatic recognition at any time. At the meeting of EU foreign ministers of 18 February 2008, the Spanish representative stated in no uncertain terms that the unilateral declaration of independence violated international law. Madrid was of course concerned that the example of Kosovo may be imitated by other secessionist movements like the Basque and Catalan nationalists. Other members of the EU – notably Romania, Bulgaria, Greece, Slovakia, and Cyprus – are similarly concerned about the impact of the Kosovo precedent on their own minorities. In particular, the Greek-Cypriot government fears that recognition of Kosovar independence might bolster the cause of Turkish-Cypriot separatists. As if to prove that such fears are not unfounded, less than a week after Kosovo's secession the Serbs of Bosnia-Herzegovina announced their intention to secede from the western Balkan country. The precedent of the unilateral secession of Kosovo was invoked again in summer 2008, in the conflict between Russia and Georgia.

That the Union's voice in the world is barely audible, even in those parts of the world of most direct and close interest to Europe, had already been made plain by the Balkan wars of the 1990s. The realization that the EU and its member states lacked the means to mount the complex interventions needed in Croatia and Bosnia, combined with American insistence that the European allies should play a larger role in maintaining the security of their own territory, in the end convinced EU leaders to accept responsibility for peacekeeping operations in Bosnia-Herzegovina. Even this limited assignment forced the Union to borrow NATO assets and capabilities. As mentioned in chapter 4, the Rapid Reaction Force of 50,000–60,000 men and women, which was supposed to be operational by 2003, should be ready by 2010 – if then. After memories of the NATO action in Kosovo (spring 1999) began to fade, it proved difficult to maintain the momentum towards an effective European Security and Defence Policy (ESDP). In the summer of 1999, when EU governments were considering the costs of implementing the Stability Pact and of preparing East European countries for eventual EU membership, there were already signs of backtracking on commitments made to Balkan countries. The reality behind the ambitious rhetoric of EU leaders is that most member states have been unwilling to invest the necessary resources for military R & D and for an adequate defence force. 'European governments spend two-thirds as much as the US on defense, but can deploy only ten per cent as many troops': this, writes William Wallace (2005: 444), was the mantra repeated continuously in prime-ministerial speeches and government statements in those years. Like a true mantra, it may have led to a higher state of spiritual awareness; certainly it did not lead to concrete actions.

Notwithstanding the growing gap between commitments and available resources, the establishment of the ESDP demonstrates that the EU leaders themselves no longer believe in the efficacy of a foreign and security policy based exclusively on 'soft power'. The first-ever European Security Strategy, *A Secure Europe in a Better World*, prepared by the EU High Representative for foreign and security policy, Javier Solana, and approved by the European Council in December 2003, referred to 'the full spectrum of instruments for crisis management and conflict prevention at our disposal, including political, diplomatic, military and civilian, trade and development activities' (cited in Manners 2006: 188). As was to be expected, some scholars now begin to worry about the 'militarization' of the EU, in spite of the fact that with the limited means at its disposal, the Union so far has focused on training and peacekeeping – not without problems in performing even these low-profile tasks. Limitations of the EU's military capabilities were again revealed in January 2008, when the twenty-seven member states struggled to find the 4,500 troops and equipment needed to send a peacekeeping force to Chad – by mid-March the EU contingent was still 1,000 short of the troop target.

If the future of Europe's new security strategy is still uncertain, the limits of a diplomacy based exclusively on dialogue, negotiations, and

economic aid are by now absolutely clear. In the 1990s the EU and its
member states supplied by far the largest proportion of economic assistance to the former socialist states, including Russia, but nonetheless
the East–West strategy was defined by the United States. In the Middle
East the EU and its members have provided the largest share of economic
aid to the Palestinians, without any tangible influence over Israeli–
Palestinian relations, and without winning respect for their humanitar-
ian efforts: after the collapse of the Palestinian–Israeli peace process at
the end of 2000, the Israelis did not hesitate to destroy much of the
civilian infrastructure the EU had financed. The dominance of US power
across the Middle East, writes William Wallace, 'left European governments able only to issue diplomatic declarations, to provide core financial assistance to the Palestinian Authority – or to pursue commercial
interests' (2005: 450). Many American analysts have reached the conclusion that the Europeans' advocacy of multilateralism in international
relations is a function of Europe's weakness; and that the rational division of labour today is one whereby 'the US does the fighting, the UN
feeds, the EU pays', or, in the shorter variant, 'The US does dinner, and
the EU does the dishes' (Pond 2004: 88–9).

One of the key principles of EU diplomacy is indeed multilateralism,
with the United Nations replacing the old League of Nations as guarantor
of world order. After World War I, the League 'was immensely popular
with war-wearied public opinion in the West, but its very creation then
permitted many the argument that there was no need for national
defense forces since the League would somehow prevent future wars'
(Kennedy 1987: 290). A rather similar public mood has prevailed in most
countries of Western Europe since the end of World War II. The EU's
low geopolitical profile mirrors a public opinion generally unwilling to
stand behind a stronger role in international affairs – and to cover
the corresponding costs. In light of this, the preference for the model
of 'civil-power' Europe is understandable: unlike diplomacy, which is
traditionally conducted by elites, 'security policy requires a public consensus; but 50 years after the Schuman plan, there still is no "European
public space" – there is only a juxtaposition of national public spaces,
capped by a jumble of intergovernmental and supranational bureaucracies' (Hoffmann 2000: 198). As other authors have also pointed out,
the dominant mode of policy-making in this area – intensive transgovernmentalism among foreign ministries within the EU and among
embassies in third countries – is such that issues of foreign and security
policy seldom get a chance to be seriously debated in public, or even in

national parliaments. Granted that the model of 'civil-power' Europe is the only one that fits the current state of public opinion, EU leaders should at least be willing to explain to their citizens the geopolitical implications of this approach, and to scale down their ambitions and commitments accordingly. Instead, official statements do not reveal any intention to face reality – quite the contrary. Article 11 of the Treaty on European Union opens with the confident statement: 'The Union shall define and implement a common foreign and security policy covering all areas of foreign and security policy.' Later on, the same article assures EU citizens that: 'The Member States shall support the Union's external and security policy actively and unreservedly in a spirit of loyalty and mutual solidarity.'

A few years after these words were written, the disintegration of the precarious foreign-policy consensus over the invasion of Iraq – the division between 'old' and 'new' Europe celebrated by policy-makers in Washington – demonstrated the illusory quality of those assurances of loyalty and mutual solidarity. Official proclamations cannot disguise the fact that in the enlarged Union it is increasingly difficult to reach a shared understanding about common European interests – as distinct from the mere algebraic sum of national interests. In particular, the new member states which feel threatened by a resurgent Russia look to the United States (and to NATO), not to 'civil-power' Europe, for protection. Indeed, some East European leaders, such as former Polish prime minister Jaroslaw Kaczynski, see the US as a useful counterweight to the EU. The importance they attach to American protection is understandable in view of the many issues still open between Russia and the former members of the Soviet bloc, or of the Soviet Union itself – including the treatment of the sizable Russian minorities in the Baltic republics. As was already noted in a previous chapter, it is to be expected that future relations between the EU and Russia will be more difficult because of the rising nationalism of the new eastern members, and their distrust of the big neighbour. What is to be feared is that, in the absence of a common position concerning relations between the EU, NATO, and Russia, East–West strategy will continue to be dictated by the United States.

Current efforts to enhance the international status of Europe deserve full respect, but it is unlikely that it will be possible to achieve concrete results without first correcting the basic flaw in the foreign and defence policy of the EU – which is the pretence of sitting at the table where the great international issues are debated without having been able to decide what the vital European interests are, if such exist. If it continues to be impossible to reach agreement on such basic matters, then the only reasonable conclusion is that a fully fledged foreign policy cannot be designed for the EU as a whole – at best only for more homogeneous subsets of its membership, as argued in the next and final chapter.

8

Unity in Diversity

Beyond Straight-Line Evolution

The traditional approach to European integration is inspired by a uni-linear evolutionary image. This notion of orthogenesis (as biologists call straight-line evolution) emerged at a time when the EC comprised a small group of fairly homogeneous West European states. In the early stages of the integration process it was not unreasonable to assume that the European Community would necessarily evolve, sooner or later, into a politically integrated bloc, perhaps even into something like a nation (see chapter 2). That assumption is no longer tenable in a Union of twenty-seven, or more, members at vastly different stages of socioeco-nomic development, with different geopolitical concerns, and corres-pondingly diverse policy priorities. Under present conditions, not orthogenesis but evolution with several side-branches seems to be the appropriate model. As a matter of fact, surveying the general pattern of European integration since the end of World War II, one can see several distinct branches – a number of, often overlapping, state groupings established for purposes of cooperation in a variety of fields: political, economic, protection of human rights, security, science, and technology. An important example is the Council of Europe founded in 1949, which at present has more than forty member countries. The Council may concern itself with all political, economic, and social matters of general European interest and thus has an even broader mandate than the European Union. True, it does not have the power to make binding laws. The two instruments at the Council's disposal are non-binding resolutions, and conventions effective only between the states that rati-fied them. The most important convention enacted under its auspices is the European Convention for the Protection of Human Rights and Fundamental Freedoms (ECHR) of 4 November 1950. With the creation of the European Court of Human Rights, located in Strasbourg, the ECHR provides an enforcement structure which subjects the states to a 'European' supervision of their compliance with the provisions of the

Convention. For this reason, it has been argued that the ECHR consti-
tutes a first expression of supranationalism in the European integration
process (Lenaerts and Van Nuffel 1999). It is interesting to note that
despite the non-binding character of the norms, levels of compliance
with the ECHR and with the decisions of the Strasbourg Court do not
appear to be at all lower than levels of compliance with European
Community law (MacCormick 1999).

The Conference for Security and Cooperation in Europe (renamed
in 1995 the Organization for Security and Cooperation in Europe, OSCE)
is another cooperative arrangement with broader scope than the EU
framework. The OSCE, with fifty-three member states, comprises virtually all European countries, including all the republics of the former
Soviet Union, as well as Canada and the United States. It consists of
several institutions and consultation mechanisms: meetings of the Heads
of State or Government; a Council of Ministers of Foreign Affairs; a
Council of Permanent Representatives to the OSCE; a Parliamentary
Assembly; an Office for Democratic Institutions and Human Rights;
and several instruments for dispute resolution. There are many other
forms of European cooperation within and without the EU framework,
e.g. Benelux – the customs union among the Netherlands, Belgium, and
Luxembourg established in 1948 and which survives within the EU
because the Treaty of Rome permits such internal regional groupings
as long as they are compatible with the EC's objectives; and the Nordic
Council, created in 1952 to promote regional, economic, and political
cooperation among Denmark, Iceland, Norway, Sweden, and Finland.
A further instance of European cooperation is provided by the association of Iceland, Norway, and Switzerland, as non-EU member states, to
the Schengen system. In addition, there are numerous functional associations cooperating in various science and technology fields, such as the
European Space Agency.

It is therefore wrong to reduce the history of European integration
after World War II to one particular approach, and wrong-headed to
insist that the EU should be the main, if not the only, forum for close
European cooperation. Neither geographically nor functionally or cultu-
rally does the 'Europe of Brussels' coincide with, or represent, the entire
continent. Actually, the variety of modes of integration and interstate
cooperation is one of the distinguishing features of European history.
As Eric Jones (1987) has stressed, for most of its history Europe formed
a cultural, economic, even a political unity. Of course, it was a special type
of unity that did not exclude frequent, if limited, wars. Not the unity of the

Chinese or Ottoman empires, rather, unity in diversity, embodied in a system of states competing and cooperating with each other. Such a system realized the benefits of competitive decision-making and the economies of scale of the centralized empire, giving Europe some of the best of both worlds. In the words of the British historian: 'This picture of a Europe which shared in salient respects a common culture ... and formed something of a single market demonstrates that political decentralisation did not mean a fatal loss of economies of scale in production and distribution. The states system did not thwart the flow of capital and labour to the constituent states offering the highest marginal return' (Jones 1987: 117). After the disastrous 'long' century of nationalism, the search for unity in diversity has been resumed along a number of paths. The idea of a manifold path to European unity is of course anathema to the believers in the dogma of orthogenesis, yet historical evidence and recent theoretical developments suggest that in complex societies the multiplication of voluntary associations, competing and cooperating with each other, need not be an element of weakness – on the contrary it can signal a positive, welfare-enhancing development.

In Search of Flexibility

To the biologist flexibility or, more precisely, 'developmental flexibility' means changes that succeed in adapting an organism to new conditions. Many students of European integration assume that the EU is developmentally flexible in this sense. Thus a legal scholar writes of 'the inherent ability of the EU integration process to constantly reinvent itself as part of an evolutionary process of political and economic survival' (Szyszczak 2006: 487). Another student of European law has contended that the approach to integration followed for half a century is still basically valid, and capable of evolving in response to changing pressures and new priorities (Dougan 2006: 869). Equally favourable prognoses have been issued by scholars and commentators who over the years have absorbed the EU's political culture of total optimism. As was argued in the preceding chapter, however, there is no basis for assuming the adaptability, let alone the continuing validity, of the traditional approaches. Even without invoking the transformation of the world economy during the last decades, and the emergence of powerful competitors which were still underdeveloped countries when the Rome Treaty was signed, it is sufficient to recall that the present EU is so heterogeneous that income inequality is now greater here than in the arch-capitalist USA. The failure to achieve a single European market for services is a prime example of the difficulty of reconciling 'widening' with 'deepening' under present conditions (see chapter 4).

The geopolitical changes since the end of the Cold War have been no less dramatic. Western Europe never seemed to be so close to being recast into a fully fledged supranational federation as in the 1950s. Beyond the Iron Curtain, communitarian Europe formed an island of democracy, with definite geographical boundaries. According to Jean-Marie Guéhenno (1993: 77) one of the unanticipated consequences of the collapse of the Soviet empire has been the discovery that Europe can no longer become a nation, even a federal one, for this would require a boundary to the east, hence the permanent exclusion of Russia from the EU. When the treaties of Paris and Rome were signed, nobody could have foreseen that the Soviet system would collapse before the end of the century, making it possible for the countries of Central and Eastern Europe to join the EU. However beneficial in so many respects, this particular mutation of the geopolitical environment has radically changed the nature of a fairly homogeneous association of mostly prosperous West European states.

Paradoxically, doubts about the capability of the European Community to adapt to the growing diversity of its members were expressed more clearly after the first, rather modest, enlargement of the EC than today, when membership has almost doubled in a decade, and diversity has reached levels unimaginable when the United Kingdom, Denmark, and Ireland joined the six founding members in 1973. These doubts provided the incentive to articulate various models of differentiated integration which will be reviewed in a later section. In the immediately following pages attention is given to attempts made by the European institutions themselves to introduce some elements of flexibility in policy-making methods. As already mentioned, the Commission's initial approach to harmonization had been to regulate exhaustively a given field, e.g. technical standards for automobile safety, to the exclusion of previously existing, or future, national laws and regulations – a sort of 'federal pre-emption' which came to be known as total harmonization. The European Court of Justice initially supported this exclusive Community competence, judging it to be necessary to the construction of the common market and, more generally, to the autonomy of the Community system – against the tendency of the member states to reduce European law to a branch of international law (Schuetze 2007). Already by the mid-1970s, however, the limit of total harmonization had become visible. The idea of a common market structured by one body of uniform European rules had to be given up once it was realized that total harmonization confers on the Community an exclusive competence which it is ill-equipped to discharge (Weatherill 1995). The same realistic assessment also explains why the notion of exclusive competence has ever since been referred to very sparingly by the ECJ, despite its obvious integrationist appeal.

The first significant effort to introduce flexibility in European regulatory policy-making was undertaken in the 1970s, when emphasis shifted from total to minimum and optional harmonization (see chapter 7). Greater autonomy for the national regulators became an issue again when the SEA replaced unanimity by Qualified Majority Voting (QMV) for harmonization measures aimed at achieving the single European market. The member states were not prepared to give up the possibility of national vetoes in such matters unless their regulatory autonomy be explicitly acknowledged. The outcome was Article 100a(4) (now Article 95(4) EC), which for the first time made opting out of a Community harmonization measure feasible. The possibility thus offered of unilateral derogation effectively acknowledged that Community legislative intervention is not of itself sufficient to exclude regulatory action by the member states. From the perspective of exclusive competence, such an acknowledgement is anathema, but this was the price that had to be paid for extending the use of QMV. Actually, opting out of harmonizing measures has been infrequent, but at first influential commentators were alarmed, considering this form of flexibility a serious backwards step in the pattern of a uniform Community legal order (see chapter 2). Various other types of options, exemptions, and derogations have been granted to the member states in order to obtain support for European directives with which they proved uncomfortable. For the sake of expanding Community competence the European institutions have been willing to run the risk that such compromises 'may fragment the directive to such an extent that the final text's claim to provide a source of common rules for the Community is a sham' (Weatherill 1995: 157).

Some thirty years later, a more radical form of flexibility was introduced with the Open Method of Coordination. The OMC employs non-binding objectives and guidelines, commonly agreed indicators, benchmarking, and persuasion, in an effort to bring about change in such areas as employment, health, migration, and pension reform – where the Community has limited or no competence. The philosophy underlying the OMC and related 'soft-law' methods is that each state should be encouraged to experiment on its own, and to craft solutions fitted to its national context. While the classic Community Method creates uniform rules member states must adopt, provides sanctions if they fail to do so, and allows challenges for non-compliance to be brought before the ECJ, the OMC provides no formal sanctions for member states that do not follow the guidelines. Advocates of the new approach to flexibility argue that the OMC can be effective despite – or perhaps because of – its open-ended, non-binding, non-justiciable qualities (Trubek and Trubek 2005). Unfortunately, the OMC seems to have fallen far short of expectations even in areas where one might have presumed it to have yielded the most significant results (see chapter 6). Because member states appear to use the method in areas where it matches domestic policy priorities, but to ignore it in areas where it conflicts with these priorities, the critics say that the OMC is at best a method of national, rather than European, policy-making. They also point out that the ECJ, as well as the EP, are completely left out of the OMC procedure. If allowed to creep into areas of existing legislative competence the new strategy would thus sap the EU's capacity to do what, according to the critics, really needs to be done, namely to pass uniform, binding, and justiciable laws (Hatzopoulos 2007). In sum, it appears that the OMC and related 'soft-law' methods can neither replace the classic Community Method nor perform more effectively the traditional tasks of international agencies like the OECD. Thus, the chances that the new methods may evolve into a viable form of developmental flexibility appear to be remote.

It has already been mentioned that the pattern of options and exceptions allowed to member states from aspects of directives with which they are uncomfortable carries the risk of a loss of legal and policy coherence. The risk becomes a great deal more serious when the loss of uniformity is not limited to specific regulatory measures, but embodied in the treaties themselves. It will be recalled that strong concerns about the loss of legal unity were expressed in connection with the 'pillar' structure introduced by the Maastricht Treaty. Behind the concerns about the internal coherence of the legal order loomed the fear that the loss of legal uniformity could be fatal to the idea that European integration must move along a single path. Other, more realistic, observers of the European scene realized that the flexibility displayed in several forms in the SEA and in subsequent treaties, as well as in particular Community measures, was no momentary aberration, but the indication of an emergent strategy for achieving progress in politically sensitive areas, even at the price of a loss of overall coherence of the system (Craig and de Búrca

2003). The question that was not raised, however, is whether the strategy of granting opt-outs to make treaty ratification possible is a viable method for adapting an increasingly diverse EU to radically new conditions, or whether it is heading in the direction, not of developmental flexibility, but of multilinear evolution.

The Selective Exit Option

In an article published in 1984, Claus-Dieter Ehlermann examined the extent to which Community law can accommodate diversity among the member states. Like other commentators before and after him, the distinguished legal scholar and influential Commission official was concerned about the long-run implications of the movement away from a strictly unitary approach to integration which was already detectable in the 1980s. A key point in his argument was a suggested criterion for distinguishing between admissible and inadmissible derogations in favour of particular member states. According to Ehlermann (1984), objective economic and social differences could in principle justify a differentiated treatment, while 'purely political phenomena' (read: different national policy preferences) could not. For instance, the circumstance that the British government, or a majority of Parliament, or of British public opinion was opposed to joining the European Monetary System (EMS) would not be a valid argument for differentiated treatment of the UK – assuming that the rules for the EMS were part of European law. In fact, the rules for monetary cooperation within the framework of the EMS were not legally binding, as Ehlermann well knew, but his prescient comments referred to a situation – the grant of exceptional status to some member states in the form of an exemption from some treaty provisions – which was to become of practical relevance several years later. The first concrete example was of course provided by Britain's opt-out from the social chapter of the Treaty on European Union; this particular opt-out was a temporary one, lasting from 1993 to 1997, when the new Labour government of Tony Blair decided to join the other member states in adopting all social-policy directives. Whereas Ehlermann had argued against granting exceptional status for political reasons, more or less permanent opt-outs for precisely such reasons have been granted with increasing frequency in recent years. The Maastricht Treaty allowed the United Kingdom and Denmark to opt out of participating in the third and final stage of monetary union. As mentioned, Sweden, not a member of the EU when the treaty was ratified, was also granted a de facto opt-out from EMU when it joined the Union on 1 January 1995. Again, the UK, Denmark, and Ireland secured various degrees of opt-out arrangements with respect to the Schengen Agreement abolishing border controls among the EU member states; while Denmark opted out of the elaboration and implementation of measures of the Common Foreign and Security Policy having defence implications.

In 2007 the UK and Poland ratified the Lisbon Treaty only after they were allowed to opt out of the Charter of Fundamental Rights. Both countries feared that the charter, if incorporated into the treaty, could be used by the Court of Justice or the Commission to extend Union competence in industrial and social legislation. Indeed, the EU legal authorities had started to take account of the charter following its proclamation at the Nice summit in December 2000, that is, before it was legally binding. In several cases an Advocate General of the ECJ referred to the charter to identify fundamental rights in the Union, while the Commission had decided to subject proposals for legislation to a charter-compatibility check as of March 2001. These precedents explain the British position, summed up by Tony Blair in a speech on the future of Europe delivered in Cardiff on 28 November 2002: 'we cannot support a form of treaty incorporation that would enlarge EU competence over national legislation. There cannot be new legal rights given by such means, especially in areas such as industrial law where we have long and difficult memories of the battles fought to get British law in proper order' (cited in Norman 2003: 88). The reasons supplied by the UK prime minister were instances of precisely those 'purely political phenomena' which some twenty years earlier Ehlermann rejected as valid justification for derogations in favour of individual member states. Positions like the one defended by the former prime minister reveal a basic disagreement about the very purpose of European integration. As such, they point to a Union too heterogeneous to support a common framework in a growing number of policy areas.

If selective opting out is becoming increasingly popular, the chance offered since the late 1990s to subsets of member states to engage in closer integration has found no takers so far. In hope of making the EU more flexible, while preserving key elements of the traditional frame-work, the 1997 Amsterdam Treaty introduced the possibility that some member states may choose to move to more advanced stages of integra-tion by setting up closer patterns of cooperation. In turn, by giving quasi-constitutional status to the principle of closer cooperation, the framers of

the treaty had acknowledged the growing diversity of national preferences as a consequence of enlargement, though they were more concerned still about the risk of fragmentation of the received model. The
consequence was a set of conditions so strict as to practically rule out
the possibility of establishing patterns of cooperation reflecting the
different policy preferences of the more integrationist member states.
The issue of closer (later called 'enhanced') cooperation was the one
where most progress was made during the negotiations leading to the
Treaty of Nice. Article 43 of this treaty provides that 'Member States
which intend to establish enhanced cooperation between themselves
may make use of the institutions, procedures and mechanisms laid
down by this Treaty and by the Treaty establishing the European
Community' – subject to a number of conditions listed in the remainder
of the article. The proposed cooperation must be aimed at furthering
the objectives of the Union and of the Community, at protecting and
serving their interests, and at reinforcing the integration process; it must
respect the treaties, the single institutional framework of the Union,
and the *acquis communautaire*; it cannot concern the areas of exclusive
Community competence; it must involve a minimum of eight member
states, be open to all members of the Union, and not constitute a barrier
to, or discrimination in, trade between the member states, nor distort
competition between them. The following Articles 43a and 43b provide,
respectively, that enhanced cooperation should be used only as a last
resort when it has been determined that the same objectives cannot be
otherwise attained within a reasonable period; and that enhanced cooperation should be open to all member states at any stage, under the
conditions specified by the treaty, and that as many members as possible
should be encouraged to take part. Decisions taken in the framework of
enhanced cooperation are not to be part of the Union *acquis* (Article 44).

Since the Treaty of Amsterdam the tendency had been to make the
use of enhanced cooperation more feasible and operational, and both
the Constitutional and the Reform (Lisbon) treaties actually meant to
reinforce this tendency. Thus, one-third of the member states would now
be sufficient to establish enhanced cooperation, as long as authorization
is granted by the EU Council; and authorization to proceed is granted
when it has been determined within the Council that the objectives of
such cooperation cannot be attained within a reasonable period by the
Union as a whole. An optimistic school of thought tends to focus attention on the potential of enhanced-cooperation clauses to regulate diversity in a principled way – in the sense that any users of these provisions

must adhere to the objectives of the Union. A more pessimistic school argues that, far from furthering the objectives of the Union, the various forms of voluntary cooperation among member states will in fact undermine the basic assumption of the Community Method: that all countries would move together along the same integration path.

This pessimistic view of selective interstate cooperation explains why the Commission's official communication presented to the Constitutional Convention in 2002 – *A Project for the European Union* (2002) – was rather hostile to the whole question of flexibility. It objected, *inter alia*, that the enhanced-cooperation provisions offer merely theoretical answers to the problems of diversity, and that it was time for a critical reappraisal of all forms of flexibility. The underlying message was that the enlarged EU needs a strengthened Community Method in order to be able to 'exercise the responsibilities of a world power'. A second, more radically federalist contribution to the Constitutional Convention – titled *Contribution to a Preliminary Project of a Constitution of the European Union* (codename: Penelope) – did not even address flexibility. Instead, the document produced at the request of President Romano Prodi by a small group of Commission officials proposed a constitutional architecture for the Union in which almost all decisions would be taken by majority vote, and enhanced-cooperation arrangements would be excluded. Member states would be allowed to conclude arrangements among themselves, however, as long as they do not make use of the institutions and procedures of the Union. While the Amsterdam and Nice treaties encouraged the member states to work within, or as closely as possible to, the framework of the Union when cooperating among themselves, the aim of the Commission proposal was to sharply separate voluntary arrangements from the mainstream integration process. In fact, the proposal seemed to admit the possibility that the objectives of closer cooperation could be unrelated to the objectives of the Union, while the previous treaties stressed that enhanced cooperation should aim to further the objectives of the Union, protect its interests and reinforce the integration process. The lowering of the participation threshold proposed by the draft Constitutional Treaty could only strengthen the Commission's fears that in a greatly enlarged Union enhanced cooperation would eventually lead to the demise of the principle of a single institutional framework for the integration process. It is true that the possibility of enhanced cooperation has never been used so far, but this is presumably due to the strict conditions imposed on the exercise of this option. If these conditions were relaxed at the

same time that national preferences became more varied as a consequence of enlargement, the temptation to form smaller, more homogeneous groupings may well become irresistible.

Differentiated Integration

Such worries are hardly new in the history of European integration.
As already mentioned, the fear of disintegration has haunted the Euro-
elites since the early 1970s. More than by the first, limited enlargement of
the Community, this fear may have been nurtured by the realization that
most European voters continued to remain indifferent to, when not
sceptical about, the integration project – a situation no amount of
federalist propaganda seemed able to change. That would explain why
Leo Tindemans, prime minister of Belgium and convinced federalist, in
his report on the future of European integration presented in December
1975 to his colleagues of the European Council, focused less on the final
goal of a federal Europe than on the model of what would be later called
'multi-speed Europe'. According to Tindemans, economic and other
differences were already so large among the (then) nine members of
the EC that it was impossible to work out a credible action programme
under the assumption that all the intermediate goals were to be reached
by all member states at the same time. Hence the proposal that different
states should be allowed to move towards deeper integration at different
speeds, depending on their ability to do so. This was the most controversial aspect of the report, and it was disliked by the smaller member
states, which objected to the prospect of first- and second-class membership, and by France and the United Kingdom, who saw the proposal as a
prelude to further losses of national sovereignty. The Tindemans Report
had no immediate impact on the integration process, but a quarter of a
century later its author could claim that his ideas had found practical
implementation in the rules of EMU, according to which only countries
satisfying certain conditions were allowed to move to the final stage of
monetary union (Tindemans 1998). The Belgian leader also emphasized
the difference between his model of multi-speed Europe – which assumes
that all the member states agree on the final goal of political integration,
and only the speed with which they move towards it may vary – and the
model of Europe à la carte.

The latter model was popularized by Ralf Dahrendorf, also in the
1970s. While still a member of the European Commission, Dahrendorf
wrote a series of newspaper articles (published in 1973 under the nom

de plume Weiland Europa) in which he severely criticized the European institutions and their strategy of integration by stealth. The first of the four principles he advocated as a means of accelerating the process of political integration was that it is more important to solve problems than to create institutions. This was a clear, if implicit, criticism of cryptofederalists like Paul-Henri Spaak and Jean Monnet, for whom what mattered most was not distant political goals, but the creation of European institutions – regardless of what these institutions might do (see chapter 3). It was his third principle that expressed the idea of integration à la carte, meaning that 'everyone does what he wants and ... no one must participate in everything', a situation that 'though far from ideal is surely much better than avoiding anything that cannot be cooked in a single pot' (cited in Gillingham 2003: 91–2). Concretely this meant that there would be common European policies in areas where the member states have a common interest, but not otherwise. This, said Dahrendorf, must become the general rule rather than the exception if we wish to prevent continuous demands for special treatment, destroying in the long run the coherence of the entire system – another prescient anticipation of the present practice of moving ahead by granting opt-outs from treaty obligations. As in the case of the Tindemans Report, Dahrendorf's arguments – especially his incisive criticism of European institutions and of the traditional integration methods – were quite controversial at the time, but had no immediate practical consequences. Today the idea of integration à la carte keeps recurring with increasing frequency, for example in the proposals advanced in 2000 by the former German foreign minister Joschka Fischer, and by other neo-federalist leaders after the constitutional debacle of 2005 (see chapter 2).

Tindemans's and Dahrendorf's contributions effectively opened the debate on differentiated integration. 'Differentiated integration' is a generic and neutral term used 'to denote variations in the application of European policies or variations in the level and intensity of participation in European policy regimes' (H. Wallace 1998: 137). In addition to those discussed so far, the label applies to several other models such as 'variable geometry', 'core and periphery', and 'concentric circles'. The distinguishing features of each model are not always spelt out. For example, Tindemans's claim that his idea of multi-speed Europe eventually found application in the design of European monetary union echoes the hope of the architects of EMU that all member states would strive to attain convergence of performance and of policy. It is far from clear, however, that the countries which opted out of the single currency, in particular the UK, intend to join the euro-zone in the foreseeable future, if ever. To speak in this case of multi-speed Europe is, at best, to express a wish: integration à la carte is the more appropriate label.

The model of multi-speed Europe is even less appropriate in the case of the British and Polish opt-outs from the Charter of Fundamental Rights of the Lisbon Treaty. The leaders of the two countries justified their refusal to support treaty incorporation of the charter by their fear that this might enlarge EU competence over national legislation, hence these opt-outs imply an outright rejection of political integration. In sum, the single most significant criterion to distinguish between various forms of differentiation is whether or not a particular model assumes that all member states must accept the political unification of Europe as the finality of the integration process. Dahrendorf's suggestion that under the mode of integration he envisaged 'everyone does what he wants' should not be taken literally, of course: even a mere free-trade area presupposes some generally accepted rules. The key point is that 'no one must participate in everything'; hence integration à la carte, although it presupposes some general rules accepted by everybody, does not assume a common final destination – not even in the sense of an open-ended process of 'ever closer union'. Beyond the common agreement to form, say, a customs union with elements of a common market, member states would be free to cooperate in specific functional areas on the basis of shared interests. This integration strategy is poles apart from the philosophy of enhanced cooperation, which as we saw allows voluntary associations of member states only to the extent that they 'further the objectives of the Union and of the Community, protect and serve their interests, and reinforce the integration process' (Art. 43 1(a) of the Treaty on European Union. See chapter 2).

A Theory of Differentiated Integration

None of the forms of differentiated integration discussed above are based on, or inspired by, any formal social-scientific theory. This is also true of more recent proposals, such as the ideas advanced by Joschka Fischer in his Humboldt University speech of May 2000, which was considered by many to have been the catalyst that led to the calling of the Convention on the Future of Europe in 2002. All concepts of differentiated integration were worked out and presented as ad hoc responses to concerns raised by the growing number and diversity of the members of the European Community, and then of the European Union. In preparation for the big bang enlargement at the beginning of the new century there was a determined attempt to minimize the risks entailed by a high level of heterogeneity among the member states. The more optimistic Euro-leaders – among whom, as we saw, figured prominently members of the German government and of the European Commission – claimed that geographical widening and policy deepening were not just compatible with, but mutually reinforcing of aspects of the integration process. Other European leaders who neither shared this view, nor wished to follow the Euro-sceptics in supporting enlargement as a way of preventing further 'deepening', tended to view enlargement primarily as an organizational or managerial problem, to be solved by better institutional design and more effective decision-making procedures. What all leaders were reluctant to admit, at least in public, was that each enlargement of the EU necessarily changes the calculus of the benefits and the costs of integration – the reduction of transaction costs made possible by harmonized rules, on the one hand, and the welfare losses entailed by rules that are less adequately tuned to the resources and preferences of each member state, on the other. To repeat an important point already emphasized in previous chapters, as long as resources and preferences are fairly similar across countries, the advantages of common rules are likely to exceed the welfare losses caused by harmonization, but when heterogeneity exceeds a certain threshold the reverse will be true.

There are indications that in the present Union this threshold has been exceeded. This may explain the growing opposition to harmonization, even of the minimum type, and also the current popularity of voluntary methods of coordination and cooperation, and other 'soft' modes of governance. In addition, recourse to mutual recognition is becoming increasingly problematic, as shown by the fierce opposition to the Bolkestein draft of the General Services Directive. As was seen in chapter 4, after the big bang enlargement to the east, trade unions and politically important sections of public opinion in the older member states became particularly sensitive to the redistributive consequences of the application of mutual recognition. The principle of mutual recognition was supposed to play a key role in the area of Justice and Home Affairs (JHA) as well. At the Tampere European Council of 1999 it had been decided that this principle should become a cornerstone of judicial cooperation in both civil and criminal matters within the EU. The first, and symbolically most important, measure to apply mutual recognition in JHA was the Framework Decision of 13 June 2002 on the European Arrest Warrant (EAW). According to this measure, a decision by the judicial authority of a member state to require the arrest and return of a person should be recognized and executed as promptly and as easily as possible in the other member states. Being based on mutual recognition, the EAW Framework Decision presupposed the essential equivalence of national standards, in this case standards of criminal law. For this reason the Ministers of Justice of the EU had initially agreed to limit the application of the Decision to the members of the old EU-15, where the assumption of equivalence of standards of criminal law was likely to be more easily satisfied. The agreement was later reversed by the Committee of Permanent Representatives on political grounds, but the initial doubts were apparently justified: recent decisions by national courts show that the necessary level of trust in each other's judicial systems cannot be assumed (Lavenex 2007).

Now, issues concerning the benefits and costs of harmonized rules or the distributive implications of mutual recognition, far from being peculiar to the EU, arise with increasing frequency in the global economy; and because of their practical importance and intrinsic interest they are attracting the attention of international economists and lawyers (Bhagwati and Hudec 1996; Trachtman 2007). Concerning the benefits and costs of harmonization, in particular, the economic theory of clubs, originally developed by James Buchanan (1965), has been applied by Alessandra Casella (1996) to study the interaction between expanding markets and the provision of standards. She argues, *inter alia*, that if we think of standards as being developed by communities of users, then 'opening trade will modify not only the standards but also the coalitions that express them. As markets ... expand and become more heterogeneous, different coalitions will form across national borders, and their number will rise' (1996: 149). The relevance of these arguments extends well beyond the narrow area of standard-setting. In fact, Casella's emphasis on heterogeneity among traders as the main force against harmonization and for the multiplication of 'clubs' suggests an attractive theoretical basis for the study of differentiated integration in the EU. Before following up this hunch, however, we need to recall a few definitions and key concepts of the theory.

Pure public goods, such as national defence or environmental quality, are characterized by two properties: first, it does not cost anything for an additional individual to enjoy the benefits of the public goods, once they are produced (*joint-supply property*); and, second, it is difficult or impossible to exclude individuals from the enjoyment of such goods (*non-excludability*). A '*club good*' is a public good from whose benefits individuals may be excluded – only the joint-supply property holds. An association established to provide excludable public goods is a *club*. Two elements determine the optimal size of a club. One is the cost of producing the club good – in a large club this cost is shared over more members. The second element is the cost to each club member of the good not meeting precisely his or her individual needs or preferences. The latter cost is likely to increase with the size of the club. The optimal size is determined by the point where the marginal benefit from the addition of one new member, i.e. the reduction in the per capita cost of producing the good, equals the marginal cost caused by a mismatch between the characteristics of the good and the preferences of the individual club members. If the preferences and the technologies for the provision of club goods are such that the number of clubs that can be formed in a society of given size is large, then an efficient allocation of such excludable public goods through the voluntary association of individuals into clubs is possible. With many alternative clubs available, each individual can guarantee herself a satisfactory balance of benefits and costs, since any attempt to discriminate against her would induce her exit into a competing club – or the creation of a new one. The important question is: what happens as the complexity of the society increases, perhaps as the result of the integration of previously separate markets? It has been shown (Casella 1996) that under plausible hypotheses the number of clubs tends to increase as well, since the greater diversity of needs and preferences makes it efficient to produce a broader range of club goods, for instance product standards. The two main forces driving the results of Casella's model are heterogeneity among the economic agents, and transaction costs – the costs of trading under different standards. Harmonization is the optimal strategy when transaction costs are high enough, relative to gross returns, to prevent a partition of the community of users into two clubs that correctly reflect their needs. Hence harmonization occurs in response to market integration, but possibly only for an intermediate range of productivity in the production of standards, and when heterogeneity is not too great.

Think now of a society composed not of individuals, but of independent states. Associations of independent states (alliances, leagues, confederations) are typically voluntary, and their members are exclusively entitled to enjoy certain benefits produced by the association, so that the economic theory of clubs is applicable to this situation. In fact, since excludability is more easily enforced in the context envisaged here, many goods that are purely public at the national level become club goods at the international level (Majone 2005: 20–21). The club goods in question could be collective security, policy coordination, common technical standards, or tax harmonization. In these and many other cases, countries unwilling to share the costs are usually excluded from the benefits of interstate cooperation. Now, as an association of states expands, becoming more diverse in its preferences, the cost of uniformity in the provision of such goods – harmonization – can escalate dramatically. The theory predicts an increase in the number of voluntary associations to meet the increased demand for club goods more precisely tailored to the different requirements of various subsets of more homogeneous states. It will be noted that the model sketched here is inspired by a pluralist philosophy according to which variety in preferences should be matched by a corresponding variety in institutional arrangements.

Of the models of differentiated integration discussed in the preceding section 'integration à la carte' and 'variable geometry' come closest to the situation modelled by the theory of clubs. The expression 'variable geometry' has been used in several senses. In the meaning most relevant to the present discussion it refers to a situation where a subset of member states undertake some project, for instance an industrial or technological project in which other members of the Union are not interested, or to which they are unable to make a positive contribution. Since, by assumption, not all member states are willing to participate in all EU programmes, this model combines the criterion of differentiation by country, as in multi-speed integration, and by activity or project – as in integration à la carte. Still, all member states are supposed to respect a core of binding rules, but no broader commitments than those implied by the rules. For some authors (e.g. Maillet and Velo 1994) variable geometry is only a temporary stage until full integration has been achieved. Monetary union and the Schengen Agreement (with the British and Irish opt-outs, and Denmark's partial opt-out) are cited as concrete examples of variable geometry. What has been said in the preceding section about Tindemans's interpretation of EMU, however, also applies to these authors' view of variable geometry. A more recent example of selective intergovernmental cooperation outside the provisions of the treaties is the so-called G-5, an intergovernmental group comprising the interior ministers of France, Germany, Italy, Spain, and the UK. This particular club seeks to circumvent the lengthy decision-making processes of the Council of Ministers, and to conclude a series of bilateral agreements which should then form the basis of future EU-wide measures (Lavenex and Wallace 2005). If EMU, Schengen, or the G-5 are to be regarded as temporary stages on the road to full integration, then the distinction between variable geometry and multi-speed integration becomes elusive. The fact is that the various models of differentiated integration discussed in the literature overlap, and the lack of an explicit theoretical basis makes systematic classification impossible.

Competition with Cooperation

Taxonomic problems are not germane to the present discussion, however. What concerns us here is the conviction, shared by most if not all advocates of differentiated integration, that in a steadily expanding Union the idea of straight-line evolution of the system is not only increasingly implausible but also a serious obstacle to future integration. In contrast to what we called the dogma of orthogenesis – the apodictic assertion that integration can be only one way – the theory of clubs shows that in an expanding polity the multiplication of voluntary associations tends to be welfare enhancing: not only because it facilitates the production of rules tailored to the resources and preferences of the club members, but also because innovation, regulatory competition, and policy learning are more likely to occur in a decentralized system. In the European context, policies that prove to be politically unfeasible in the EU at large – e.g. the full liberalization of the services sector – might be acceptable to the members of a smaller, more homogeneous subset. Instead of compromise solutions that do not really satisfy anyone, genuine policy innovations would thus become viable – albeit on a smaller scale – and other members of the Union could later draw lessons from the practical experience of the pioneering states. In this way the clubs forming within the Union could effectively become policy laboratories, without the bureaucratic complications and background noise that necessarily arise when all the thirty or so member states participate in the experiment, as in the case of the OMC.

Rules on market competition are a constituent part of the EU economy, but I have argued that the reason for the importance attached to them by the founding fathers was utilitarian, rather than a commitment to a genuine free-market philosophy. The narrowly utilitarian philosophy of European competition rules is also demonstrated by the fact that inter-jurisdictional competition – competition between different national approaches to economic and social regulation, or between national currencies – has played no role in the integration process. Indeed, well-known EU lawyers like Stephen Weatherill maintain that competition among regulators is incompatible with the notion of undistorted competition in the internal European market to which reference is made in Article 3(g) of the EC Treaty. Hence the UK – the member state which has most consistently defended the benefits of interstate competition – has been accused of subordinating individual rights and social protection to a free-market philosophy incompatible with the basic aspirations of the European Community/Union: 'Competition between regulators on this perspective is simply incompatible with the EC's historical mission' (Weatherill 1995: 180). Widespread opposition to inter-jurisdictional competition explains why the principle of mutual recognition has played a more limited role in the process of European integration than originally expected.

Not surprisingly, André Breton – whose economic theory of politics and public finance based on a model of competitive governments has already been mentioned – thinks that, in the EU, inter-country competition has been virtually suppressed through excessive policy harmonization. His conclusion is worth repeating in the present discussion: 'competition is minimized through excessive harmonization of a substantial fraction of social, economic, and other policies … if one compares the degree of harmonization in Europe with that in Canada, the United States, and other federations, one is impressed by the extent to which it is greater in Europe than in the federations' (Breton 1996: 275–6). The same author points out that part of the opposition to the idea that governments, national and international agencies, clubs, vertical and horizontal networks, and so on, should compete among themselves derives from the widespread notion that competition is incompatible with, even antithetical to, cooperation. Breton cogently argues that this perception is mistaken. Excluding the case of collusion, cooperation and competition can and generally do coexist, so that the presence of one is no indication of the absence of the other. In particular, the observation of cooperation and coordination does not per se disprove that the underlying determining force may be competition. If one thinks of competition not as the *state* of affairs neoclassical theory calls 'perfect competition', but as an *activity* – à la Schumpeter, Hayek, and other Austrian economists who developed the model of *entrepreneurial competition* – then it becomes plain that 'the entrepreneurial innovation that sets the competitive process in motion, the imitation that follows, and the Creative Destruction that they generate are not inconsistent with cooperative behavior and the coordination of activities' (Breton 1996: 33). Given the appropriate competitive stimuli, political entrepreneurs, like their business counterparts, will consult with colleagues at home and abroad, collaborate with them on certain projects, harmonize various activities, and in the extreme case integrate some operations – all actions corresponding to what is generally meant by cooperation and coordination.

In some governmental systems the potential movement of citizens from one jurisdiction to another offering comparable services at lower cost may act as a stimulus to intergovernmental competition. According to the so-called Tiebout hypothesis, inter-jurisdictional competition results in communities supplying the goods and services individuals demand, and producing them in an efficient manner (Stiglitz 1988). We might try to extend this hypothesis to governmental systems where Tiebout's potential entry and exit mechanisms do not work effectively, for instance because mobility is limited by language and/or cultural and social cleavages, as in the EU. The extension consists in assuming that the citizens of a jurisdiction can use information about the goods and services supplied in other jurisdictions as a benchmark to evaluate the performance of their own government. This is of course the idea underlying the OMC, but we saw that the results so far have been disappointing. The excessive bureaucratization of the approach is one problem; another problem is that the OMC is under the complete control of the national executives. The crucial point, however, is that citizens are unable in practice to use information about the performance of other member states to induce their government to improve its own – the reason being that national parliaments are largely excluded from the OMC process. Thus, the stimulus to intergovernmental competition, which is assumed by the proposed extension of the Tiebout hypothesis, is missing.

The theory of clubs suggests that competition is more likely to take place between private associations, local communities, or transnational networks, than between monolithic national governments. In the next section I review some historical evidence that supports this hypothesis, and submit that the opposition to inter-jurisdictional competition can be traced to the persistence of state-centred thinking even among people who see the EU as the model of post-national Europe.

The Tenacity of a Flawed Paradigm

Such is the hold on people's minds of the paradigm of the nation state, with its claim to omnicompetence, undivided sovereignty, and territorial exclusivity, that the best-known theories of European integration attempt to locate the EC/EU along a single dimension going from an intergovernmental arrangement among sovereign states at one end to a state writ large – a multinational (quasi-)federation – at the other. Intergovernmentalist scholars view the EU as an international regime not essentially different – despite some special features – from other regimes of international policy coordination. According to them, the sovereignty of the nation state is preserved and actually strengthened by membership of the Union, while the European institutions are the creatures of national governments, having been established by their political principals in order to perform specific tasks. The other major theoretical approach to European integration occupies the opposite pole on the intergovernmentalism–supranationalism dimension. Neofunctionalists, as we know, predicted that economic integration would be self-sustaining, and would eventually lead to political integration: if national governments wish to secure the advantages of an initial agreement to integrate some sector of their economies, they would have to expand the scope of integration to include new sectors. It follows that any intermediate position between undiminished state sovereignty and full political integration would be inherently unstable. European institutions were to play a crucial role in transforming functional spillovers into political ones; more than that, they were to constitute the kernel of the future European government, which would largely replace the national governments – not so long ago Jacques Delors predicted that 80 per cent of all laws and regulations of the member states eventually would be coming from Brussels.

The same dichotomy – nation state or federal super-state – lurks behind many other, less theoretically articulate, positions. Thus the claim that the process of European integration must necessarily move along a single trajectory if it is not to dissolve in chaos, reflects the belief that no stable intermediate position can exist between the nation state and a large-scale replica of the same. The principle of subsidiarity, as stated in Article 5 of the EC Treaty, reveals similarly dichotomous thinking. As suggested in chapter 6, those national leaders who opposed further movement towards a pre-federal Union considered subsidiarity a barrier designed to halt Brussels's centralizing tendencies. At the other extreme, Commission president Delors maintained that subsidiarity had to be authorized in Brussels before taking effect (Gillingham 2003: 161). In any case, the explication of the principle in terms of comparative efficiency ('the Community shall take action ... only if and in so far as the objectives of the proposed action cannot be sufficiently achieved by the Member States') considers only two alternatives: again, the nation state and a pre-federal polity. But this is a much narrower enunciation of subsidiarity than that of the social doctrine of the Catholic Church, where the term originated. In its original meaning the principle acts as a constraint limiting intervention by public authorities to such matters with which individuals, families, local communities, or voluntary associations (national or transnational like the Church itself) cannot themselves deal.

This broader view of subsidiarity has deep roots in European history, while the paradigm of the nation state – or its supranational transfiguration – is flawed precisely because it takes the modern notion of statehood as an invariant unit of historical and political analysis. Starting from the symbolic level, it was noted in an earlier chapter that the EU seems to be unable to go beyond the traditional trappings of the nation state: a European logo and flag, an EU anthem, a standardized European passport, an official 'Europe Day' public holiday, etc. The phenomenon of Eurocentricity discussed in chapter 3 is another manifestation of the persistence of state-centred ways of thinking at EU no less than at national level. It may be remembered, for instance, that the Commission's 1990 Green Paper on European standardization was severely criticized for its exclusive focus on EC-mandated standards, neglect of international standardization, and 'an almost cavalier disregard of all interests other than the Community's', as the Dutch Interdepartmental Committee for Standardization (see chapter 3) put it. Monetary union and some of the more ambitious plans for a 'Social Europe' reveal quite clearly the attempt to present the EU as the logically subsequent stage in a straight-line evolution from the national to the European state. As we saw in the introduction, the tendency to imagine the united Europe of the future as a large-scale replica of the modern nation state was already evident in the writings of the federalists of the period between the two world wars. In addition to Ortega y Gasset, one may mention the French writer Julien Benda, who hoped that a European nationalism might replace the nationalism of many nation states. The symbols of a European nation, he maintained, must supplant the myths of the individual nations (cited in Holmberg 1994: 98).

The irony of it all is that both the idea of nation and the doctrine of undivided sovereignty and territorial exclusivity as essential marks of statehood, although fairly recent inventions, are not well adapted to the post-modern world of devolution, regional integration, and globalization (MacCormick 1999). The affirmation of indivisible and unlimited sovereignty by Bodin and other theorists of absolutism (cited in Holmes 1995) was aimed at the various restraints which hampered and limited the state of medieval and early modern Europe: the overriding claims of the empire, the demands of the Church, the constraints on the government's will set by natural law, by custom, feudal privilege, or common law. Such restraints no longer operate today, so we run the double risk of judging contemporary developments in light of inappropriate standards; and, conversely, of overlooking the array of institutional solutions that propose themselves to our attention once the relativity of the nation state paradigm is recognized. The limitations on the powers of the pre-absolutist state made a variety of alternative institutional arrangements possible, which variety, in turn, favoured inter-jurisdictional competition, imitation, and learning. The diffusion of different models of urban law provides a good illustration of the process.

The laws of a dozen major German cities were replicated in hundreds of new towns that were founded in Eastern Europe between the twelfth and the fourteenth centuries. The laws of Luebeck were adopted by forty-three towns, those of Frankfurt by forty-nine, of Munich by thirteen, of Freiburg by nineteen. Most important was the dissemination of the laws of Magdeburg to over eighty new towns. The *Magdeburger Recht* became the predominant basis of written law for Central and Eastern Europe (Berman 1983). Likewise, the laws of the Norman town of Breteuil became the model for Norman settlements in Wales, Scotland, and Ireland. The emergence of a limited number of standard models (which were often updated to reflect new legal developments in the mother town) suggests a competitive process leading to a portfolio of types of urban law, each type offering a different combination of advantages and disadvantages. At the same time, imitation and learning ensured that the everyday rights, privileges, liberties, and immunities of English, French, German, or Polish burghers did not differ essentially from those of burghers in other parts of Europe: a very early example of ex post, (political) market-driven harmonization (see chapter 7). Another consequence was that in many respects urban communities in different countries had more in common with one another than they had with the respective countries in which they were situated. In some cases judges in the mother town would hear judicial appeals from the courts of a daughter town. Such transregional networks of urban judicial authorities were not always favoured by territorial rulers, who considered the existence of an alternative and external jurisdiction a threat to their own position. The aspiration of the princes to have a single hierarchy of judicial authority within their territories is a manifestation of that striving to achieve legal homogeneity typical of the modern conception of national sovereignty. In the thirteenth century and later, however, 'that aspiration faced the powerful alternative of an international urban network that drew the lines more widely and fluidly from mother city to daughter city along the trade routes and the migratory paths rather than within the tight boundaries of the monarchical domain' (Bartlett 1993: 176). The consequence was a unique feature of medieval law: the individual lived under a plurality of legal systems, each governing one of the overlapping subcommunities of which he was a member. Because none of the coexisting legal systems – canon, feudal, mercantile, urban, and royal law – had a claim to be all-inclusive or omnicompetent, each had to develop constitutional standards for limiting sovereignty. In medieval Europe 'checks and balances' were provided mainly by competing and cooperating polities rather than by concurrent branches of the same polity, as in modern separation-of-powers systems.

The European state system of the early modern age preserved important aspects of the competition and cooperation of rival jurisdictions which characterized the previous age. Individuals and whole populations sometimes 'voted with their feet' by shifting their allegiance to that country which was governed best. The ever present possibility that people and capital might move to another country acted as a restraint on excessive taxation and the use of arbitrary power. A large empire which was not threatened by more advanced neighbours had little incentive to adopt new methods. The states of Europe, on the other hand, were surrounded by actual or potential competitors. Hence the fairly rapid diffusion of policy and institutional innovations throughout the continent in the period preceding the full development of the nation-state. In its state system, writes Eric Jones (1987: 115), 'Europe had a portfolio of competing and colluding polities whose spirit of competition was adapted to diffuse best practice'. But as the European nation states became more self-conscious they began to impede the movement of capital and people by closing their borders and enforcing cultural and legal homogeneity on their people. The long century of nationalism that followed was an aberration in European history, and the integration process that succeeded it, a healthy reaction to the catastrophic consequences of nationalist ideology. The mistake was to assume a unilinear development from the nation state to something fulfilling much the same functions, on a grander scale and allegedly more effectively. When it became clear that a large majority of Europeans rejected the federalist solution, the 'f-word' was replaced by the hazy teleology of 'ever closer union'; but, as we saw, patterns of unilinear thinking still survive in the institutions and policies, and in the political culture, of the EC/EU.

The survival of this mode of thinking has so far precluded the development and testing of institutional alternatives even remotely comparable to the richness and variety of those which emerged from the crisis of the feudal state: legal pluralism, competing city-states, city-leagues like the Hanseatic and Swabian-Rhenish leagues, and so on. True, the sovereign territorial state eventually emerged as the winner in the competition between different patterns of governance (Spruyt 1994), but its final victory was made possible by the institutional innovations developed by its competitors. We can show this through Trevor-Roper's well-known thesis that the crisis of the monarchical states in the years 1620–50 was overcome by the adoption, on the much larger scale of the new national states, of the practices and civic traditions of the medieval city-states. In order to adapt successfully to the new conditions of the seventeenth century, the monarchies of the late Renaissance had to solve two key problems: how to achieve a drastic improvement in administrative efficiency; and how to devise new economic policies capable of providing a stable financial support for the greatly expanded activities of the national states. The two great achievements of the city-state – the transformation of self-sufficient agricultural societies into interdependent commercial and industrial societies, and the introduction of a new standard of business-like efficiency in the conduct of both economics and politics – represented precisely the solutions sought by the national states of the seventeenth century. The states that were able to adapt the social inventions which the Italian and Flemish city-states had devised, so as to make them workable on the enlarged scale, prospered. In Holland, France, and England, the crisis marked the end of sixteenth-century extravagance, and a return to more rational forms of state organization. Spain proved unable to adapt its administrative institutions and to design suitable economic policies. Consequently, the crisis of the 1640s led to the permanent loss of Portugal, and to the accelerated decline of the unreformed state (Trevor-Roper 1968).

The economic theory of clubs emphasizes the advantages of institutional pluralism, and implies that an efficient assignment of tasks between different levels of governance need not coincide with existing national boundaries: there may be significant externalities and a need for coordination between some, but not all, regions within a country or group of countries. For instance, the existence of transboundary externalities is often cited as a justification for EU-wide harmonization. The Commission has affirmed that where there is a potential for trans-boundary pollution there is often justification for the EU to act. This is far from being generally true. For most environmental problems, the EU is not an optimal regulatory area, being either too large or too small. In a number of cases – e.g. the Mediterranean, the Baltic Sea, or the Rhine – the scope of the problem is regional rather than EU-wide, and is best tackled through regional arrangements tailored to the scope of the relevant environmental externality. Self-regulatory organizations encompassing only some states ('regional compacts', such as the Delaware River Basin Commission or the Appalachian Regional Commission) have been used in the United States since the 1960s, and even earlier. The central government is represented by a federal coordinator who sometimes is appointed jointly by the US president and by the governors of the states making up the particular interstate compact (Derthick 1974). More recently, organizations including some US states and Canadian provinces have been created in order to control pollution in the Great Lakes region. By pooling their financial, technical, and administrative resources, these consortiums are in a better position to deal effectively with their regulatory problems than each jurisdiction either acting alone or relying exclusively on centralized regulation which could not be closely tailored to their specific needs.

Again, the theory of clubs explains why a number of tasks which used to be assigned to central governments are today performed by private, increasingly transnational, organizations. Although there is a strong historical correlation between standardization and the emergence of the sovereign territorial state (Spruyt 1994), current views on standardization have changed radically as a result of the advance of globalization, the development of technology, and the growing variety and sophistication of technical standards. Standards are public goods – in that they fulfil specific functions deemed desirable by the community that shares them – but this does not mean that they must be established by government fiat. A good standard must reflect the needs, preferences, and resources of the community of users, rather than some centrally defined vision of the 'common interest'. As Alessandra Casella (1996) has written, the fact that in today's integrating world economy the relevant community of standards users need not be territorially defined, distinguishes the traditional approach from the contemporary understanding of standards as a special class of club goods. The general implication of Casella's model, we saw, is that top-down harmonization is desirable when the market is relatively small and homogeneous. In a large market, harmonization tends to be brought about by the recognition of similar demands, rather than by a policy imposed from the top. This conclusion is supported by empirical evidence. Already some years ago the OECD noticed that all industrialized countries tend to converge towards a greater emphasis on self-regulation and non-mandatory standards – that is, towards a plurality of standards and standard-setting organizations. A large market like the United States, Casella adds, is remarkable for the high decentralization of its standardization system. There are literally hundreds of organizations involved in the development of standards. The American National Standards Institute (ANSI), a private organization, coordinates private standards, approves standards as American National Standards, and represents the United States in international standards organizations. In practice, however, only about one-half of all standard-setting organizations participate in the ANSI system, and several organizations which do not participate, such as the American Society of Testing, are as internationally well known as ANSI. Europe is slowly moving in the same direction, though the temptation to think of standards in EU-territorial terms is still strong in Brussels, as demonstrated by the above-mentioned Commission Green Paper on standardization.

A Post-Modern Empire?

A question of some significance for the future configuration of the EU is whether the theory of clubs may also be applicable to the area of foreign, security, and defence policy. The answer is a resounding YES – in theory. As pointed out above, excludability from the benefits of public goods is often more easily enforced at international than at the domestic level. Therefore many goods which are purely public at the national level, such as collective security, can be treated as club goods at the international level: countries that are unwilling to share the costs of producing the goods are simply excluded from the benefits of interstate cooperation. It follows that countries which broadly agree on the definition of their vital interests, and on the appropriate means of protecting them against actual or potential threats, have an incentive to form a club – an alliance, league, or confederation – in order to share the benefits and costs of a common foreign and security policy. Unfortunately, the examples mentioned in the preceding chapter indicate that on many important issues the EU as a whole is incapable of reaching a common position. The Iraq war revealed the existence of a serious cleavage separating the majority of member states which supported Washington's initiative – a group including Britain, Spain, Italy, Portugal, and all the new EU members from Central and Eastern Europe – from the governments of France, Germany, and Belgium, which made active efforts to oppose it. The stance of the 'Atlanticists' was clearly expressed by the British prime minister when he said that his goal was to have a united Europe that was pro-American, but if that proved impossible, he would have preferred a divided Europe that was partly pro-American to a united Europe lined up against the United States (Gordon and Shapiro 2004: 131). Today EU leaders tend to present that disagreement over Iraq as a limited episode, but there are strong reasons to believe that both the special relation between the UK and the US, and the reliance of most new member states on the kind of protection and support which only the US can assure, will persist in the foreseeable future.

In April 2003 the three countries opposed to the American position on Iraq held a mini-summit in Brussels – sarcastically called by some observers the 'praline summit' – to launch a core European 'defence union'. French president Chirac hoped that this avant-garde would become a rival of NATO and help shape a multipolar rather than uni-polar world, while the position of the German government was much more cautious. In the end, the praline summit achieved nothing besides the establishment of an autonomous planning staff, too tiny to seriously concern either NATO or the US government (Pond 2004: 87). More recent issues, such as the secession of Kosovo and the eastward expansion of NATO, are additional evidence of the difficulty of reaching EU-wide consensus even on problems of immediate interest to Europe. There is, too, the perennial problem of matching commitments and resources – a problem exacerbated by EMU. The strict budgetary dis-cipline imposed by monetary union, no matter how beneficial in other respects, makes it impossible even for the larger member states to keep up with the revolution in military technology initiated by the United States in the 1980s. This is a prime example of the phenomenon of unintended consequences discussed in chapter 4: EMU, which in the words of Dutch prime minister Wim Kok was supposed to be 'the foundation for Europe's increased power in the world' (cited in Zimmerman 2004: 244), has actually contributed to the loss of status of the EU as a global actor.

Integrationist leaders of course continue to hope that the situation will eventually improve. After five decades of poorly coordinated and partly contradictory efforts to approach the open-ended goal of 'ever closer union', they should be reminded of Edward Carr's shrewd comment to the effect that the conception of politics as an infinite process is, in the long run, incomprehensible to the human mind (Carr 1964). What is urgently needed is a practical demonstration that the hopes of these leaders have some basis in reality. For instance, a club comprising Germany, France, Belgium, and a few other countries of continental Europe, would have sufficient political and material resources to play a significant international role – were they capable of adopting a truly common foreign policy. Sadly, the three governments of the 'praline summit' were unable to take operational decisions even on an issue where domestic public opinion supported them in their anti-war attitude. Even the members of Benelux – the customs union of Belgium, the Netherlands, and Luxembourg, which is older than the EU, having been established in 1948 – were divided over the Iraq war, with Belgium opposing and the Netherlands supporting the American position. Nevertheless, neo-federalist leaders like the Belgian Guy Verhofstadt should be taken at their word when they propose the formation of an avant-garde of the more integration-minded countries (see chapter 2). They should be encouraged to move as fast and as far as possible in that direction, taking advantage of the option of enhanced cooperation offered by the European treaties. Article 43a of the Nice Treaty, it will be recalled, states that enhanced cooperation should be adopted when it has been determined that some objectives of the Union cannot be otherwise attained within a reasonable period. It seems by now fairly clear that key objectives of EU foreign, security, and defence policies will not be attained 'within a reasonable period'. Empirical proof that a subset of integration-minded countries are able to effectively pursue such policy objectives would demonstrate the feasibility of the broader integrationist project, at least in principle: it would provide what mathematicians call an 'existence proof'. If, on the other hand, the experiment were to fail, then EU leaders should draw the conclusion that institution-building, such as the establishment of a 'High Representative' for foreign affairs, and confident announcements of common policies, unsupported by political will, a shared understanding of Europe's vital interests, and adequate resources, can only undermine the credibility of the Union as a global actor. The abandonment of overly ambitious aspirations, however discouraging initially, would facilitate a more experimental approach to integration.

In a once famous book on *De Statu Imperii Germanici*, published in 1667, Samuel von Pufendorf argued that any attempt to transform the

Holy Roman Empire of the German Nation into a more cohesive polity, on the French or English model, was bound to fail. As an association of sovereign states, however, the empire could and did perform a number of very useful tasks for its members. In fact, while nationalist historians of the nineteenth century considered the empire a monstrosity, modern scholarship has rediscovered the virtues of an institutional arrangement which, for all its limitations, fulfilled important functions and exerted a profound influence on the historical and political culture of Germany (Schilling 1989). Thus, contemporary historians find that the competition between the two main imperial courts (the Reichskammergericht and the Reichshofrat), far from being dysfunctional, served the interest of different corporate groups. Furthermore, the imperial parliament – the (in)famous Immerwaehrender Reichstag, or Permanent Parliament – was an ideal venue for interest mediation among the territorial members of the empire. Again, the various 'Circles' (*Reichskreise*) – clubs or associations operating between the sovereign states and the empire – represented a useful intermediate level of policy-making for a number of issues, including defence.

State-like ambitions are bound to be counterproductive for a *sui generis* polity like the EU as well. Within the general framework of a customs union and a common market for goods – a degree of integration most Europeans seem willing to support – different, often overlapping, clubs would form, according to the preferences and needs of their members. Broader popular support than is available to the EU today – elicited by a few concrete examples of successful interstate cooperation – would of course make it possible to set more ambitious goals than a customs union-cum-common market. The guiding principle should always be that each new commitment must be matched by corresponding material and normative resources. This means that the strategy of fait accompli must be abandoned once and for all. If one clear lesson emerges from the experience of the last fifty years, it is that in the age of mass democracy elite-led integration can only go so far.

REFERENCES

Ackerman, B. (1991) *We The People*. Cambridge, MA: The Belknap Press.

Agence France-Presse (2008) 'IMF Head Sees Euro Overvalued, Says ECB Needs Political Counter Weight', http://afp.google.com/article/ALeqM5jGolqIec PwSa-vhb3nOB6INBbVzQ (accessed 10 February 2009).

Allen, D. (2005) 'Cohesion and the Structural Funds', in Wallace, H., Wallace, W., and Pollack, M. A. (eds.) *Policy-Making in the European Union*. Oxford: Oxford University Press, fifth edition, pp. 213–41.

Balassa, B. (1967) 'Trade Creation and Trade Diversion in the European Common Market', *Economic Journal*, Vol. 77, March, pp. 13–24.

Barnett, R. J. (1983) *The Alliance*. New York: Simon & Schuster.

Bartlett, R. (1993) *The Making of Europe*. London: Penguin Books.

Berman, H. J. (1983) *Law and Revolution*. Cambridge, MA: Harvard University Press.

Berschens, Ruth (2007) 'Nuen Fragen an Jean-Pierre Jouyet: "Uns liegt sehr viel an einer europaeischen Wirtschaftspolitik"', *Handelsblatt*, 29/30 June.

Beste, R., Schlamp, H.-J., and Simons, S. (2008) 'EU in Chaos after Ireland's "No" Vote', *Spiegel On Line International*, 6 September (accessed 1 October 2008).

Beyerle, H. (2008) 'Ostdeutschland in 320 Jahre auf Westniveau', *Financial Times-Deutschland*, 19 June.

Bhagwati, J. N. and Hudec, R. E. (eds.) (1996) *Fair Trade and Harmonization*. Cambridge, MA: The MIT Press.

Brenner, M. J. (2002) *Europe's New Security Vocation*. McNair Paper 66. Washington, DC: Institute for National Strategic Studies.

Breton, A. (1996) *Competitive Governments*. Cambridge: Cambridge University Press.

Brodie, B. (1973) *War and Politics*. New York: Macmillan Publishing Co.

Buchanan, J. M. (1965) 'An Economic Theory of Clubs', *Economica*, Vol. 32, No. 1, pp. 1–14.

Buchanan, J. M. and Tullock, G. (1962) *The Calculus of Consent*. Ann Arbor, MI: The University of Michigan Press.

Carr, E. H. (1961) *What Is History?* New York: Vintage Books.

(1964 [1939]) *The Twenty Years' Crisis, 1919–1939*. New York: Harper & Row.

Casella, A. (1996) 'Free Trade and Evolving Standards', in Bhagwati, J. N. and Hudec, R. E. (eds.) *Fair Trade and Harmonization*, Vol. I. Cambridge, MA: The MIT Press, pp. 119–56.

Castle, S. (2007) 'EU Leaders Want to Try Again with Subsidies – Wealthy Landowners Stand to Lose Most from Suggested Cuts', *International Herald Tribune*, 8 November, p. 1 (continued on p. 8).

(2008) 'After Irish No Vote, EU Seeks Damage Control', *International Herald Tribune*, 19 June, p. 3.

Choper, J. H. (1983) *Judicial Review and the National Political Process*. Chicago, IL: The University of Chicago Press.

Christiansen, T., Joergensen, K. E., and Wiener, A. (1999) 'The Social Construction of Europe', special issue, *Journal of European Public Policy*, Vol. 6, No. 4, pp. 528–44.

Cingolani, S. (2006) 'Chi dice bye bye Italia', *Il Mondo Economico*, 20 October, pp. 21–4.

Coase, R. H. (1988 [1937]) *The Firm, the Market and the Law*. Chicago IL: The University of Chicago Press.

Cohen, R. (2008) 'The EU in an Irish Bog', *International Herald Tribune*, 19 June, p. 5.

Commission of the European Communities (1985) *Completing the Internal Market: White Paper from the Commission to the European Council*. COM (85) 310 final.

(1990a) *One Market, One Money*. (*European Economy* 44).

(1990b) Green Paper on 'The Development of European Standardisation: Action for Faster Technological Integration in Europe', COM (90) 456 final.

(2000) *Communication from the Commission on the Precautionary Principle*. COM (2000) 1.

(2001a) *European Governance*. Luxembourg: Office for Official Publications of the European Communities.

(2001b) 'How Europeans See Themselves. Looking through the Mirror with Public Opinion Surveys', http://ec.europa.eu/publications/booklets/ eu_documentation/05/txt_en.pdf (accessed 11 February 2009).

(2002) *The Operating Framework for the European Regulatory Agencies*. COM (2002) 718 final.

(2003) 'Choosing to Grow: Knowledge, Innovation and Jobs in a Cohesive Society: Report to the Spring European Council, 21 March 2003 on the Lisbon Strategy of Economic, Social and Environmental Renewal', COM (2003) 5 final, p. 17.

(2006) *The Future of Europe*, Special EUROBAROMETER 251, http://ec.europa. eu/public_opinion/archives/ebs/ebs_251_en.pdf (accessed 11 February 2009).

Craig, G. A. (1978) *Germany 1866–1945*. New York: Oxford University Press.

Craig, P. and de Búrca, G. (2003) *EU Law: Text, Cases, and Materials*. Oxford: Oxford University Press, third edition.

Curtin, D. (1993) 'The Constitutional Structure of the Union: A Europe of Bits and Pieces', *Common Market Law Review*, Vol. 30, No. 1, pp. 17–69.

Dahl, R. A. (1989) *Democracy and its Critics*. New Haven, CT: Yale University Press.

Dashwood, A. (1983) 'Hastening Slowly: The Communities' Path towards Harmonization', in Wallace, H., Wallace, W., and Webb, C. (eds.) *Policy-Making in the European Community*. Chichester, UK: Wiley, second edition, pp. 177–208.

(1996) 'The Limits of European Community Powers', *European Law Review*, Vol. 21, pp. 113–28.

De Grauwe, P. (2004) 'Challenges for Monetary Policy in Euroland', in Torres, F., Verdun, A., Zilioli, C., and Zimmerman, H. (eds.) *Governing EMU*. Florence: European University Institute, pp. 363–88.

Dehousse, R. (2005) *La fin de l'Europe*. Paris: Flammarion.

Delors, J. (1989) 'Statement on the Broad Lines of Community Policy', *Bulletin of the European Communities*, supplement 1/89, p. 21 (full text of Presidency Conclusions since 1994 can be found at the Commission website 'Europa' (http://europa.eu)).

Derthick, M. (1974) *Between State and Nation: Regional Organizations of the United States*. Washington, DC: The Brookings Institution.

Dohmen, F. and Schlamp, H.-J. (2005) 'Club im Club', *Spiegel Online*, 19 December.

Dougan, M. (2006) ' "And Some Fell on Stony Ground ..." – A Review of G. Majone's *Dilemmas of European Integration*', *European Law Review*, Vol. 31, No. 4, pp. 865–72.

Downs, A. (1957) *An Economic Theory of Democracy*. New York: Harper & Row.

Duchêne, F. (1972) 'Europe's Role in World Peace', in Mayne, R. (ed.) *Europe Tomorrow: Sixteen Europeans Look Ahead*. London: Fontana, pp. 32–47.

Ehlermann, C.-D. (1984) 'How Flexible is Community Law? An Unusual Approach to the Concept of "Two Speeds"', *Michigan Law Review*, Vol. 82, No. 3, pp. 1274–93.

Eichengreen, J. and Frieden, J. A. (1995) 'The Political Economy of European Monetary Unification: An Analytical Introduction', in Frieden, J. A. and Lake, D. A. (eds.) *International Political Economy*. London: Routledge, third edition, pp. 267–81.

Eilstrup-Sangiovanni, M. (2006) *Debates on European Integration*. New York: Palgrave Macmillan.

Ellis, E. (1998) *EC Sex Equality Law*. Oxford: Clarendon Press.

Engel, C. (2002) 'European Telecommunications Law: Unaffected by Globalization?', Working Paper. Bonn: Max Planck Institute.

European Council (2005) *Presidency Conclusion, Part 1*, Brussels, June (full text of Presidency Conclusions since 1994 can be found at the Commission website 'Europa' (http://europa.eu.int)).

European Union (2007). 'The Spring European Council: Integrated Climate Protection and Energy Policy, Progress on the Lisbon Strategy', http://europa.eu, 12 March (accessed 6 April 2007).

Feldstein, M. (1992) 'The Case against EMU', *Economist*, 13 June, pp. 19–22.

Ferrera, M., Hemerijck, A., and Rhodes, M. (2001) 'The Future of the European "Social Model" in the Global Economy', *Journal of Comparative Policy Analysis*, Vol. 3, No. 2, pp. 163–90.

Fischer, J. (2000) 'Vom Staatenverbund zur Foederation – Gedanken ueber die Finalitaet der Europaeischen Integration'. Lecture given at Humboldt University, Berlin, 22 May.

Frankenberger, K.-D. (2005) 'Aufstand in Europa', *FAZ.NET-Politik-EU-Verfassungsvertrag*, 17 June (accessed 12 October 2005).

Gall, L. (1981) *Bismarck Der Weisse Revolutionär*. Frankfurt: Ullstein, fifth edition.

Gay, P. (1962) *The Dilemma of Democratic Socialism*. New York: Collier Books.

Gillingham, J. (1991) *Coal, Steel, and the Rebirth of Europe, 1945–1955*. Cambridge: Cambridge University Press.

(2003) *European Integration, 1950–2003*. Cambridge: Cambridge University Press.

Gordon, P. H. and Shapiro, J. (2004) *Allies At War*. New York: McGraw-Hill.

Gormley, L. and de Haan, J. (1996) 'The Democratic Deficit of the European Central Bank', *European Law Review*, Vol. 21, pp. 95–111.

Goyder, D. G. (2003) *EC Competition Law*. Oxford: Oxford University Press, fourth edition.

Grant, R. W. and Keohane, R. O. (2005) 'Accountability and Abuses of Power in World Politics', *American Political Science Review*, Vol. 99, No. 1, pp. 29–43.

Greider, W. (1987) *Secrets of the Temple*. New York: Simon & Schuster.

Guéhenno, J.-M. (1993) *La fin de la démocratie*. Paris: Flammarion.

Haas, E. B. (1958) *The Uniting of Europe: Political, Social and Economic Forces 1950–1957*. Stanford, CA: Stanford University Press.

(1971) 'The Study of Regional Integration', in Lindberg, L. N. and Scheingold, S. A. (eds.) *Regional Integration*. Cambridge, MA: Harvard University Press, pp. 3–42.

Habermas, J. (2000) 'Il y aura toujours des Etats nations', *Le Figaro*, 28 June.

(2005) 'Europa ist uns ueber die Koepfe hinweggerollt', *Sueddeutsche Zeitung*, 9 June.

Hartley, T. C. (1991) *The Foundations of European Community Law*. New York: Oxford University Press, second edition.

Hatzopoulos, V. (2007) 'Why the Open Method of Coordination Is Bad For You: A Letter to the EU', *European Law Journal*, Vol. 13, No. 3, pp. 309–42.

Hayek, F. A. (1948 [1939]) 'The Economic Conditions of Interstate Federalism', in Hayek, F. A. *Individualism and Economic Order*. Chicago, IL: The University of Chicago Press, pp. 255–72.

(1969) *Studies in Philosophy, Politics and Economics*. New York: Simon & Schuster.

Hayes-Renshaw, F. and Wallace, H. (1997) *The Council of Ministers*. London: Macmillan Press.

Henning, C. R. (2000) 'U.S.–EU Relations after the Inception of the Monetary Union: Cooperation or Rivalry?', in Henning, C. R. and Padoan, P. C. *Transatlantic Perspectives on the Euro*. Washington, DC: The Brookings Institution, pp. 5–63.

Hillgruber, A. (1981) *Europa in der Weltpolitik der Nachkriegszeit 1945–1963*. Munich: Oldenbourg Verlag.

Hirschman, A. O. (1981) 'Three uses of Political Economy in Analyzing European Integration', in Hirschman, A. O. *Essays in Trespassing*. Cambridge: Cambridge University Press, pp. 266–84.

Hoffmann, S. (2000) 'Towards a Common Foreign and Security Policy?', *Journal of Common Market Studies*, Vol. 38, No. 2, pp. 189–98.

Holmberg, A. (1994) 'The Holy European Empire', in Loennroth, E., Molin, K. and Bjoerk, R. (eds.) *Conceptions of National History*. Berlin: Walter de Gruyter, pp. 98–113.

Holmes, S. (1995) 'The Constitution of Sovereignty in Jean Bodin', in *Passions and Constraint*. Chicago, IL: The University of Chicago Press, pp. 100–133.

Hrbek, R. (1981) 'Europa', in Greiffenhagen, M., Greiffenhagen, S., and Praetorius, R. (eds.) *Handwoerterbuch zur politischen Kultur der Bundesrepublik Deutschland*. Opladen: Westdeutscher Verlag, pp. 147–9.

Hufbauer, G. (ed.) (1990) *Europe 1992 – An American Perspective*. Washington, DC: The Brookings Institution.

Hyde-Price, A. (2006) '"Normative" Power Europe: A Realist Critique', *Journal of European Public Policy*, Vol. 13, No. 2, pp. 217–34.

Idema, T. and Kelemen, R. D. (2006) 'New Modes of Governance, the Open Method of Co-ordination and Other Fashionable Red Herrings', *Perspectives in European Politics and Society*, Vol. 7, No. 1, pp. 108–23.

Ipsen, H. P. (1972) *Europäisches Gemeinschaftsrecht*. Tuebingen: J. C. B. Mohr/ Paul Siebeck.

Jacqué, J. P. (1991) 'Cours général de droit communautaire', in Clapham, A. (ed.) *Collected Courses of the Academy of European Law*, Vol. I, Book 1. Dordrecht, The Netherlands: Martinus Nijhoff Publishers, pp. 247–360.

Jaeger, W. (1976) *Paideia – The Ideals of Greek Culture*. New York: Oxford University Press.

Joerges, C., Schepel, H., and Vos, E. (1999) 'The Law's Problems with the Involvement of Non-Governmental Actors in Europe's Legislative Processes: The Case of Standardization Under the New Approach', EUI Working Papers, Law No. 99/9. Florence: European University Institute.

Johnson, H. G. (1972) *Aspects of the Theory of Tariffs*. Cambridge, MA: Harvard University Press.

Jones, E. L. (1987) *The European Miracle: Environments, Economies and Geopolitics in the History of Europe and Asia*. New York: Cambridge University Press, second edition.

Judge, D. and Earnshaw, D. (2002) 'The European Parliament and the Commission Crisis: A New Assertiveness', *Governance: An International Journal of Policy, Administration, and Institutions*, Vol. 15, No. 3, pp. 345–74.

Kahler, M. (1995) *International Institutions and the Political Economy of Integration*. Washington, DC: The Brookings Institution.

Kennedy, P. (1987) *The Rise and Fall of the Great Powers*. New York: Random House.

Keohane, R. O. (1995) 'Comments', in Kahler, M. *International Institutions and the Political Economy of Integration*. Washington, DC: The Brookings Institution, pp. 135–44.

Ketcham, R. (1990) *James Madison*. Charlottesville, VA: The University Press of Virginia.

Kettle, D. F. (1986) *Leadership at the Federal Reserve System*. New Haven, CT: Yale University Press.

Klabbers, J. (1998) 'The Netherlands', in Dinan, D. (ed.) *Encyclopedia of the European Union*. Boulder, CO: Lynne Rienner Publishers, pp. 355–7.

Knudsen, J. S. (2005) 'Is the Single European Market an Illusion? Obstacles to Reform of EU Takeover Regulation', *European Law Journal*, Vol. 11, No. 4, pp. 507–24.

Kohnstamm, M. (1989) 'Jean Monnet face à l'Union Européenne', in Majone, G., Noël, E., and Van den Bossche, P. (eds.) *Jean Monnet et l'Europe d'aujourd'-hui*. Baden-Baden: Nomos, pp. 39–44.

Kolakowski, L. (1978) *Main Currents of Marxism – The Golden Age*. Oxford: Oxford University Press.

Kostoris Padoa Schioppa, F. (2007) 'Dominant Losers: A Comment on the Services Directive from an Economic Perspective', *Journal of European Public Policy*, Vol. 14, No. 5, pp. 735–42.

Ladeur, K.-H. (2008) '"We, the European People ..." – Relache?', *European Law Journal*, Vol. 14, No. 2, pp. 147–67.

Laqueur, W. (1982) *Europe Since Hitler*. New York: Penguin Books, revised edition.

Lavenex, S. (2007) 'Mutual Recognition and the Monopoly of Force: Limits of the Single Market Analogy', *Journal of European Public Policy*, Vol. 14, No. 5, pp. 762–79.

Lavenex, S. and Wallace, W. (2005) 'Justice and Home Affairs', in Wallace, H., Wallace, W., and Pollack, M. A. (eds.) *Policy-Making in the European Union*. Oxford University Press, fifth edition, pp. 457–80.

Leibenstein, H. (1980) *Beyond Economic Man*. Cambridge, MA: Harvard University Press.

Leibfried, S. (2005) 'Social Policy – Left to the Judges and the Market?', in Wallace, H., Wallace, W., and Pollack, M. A. (eds.) *Policy-Making in the European Union*. Oxford: Oxford University Press, fifth edition, pp. 243–78.

Le Monde – Éditorial (2006) 'Test européen', 15 February.

Lenaerts, K. (1990) 'Constitutionalism and the Many Faces of Federalism', *American Journal of Comparative Law*, Vol. 38, pp. 205–63.

Lenaerts, K. and Van Nuffel, P. (1999) *Constitutional Law of the European Union*. London: Sweet & Maxwell.

Lijphart, A. (1984) *Democracies*. New Haven, CT: Yale University Press.

Lippmann, W. (1943) *U.S. Foreign Policy*. Boston, MA: Little, Brown and Company.

Lipset, S. M. (1963) *Political Man*. Garden City, NY: Anchor Books.

Lucas, N. J. D. (1977) *Energy and the European Communities*. London: Europa Publications.

MacCormick, N. (1999) *Questioning Sovereignty: Law, State, and Nation in the European Commonwealth*. New York: Oxford University Press.

Magnette, P. (2001) 'Appointing and Censuring the Commission: The Adaptation of Parliamentary Institutions to the Community Context', *European Law Journal*, Vol. 7, No. 3, pp. 292–310.

Maillet, P. and Velo, D. (1994) *L'Europe à gèometrie variable. Transition vers l'intégration*. Paris: L'Harmattan.

Mair, P. (2007) 'Political Opposition and the European Union', *Government and Opposition*, Vol. 42, No. 1, pp. 1–17.

Majone, G. (1993) 'The European Community Between Social Policy and Social Regulation', *Journal of Common Market Studies*, Vol. 31, No. 2, pp. 153–70.

(1996) *Regulating Europe*. London: Routledge.

(1998) 'Europe's "Democratic Deficit": The Question of Standards', *European Law Journal*, Vol. 4, No. 1, pp. 5–28.

(2005) *Dilemmas of European Integration: The Ambiguities and Pitfalls of Integration by Stealth*. Oxford: Oxford University Press.

Manners, I. (2006) 'Normative Power Europe Reconsidered: Beyond the Crossroads', *Journal of European Public Policy*, Vol. 13, No. 2, pp. 182–99.

Marc, A. (1989) 'Fédéralisme contre fonctionnalisme', in Majone, G., Noël, E., and Van den Bossche, P. (eds.) *Jean Monnet et l'Europe d'aujourd'hui*. Baden-Baden: Nomos, pp. 83–90.

Marshall, T. H. (1975) *Social Policy*. London: Hutchinson.

Mayne, R. (1989) 'Jean Monnet and the United Kingdom', in Majone, G., Noël, E., and Van den Bossche, P. (eds.) *Jean Monnet et l'Europe d'aujourd'hui*. Baden-Baden: Nomos, pp. 121–7.

McCubbins, M. D. and Noble, G. W. (1995) 'The Appearance of Power: Legislators, Bureaucrats, and the Budget Process in the United States and Japan', in Cowhey, P. F. and McCubbins, M. D. (eds.) *Structure and Policy in Japan and the United States*. New York: Cambridge University Press, pp. 56–80.

Menon, A., Nicolaïdis, K., Welsh, J. (2004) 'In Defence of Europe – A Response to Kagan', *Journal of European Affairs*, Vol. 3, No. 2, pp. 5–14.

Merk, F. (1963) *Manifest Destiny and Mission in American History*. New York: Vintage Books.

Merkel, A. (2007) 'Politik-Im Wortlaut Die Berliner Erklaerung', *Spiegel On Line*, 25 March (accessed 25 March 2007).

Merton, R. K. (1949) *Social Theory and Social Structure*. New York: The Free Press.

Meunier, S. (2005) *Trading Voices*. Princeton, NJ: Princeton University Press.

Michels, R. (1962) *Political Parties: A Sociological Study of the Oligarchical Tendencies of Modern Parties*. Trans. E. Paul, and C. Paul. New York: Collier Books (first published in Germany in 1911).

Micossi, S. and Gros, D. (2006) 'Confronting Crisis in the European Union: A Fresh Start', CEPS Policy Brief No. 117, December. Brussels: Centre for European Policy Studies.

Milgrom, J. and Roberts, P. (1992) *Economics, Organization and Management*. Englewood Cliffs, NJ: Prentice-Hall.

Milward, A. S. (1992) *The European Rescue of the Nation State*. London: Routledge.

Milward, A. S. and Sørensen, V. (1994) 'Interdependence or Integration? A National Choice', in Milward, A. S., Lynch, F. M. B., Ranieri, R., Romero, F. and Sørensen, V. *The Frontier of National Sovereignty*. London: Routledge.

Mishan, E. J. (1969) *21 Popular Economic Fallacies*. Harmondsworth, UK: Penguin Books.

Moravcsik, A. (2005) 'The European Constitutional Compromise and the Neofunctionalist Legacy', *Journal of European Public Policy*, Vol. 12, No. 2, pp. 349–86.

Morgan, E. S. (1988) *Inventing the People: The Rise of Popular Sovereignty in England and America*. New York: W. W. Norton.

Morgan, G. (2005) *The Idea of a European Superstate*. Princeton, NJ: Princeton University Press.

Mosse, G. L. (1975) *The Nationalization of the Masses*. New York: New American Library.

Mueller, H. (2006) 'Dann wird die Eurozone explodieren', *Spiegel Online*, 20 December 2006 (accessed 3 January 2007).

Muenchau, Wolfgang and Atkins, Ralph (2004) 'Working Longer to Save Jobs: But Will it Help Europe to Close the Productivity Gap?', *Financial Times*, 23 July.

Murray Brown, J. (2008) 'Businessman Proves a Thorn in the Side of the Irish Yes Vote Campaign', *Financial Times*, 7/8 June.

Nicolaïdis, K. and Schmidt, S. K. (2007) 'Mutual Recognition "On Trial": The Long Road to Services Liberalization', *Journal of European Public Policy*, Vol. 14, No. 5, pp. 717–34.

Norman, P. (2003) *The Accidental Constitution*. Brussels: EuroComment.

Obinger, H., Leibfried, S., and Castles, F. G. (2005) 'Bypasses to a Social Europe? Lessons from Federal Experience', *Journal of European Public Policy*, Vol. 12, No. 3, pp. 545–71.

OECD (Organisation for Economic Co-operation and Development) (2007) *Economic Survey of the European Union*. Paris: OECD.

Ortega y Gasset, Jose (1932) *The Revolt Of The Masses*. New York: W. W. Norton (authorized translation of the Spanish original published in 1930).

Ostner, I. and Lewis, J. (1995) 'Gender and the Evolution of European Social Policies', in Leibfried, S. and Pierson, P. (eds.) *European Social Policy: Between Fragmentation and Integration*. Washington, DC: The Brookings Institution, pp. 159–93.

Padover, S. K. (ed.) (1953) *The Forging of American Federalism – Selected Writings of James Madison*. New York: Harper Torchbooks.

Paolini, E. (1988) *Altiero Spinelli*. Bologna: Il Mulino.

Pelkmans, J. (2007) 'Mutual Recognition in Goods. On Promises and Disillusions', *Journal of European Public Policy*, Vol. 14, No. 5, pp. 699–716.

Peterson, P. E. and Rom, M. C. (1990) *Welfare Magnets*. Washington, DC: The Brookings Institution.

Pilz, F. and Ortwein, H. (1995) *Das Politische System Deutschlands*. Munich: Oldenbourg.

Poehl, K. O. (1990) 'Towards Monetary Union in Europe', in Institute of Economic Affairs, *Europe's Constitutional Future*. London: Institute of Economic Affairs, pp. 35–42.

Pollack, M. A. (1997) 'Delegation, Agency, and Agenda Setting in the European Community', *International Organization*, Vol. 51, pp. 99–134.

Pond, E. (2004) *Friendly Fire*. Washington, DC: Brookings Institution Press.

Popper, K. R. (1969) *Conjectures and Refutations*. London: Routledge and Kegan Paul, third edition.

Rasmussen, H. and Hoekkerup, N. (1998) 'Denmark', in Dinan, D. (ed.) *Encyclopedia of the European Union*. Boulder, CO: Lynne Rienner Publishers, pp. 134–7.

Revesz, R. L. (1992) 'Rehabilitating Interstate Competition: Rethinking the "Race-to-the-Bottom" Rationale for Federal Environmental Regulation', *New York University Law Review*, Vol. 67, pp. 1210–54.

Roessler, F. (1996) 'Diverging Domestic Policies and Multilateral Trade Integration', in Bhagwati, J. N. and Hudec, R. E. (eds.) *Fair Trade and Harmonization*, Vol. II. Cambridge, MA: The MIT Press, pp. 1–56.

Rosenthal, D. E. (1990) 'Competition Policy', in Hufbauer, G. C. (ed.) *Europe 1992: An American Perspective*. Washington, DC: The Brookings Institution, pp. 293–344.

Ross, G. (1995) *Jacques Delors and European Integration*. London: Polity Press.

Rostow, W. W. (1982) *The Division Of Europe after World War II: 1946*. London: Gower Publishing Company.

Ryle, G. (1949) *The Concept of Mind*. New York: Barnes & Noble.

Sapir, A. (1996) 'Trade Liberalization and the Harmonization of Social Policies: Lessons from European Integration', in Bhagwati, J. N. and Hudec, R. E. (eds.) *Fair Trade and Harmonization*, Vol. I. Cambridge, MA: The MIT Press, pp. 543–70.

Sapir, A., Aghion, P., Bertola, G., Hellwig, M., Pisani-Ferry, J., Rosati, D., Vinals, J., and Wallace, H. (2004) *An Agenda for a Growing Europe*. Oxford: Oxford University Press.

Scharpf, F. W. (1999) *Governing in Europe: Effective and Democratic?* Oxford: Oxford University Press.

Scherer, F. M. (1994) *Competition Policies for an Integrated Economy*. Washington, DC: The Brookings Institution.

Schilling, H. (1989) *Hoefe und Allianzen. Deutschland 1648–1763*. Berlin: Siedler.

Schlamp, H.-J. (2008) 'Europa versagt als Krisenhelfer', *Spiegel Online*, 13 August.

Schmitter, P. C. (2005) 'Ernst B. Haas and the Legacy of Neofunctionalism', *Journal of European Public Policy*, Vol. 12, No. 2, pp. 255–72.

Schneider, L. (ed.) (1967) *The Scottish Moralists*. Chicago, IL: The University of Chicago Press.

Schuetze, R. (2007) 'Dual Federalism Constitutionalised: The Emergence of Exclusive Competences in the EC Legal Order', *European Law Review*, Vol. 32, No. 1, pp. 3–28.

Schwarz, H.-P. (1994) *Adenauer*, Volume I. Munich: DTV.

Sedelmeier, U. (2005) 'Eastern Enlargement: Towards a European EU', in Wallace, H., Wallace, W., and Pollack, M. A. (eds.) *Policy-Making in the European Union*. Oxford: Oxford University Press, fifth edition, pp. 401–28.

Selznick, P. (1966 [1949]) *TVA and the Grass Roots*. New York: Harper & Row.

Shackleton, M. (1998) 'Democratic Deficit', in Dinan, D. (ed.) *Encyclopedia of the European Union*, Boulder, CO: Lynne Rienner Publishers, pp. 130–34.

Shore, C. (2006) 'Government Without Statehood? Anthropological Perspectives on Governance and Sovereignty in the European Union', *European Law Journal*, Vol. 12, No. 6, pp. 709–24.

Sjursen, H. (2006) 'The EU as a "Normative" Power: How Can This Be?', *Journal of European Public Policy*, Vol. 13, No. 2, pp. 235–51.

Sked, A. and Cook, C. (1979) *Post-War Britain*. Harmondsworth, UK: Penguin Books.

Spiegel On Line International (2007) 'Haelfte der Deutschen will EU bremsen', 19 March (accessed 19 March 2007).

Spruyt, H. (1994) *The Sovereign State and Its Competitors*. Princeton, NJ: Princeton University Press.

Stiglitz, J. E. (1988) *Economics of the Public Sector*. New York: W. W. Norton, second edition.

Symes, D. and Crean, K. (1995) 'Historic Prejudice and Invisible Boundaries: Dilemmas for the Development of the Common Fisheries Policy', in Blake, G., Hildesley, W., Pratt, R., Ridley, R., and Schofield, C. (eds.) *The Peaceful Management of Transboundary Resources*. London: Graham and Trotman.

Szyszczak, E. (2006) 'Experimental Governance: The Open Method of Coordination', *European Law Journal*, Vol. 12, No. 4, pp. 486–502.

Taylor, A. J. P. (1971) *The Struggle for Mastery in Europe*. Oxford: Oxford University Press.

Tilly, C. (ed.) (1975) *The Formation of National States in Western Europe*. Princeton, NJ: Princeton University Press.

Tindemans, L. (1998) 'Dreams Come True, Gradually. The Tindemans Report a Quarter of a Century Later', in Westlake, M. (ed.) *The European Union Beyond Amsterdam*. London: Routledge, pp. 131–44.

Trachtman, J. P. (2007) 'Embedding Mutual Recognition at the WTO', *Journal of European Public Policy*, Vol. 14, No. 5, pp. 780–99.

Trechsel, A. H. (2005) 'How to Federalize the European Union ... and Why Bother', *Journal of European Public Policy*, Vol. 12, No. 3, pp. 401–18.

Trevor-Roper, H. R. (1968) *The Crisis of the Seventeenth Century: Religion, the Reformation and Social Change*. New York: Harper & Row.

Trubek, D. M. and Trubek, L. G. (2005) 'Hard and Soft Law in the Construction of Social Europe: The Role of the Open Method of Co-ordination', *European Law Journal*, Vol. 11, No. 3, pp. 343–64.

Tsoukalis, L. (1993) *The New European Economy*. Oxford: Oxford University Press, second revised edition.

 (2000) 'Economic and Monetary Union', in Wallace, H. and Wallace, W. (eds.) *Policy-Making in the European Union*. Oxford: Oxford University Press, fourth edition, pp. 149–78.

Uri, P. (1989) 'Réflexion sur l'approche fonctionaliste de Jean Monnet et suggestions pour l'avenir', in Majone, G., Noël, E., and Van den Bossche, P. (eds.) *Jean Monnet et l'Europe d'aujourd'hui*. Baden-Baden: Nomos, pp. 75–82.

Urmson, J. O. (1968) *The Emotive Theory of Ethics*. Oxford: Oxford University Press.

Vernet, Daniel (2005) 'M. Douste-Blazy souhaite une "avangarde européenne"', *Le Monde*, 23 September, p. 2.

Volkery, C. (2008) 'No EU Expansion Without Treaty, Says Sarkozy', *Spiegel On Line International*, 20 June (accessed 28 June 2008).

von der Groeben, H. (1987) *The European Community – The Formative Years*. Luxembourg: Office for Official Publications of the European Communities.

Wallace, H. (1998) 'Differentiated Integration', in Dinan, D. (ed.) *Encyclopedia of the European Union*. Boulder, CO: Lynne Rienner Publishers, pp. 137–40.

    (2005) 'An Institutional Anatomy and Five Policy Models', in Wallace, H., Wallace, W., and Pollack, M. A. (eds.) *Policy-Making in the European Union*. Oxford: Oxford University Press, fifth edition, pp. 49–90.

Wallace, W., (2005) 'Foreign and Security Policy', in Wallace, H., Wallace, W., and Pollack, M. A. (eds.) *Policy-Making in the European Union*. Oxford: Oxford University Press, fifth edition, pp. 429–56.

Weatherill, S. (1995) *Law and Integration in the European Union*. Oxford: Clarendon Press.

Weiler, J. H. H. (1999) *The Constitution of Europe*. Cambridge: Cambridge University Press.

Williams, S. (1991) 'Sovereignty and Accountability in the European Community', in Keohane, R. O. and Hoffmann, S. (eds.) *The New European Community: Decisionmaking and Institutional Change*. Boulder, CO: Westview Press, pp. 155–76.

Winkler, H. A. (2005) 'Europas Bonapartismus', *Frankfurter Allgemeine Sonntagszeitung*, 17 April.

Wolfe, C. (1986) *The Rise of Modern Judicial Review*. New York: Basic Books.

Zimmermann, H. (2004) 'Ever Challenging the Buck? The Euro and the Question of Power in International Monetary Governance', in Torres, F., Verdun, A., Zilioli, C., and Zimmerman, H. (eds.) *Governing EMU*. Florence: European University Institute, pp. 233–48.

INDEX